LINDBERGH

vs.

ROOSEVELT

LINDBERGH

vs.

ROOSEVELT

THE RIVALRY THAT DIVIDED AMERICA

JAMES P. DUFFY

Since 1947
REGNERY
PUBLISHING, INC.
An Eagle Publishing Company • Washington, DC

Library of Congress Cataloging-in-Publication Data

    Duffy, James P., 1941-
      Lindbergh vs. Roosevelt / by James P. Duffy.
        p. cm.
      Includes bibliographical references and index.
      ISBN 978-1-59698-601-5
      1. Roosevelt, Franklin D. (Franklin Delano),
1882-1945—Adversaries. 2. Lindbergh, Charles A. (Charles Augustus),
1902-1974. 3. United States—Politics and government—1933-1945. 4.
Right and left (Political science)—United States—History—20th
century. 5. United States—Military policy. 6. World
politics—1900-1945. I. Title. II. Title: Lindbergh versus Roosevelt.
    E807.D86 2010
    973.917--dc22

2010036142

Published in the United States by
Regnery Publishing, Inc.
One Massachusetts Avenue, NW
Washington, DC 20001
www.regnery.com

Manufactured in the United States of America
10 9 8 7 6 5 4 3 2 1

Books are available in quantity for promotional or premium use. Write to Director of Special Sales, Regnery Publishing, Inc., One Massachusetts Avenue NW, Washington, DC 20001, for information on discounts and terms or call (202) 216-0600.

Distributed to the trade by:
Perseus Distribution
387 Park Avenue South
New York, NY 10016

For Kathy

CONTENTS

PREFACE

I began thinking about writing this book more than thirty years ago. I started collecting various research items including books, magazine and journal articles, and newspaper reports. I hunted in libraries and archives for bits of information. Anything relating to Charles Lindbergh found its way into several file boxes that I lugged with me as I moved from place to place over these many years.

Why bother, you might ask. Well, something about Lindbergh troubled me deeply. But it was not Lindbergh himself I found disconcerting—it was what happened to him.

Over the intervening years, I wrote and published fifteen books. Between working on each book, I would return to Lindbergh, even if only for brief periods. I read biographies of Lindbergh and the published diaries of his wife, Anne Morrow Lindbergh, as well as his autobiographical volumes and books on the noninterventionist movement in the pre-World War II years. I also waded through numerous biographies of Lindbergh's arch-opponent, President Franklin D. Roosevelt, and books by and about members of FDR's administration.

In all that time, however, I made no serious effort to obtain a publishing contract for a book about the rivalry that rocked America twice during the first half of the twentieth century. For one thing, I was not sure anyone else cared about what happened to Lindbergh's reputation. Just mentioning Lindbergh's name usually brought a quizzical look and the question, "Wasn't he a Nazi?"—or equally devastating, "Wasn't he an anti-Semite?"

A better question is: how could a true American hero have been slandered the way Lindbergh was? I believe the explanation lies in the fact that twice he opposed the most powerful man in America, President Roosevelt. Because of that, he became the target of a venomous smear campaign by the White House and the president's supporters. I expected it would be difficult to make people understand that FDR and those around him could stoop so low as to outright demonize someone for simply taking an opposing position—especially because many people were raised to think FDR was the country's savior, the man who pulled us out of the Great Depression and won the greatest war in history.

But the public's opinion of Roosevelt has changed over the last two decades. Many serious writers have published somber analyses concluding that Roosevelt's big spending programs actually prolonged the Depression.[1] It was only ended by a world war that put millions of men and women to work and got factories running around the clock.

Then in 2008, a presidential candidate widely fancied as a new FDR won the White House. He had issued a clarion call for "change," and millions responded to it. But soon, many began to question what it was he wanted to change. They thought he was going to change Washington and the way business is conducted there, but discovered they were wrong. President Obama, like FDR, is an elitist who has filled his administration with other elitists and his favorite "experts." This president doesn't want to change Washington, but America itself. The response was powerful as tens of thousands of voters attended townhall meetings with their senators and congressional representatives and spoke out against policies they believed were driving the country into bankruptcy. Hundreds of thousands united in the grassroots tea party movement and attended rallies across the country.

Then the name-calling and demonizing began by the White House, the congressional leadership, and the mainstream media that supported the president. People who protested Obama's policies were "racists," "Nazis," and "unpatriotic." Speaker of the House Nancy Pelosi called tea parties an "Astroturf" operation, implying its adherents were shills being organized and manipulated by some higher authority. Meanwhile, other critics made the opposite charge—that tea partiers were an unruly, violence-prone mob.

A special dose of malice was reserved for former governor and vice presidential candidate Sarah Palin, radio and TV host Glenn Beck, and talk radio king Rush Limbaugh. The vindictive attitude underlying the whole campaign, and the desire to see the Left's political opponents not just proved wrong but destroyed, was encapsulated in a post about Limbaugh on JournoList. In that forum for leftwing journalists and commentators, Sarah Spitz, producer for an affiliate of National Public Radio, testified she would "laugh loudly like a maniac and watch his eyes bug out" if Limbaugh had a heart attack. "I never knew I had this much hate in me," she wrote. "But he deserves it."

For me, it was Lindbergh's fate playing out again, but with different victims. He had dared to speak out against the policies of a president the Left revered, and he was maligned in much the same way as Obama's opponents are today.

Now, I thought, readers might be interested in what happened to Lindbergh, because they are witness to the same thing happening again. Today's slanders must not be allowed to become accepted historical fact as the attacks on Lindbergh became. Lindbergh never really fought back against his attackers, which is a shame, because he had truth on his side, and truth is always a powerful ally.

I tell here the story of Charles Lindbergh's words, deeds, and beliefs, how they were deliberately misrepresented in order to smear him, and who attacked him and why. I hope to prompt readers once again to view Lindbergh for what he really was: an American patriot who had the audacity to stand up to a president whose policies he believed would damage the country.

James P. Duffy

INTRODUCTION

❦

THE LINDBERGH LEGACY

N oted historian and best-selling author David McCullough called Charles Lindbergh "one of the most celebrated figures of the century, a man more complicated and contradictory than often portrayed." He added, "For all that has been written and said about him, he remains, in many ways, a mystery."

Following his historic non-stop flight from New York to Paris on May 20–21, 1927, the shy, handsome young aviator became the most honored private citizen on earth. Nations showered him with decorations, and crowds followed him wherever he went. *Time* magazine put his image on its cover and made him its first Man of the Year. He had undoubtedly become the most famous man in the world with his flight across the Atlantic—a feat that six aviators had already perished trying to achieve. His flight out of France to Belgium on May 28, 1927, the first leg of his return trip to America, was watched by uncounted hundreds of thousands of people crammed into the streets of Paris looking up at the great aviator circling the Eiffel Tower. When he landed in Belgium, it took most of the Brussels police force and some five thousand troops with fixed bayonets to keep the cheering throng from rushing him and his now-famous single-engine airplane, the *Spirit of St. Louis*. In Britain, 150,000 people turned out to welcome him. In Belgium, he met privately with the King and Queen and in London with the King and the Prince of Wales.

When he arrived back in America, tens of thousands turned out at a time to greet "the Lone Eagle," as the press called him. Offers poured in of financial rewards for speaking tours, product endorsements, and just about anything else to which some promoter could attach Lindbergh's name. He was not wealthy by a long shot, so he had to find some way to earn a living. It was, he said, "essential that I find ways of earning more money that would leave me as free as possible to pursue the development of aviation."[1]

As a way to both earn a living and to further the cause of aviation, he accepted an invitation from the Guggenheim Fund for the Promotion of Aeronautics to tour the country "for the primary purpose of stimulating popular interest in the use of air transport."[2]

Fame, however, brought Lindbergh and his wife Anne unimaginable tragedy. On March 1, 1932, one or possibly two individuals placed a homemade ladder against the side of the Lindbergh home in semi-rural East Amwell, New Jersey, and snatched 20-month-old Charles A. Lindbergh Jr. from his crib, leaving a note demanding a $50,000 ransom. The abduction spurred an intense search for the baby and his kidnappers, with President Hoover ordering the Bureau of Investigation (later renamed the FBI) to support state and local police forces. The kidnapping, involving numerous subsequent ransom notes, shadowy intermediaries working for Lindbergh, the suicides of several suspects, and a possible connection to organized crime, sparked a media frenzy. The original ransom note was even leaked to the press, creating the possibility that some of the later notes were not sent by the actual kidnappers.

Despite Lindbergh's payment of $50,000 in gold certificates to someone purporting to be one of the kidnappers, two months after the abduction, the baby's partially buried body was discovered by a truck driver less than five miles from his home. His head had been crushed. The nation was horrified by what was dubbed "the crime of the century," and Congress quickly passed a law making kidnapping a federal offense (referred to as the "Lindbergh Law"). Police eventually found the killer, German immigrant Bruno Hauptmann, by tracking one of the gold certificates Lindbergh had used to pay the ransom. With more than $10,000 in ransom certificates found at his home, Hauptmann was arrested, tried, and executed in the electric chair. He proclaimed his innocence to the end.

Afraid the baby's grave would become a macabre tourist attraction, Lindbergh had his son's remains cremated and spread the ashes over the Atlantic Ocean from an airplane.[3]

———

Reviewing the histories of the families that produced Charles—the Lindberghs, the Lodges, and the Lands—Scott Berg wrote, "And so this third-generation Lindbergh was born with a deeply private nature and bred according to the principles of self-reliance—nonconformity and the innate understanding that greatness came at the inevitable price of being misunderstood."[4]

In 1906 Charles' father, Charles August Lindbergh, called "C. A.," won the Republican nomination for Minnesota's sixth congressional district over a scandal-ridden incumbent. C. A.'s reputation for honesty, his noted concern for the financial condition of farmers and small business owners, and his attacks on what he called the "favored class" gave him a 3,600-vote margin of victory over his Democratic opponent in the predominantly rural district. He left his lucrative law practice in Little Falls and moved his family to Washington.

In Congress, C. A. won a reputation as an outspoken critic of the big bankers who had organized trusts to gain control over the nation's commerce. In 1912, he supported Theodore Roosevelt's third party campaign to return to the White House. Democrat Woodrow Wilson eventually won the election.

The following year, C. A.'s stature grew among Progressives and money trust conspiracy believers when an article in the *American Magazine* declared, "It was a Swede from Minnesota who first raised in Congress the hue-and-cry of the MONEY TRUST HUNT—'a Swede who dreams,' a fellow member describes him—Charles A. Lindbergh."[5]

C. A. fought with Charles' mother, Evangeline, throughout much of Charles' boyhood. Evangeline often threatened C. A. with divorce, knowing he would cave in to her demands out of fear a divorce would cost him his congressional seat. His mother had a hard time raising C. A.'s two daughters by a previous marriage. Eventually they both moved away.

As a young boy, Charles was shy and withdrawn, making few friends. He was further isolated from his peers in 1909, when Evangeline established a separate residence from her husband. This turned out to be a series of boardinghouses in which Charles was usually the only child in residence. Berg reports, "The boardinghouses constricted his already constrained personality; and at an early age, he became an overly polite silent sufferer."[6]

When World War I broke out in Europe in 1914, C. A. regularly warned against allowing America to be dragged into the conflict. Two years later, C. A. ran for the U.S. Senate. He lost to a candidate who called for preparing for the possibility of war.

In 1916, President Wilson was reelected based largely on his boast that he had kept America out of the war. No sooner was he inaugurated into his second term than the country began moving toward a war footing. In March 1917 a bill authorizing the arming of U.S. merchant ships passed the House by a vote of 403 to 14, with C. A. voting in the minority. As the federal government successfully whipped up war fever in the country, there were only a few so-called "isolationists" who spoke out for peace. The following month a new Congress granted Wilson's call for a declaration of war against Germany. America thus entered "the war to end all wars," as its supporters called it.

In 1918, Charles served as his father's driver during C. A.'s campaign for governor of Minnesota. Because of C. A.'s earlier opposition to U.S. intervention in the war, and the fact that he was supported by the Farmers Nonpartisan League, which called for government ownership of certain productive enterprises such as mills, plants, and grain elevators, crowds of townspeople regularly pelted him with eggs and rocks during his campaign speeches. Although his rallies were attended by thousands of well-wishers, local sheriffs usually found enough townspeople to deputize and break up the meetings. Charles likely never forgot the hostile crowds that harassed his father, or the way the press derided him.

That same year, men identifying themselves as federal agents entered the plant of the National Capital Press in Washington and ordered the owner to "destroy all the Lindbergh plates in your plant." They were after the plates for a book C. A. had written titled *Why Is Your Country at War?* They also demanded the destruction of an earlier book written by the senior Lindbergh attacking the Federal Reserve system and big banks, titled *Banking and Currency.* The printer complied, though several hundred copies of *Why is Your Country at War?* had already been shipped to Minnesota. The book was reprinted and issued in 1934, a decade after C. A.'s death from brain cancer, with the title *Your Country at War, and What Happens to You After a War.*[7]

In the first chapter of that book, C. A. wrote, "It is impossible according to the big press to be a true American unless you are pro-British. If you are really for America first, last and all time, and solely for America and for the masses primarily, then you are classed as pro-German by the big press which is supported by the speculators."[8] It was a passage that surely resonated with his son years later, as another world war drew near and Charles found himself subjected to a campaign of vituperation that historians, to this very day, have failed to rectify.

Chapter One

❦

"DON'T WORRY ABOUT LINDBERGH. WE WILL GET THAT FAIR-HAIRED BOY."

O n a chilly March morning in 1934, four Western Union messenger boys trotted up the front steps of four different homes across the United States. Each delivered a telegram similar to the one handed to the woman who answered the door at 15 Baker Street in the small eastern Long Island town of Patchogue, New York:

> Deeply regret to advise you that your son, Lieut. Otto Wienecke, died at 5 A.M. March 9, as a result of an airplane accident at Burton, Ohio, while flying the air mail. No details of accident are available.
> (Col. John) Howard.

Lieutenant Wienecke, flying a Curtiss 0-39 army observation plane, had taken off from the Newark, New Jersey airport with a load of airmail shortly before midnight on Friday, March 9. His destination was to be

Cleveland, Ohio. Investigators later described the weather over his planned route as "not good, but flyable." Wienecke made a brief stop at Kylertown, Pennsylvania, for fuel. The landing damaged his rear skid, which was quickly repaired and he lifted off into the dark night to continue his trip.

Meanwhile, John Hess was awakening and preparing for another day of work on his farm one mile northwest of Burton, Ohio, about halfway between the Pennsylvania state line and the city of Cleveland. He was preparing for the morning chores when he heard the unmistakable sound of an airplane's engine overhead. He thought it sounded like the plane was flying very low, so he grabbed his lantern and ran out of the house just in time to hear the deafening roar of a crash. Blinded by the darkness and falling snow, he headed in the direction of what he presumed to be a downed aircraft. He found Wienecke's Curtis airplane standing straight up in the air on its nose. Peering into the cockpit, Hess could clearly see the pilot was dead. His neck was broken.[1]

The 32-year-old U.S. Army pilot's fatal crash brought the death toll of such airmail related accidents to ten in less than three weeks. Two more would perish in fiery crashes before the Army finally abandoned all airmail flights. *Newsweek* estimated the cost to the army of the airmail crashes at $575,000[2]—roughly $9 million in 2010 dollars.[3]

After the third pilot was killed, and amidst rising public indignation at the pilots' deaths, World War I flying ace Captain Eddie Rickenbacker told reporters it was "legalized murder" to use army pilots to transport the airmail.[4]

The story of why the U.S. Army Air Corps—the predecessor of the U.S. Air Force—came to be delivering the airmail, and the ensuing deaths of a dozen army pilots, is the starting point of a bitter, decade-long rivalry between two public figures who in the early 1930s were the two most famed and popular men in America. They were Franklin D. Roosevelt, President of the United States in the second year of his first term, and Charles A. Lindbergh, world-renowned pilot, aviation expert, and colonel in the U.S. Army Officers' Reserve Corps.

———

The U.S. Air Mail Service began inauspiciously on May 15, 1918, when Lieutenant George L. Boyle, pilot of a single engine Curtiss JN-4H trainer carrying four bags of mail from Washington, D.C. to New York via Philadelphia lost his way trying to follow a railroad line north. He landed in a farmer's field to ask directions and flipped his plane onto its back. Luckily, Boyle walked away uninjured.[5]

Army pilots handled the first airmail deliveries in army planes. Within a few months, however, the Post Office began employing civilian planes and pilots in an effort to expand the service. The first crew of airmail pilots had dangerous jobs—due to bad weather, inferior aircraft, and myriad other causes, thirty-one of the first forty airmail pilots died in crashes.[6] During those first few years, the average airmail pilot had a life expectancy of less than two years.

The pilots themselves showed a unique combination of reckless daring and great resourcefulness. Tales of pilots flying blindly through snowstorms or thick clouds to get their mail delivered on time fills the history of the airmail. Recall that this was a time when pilots flew without the aid of instruments or even lighted landing fields. In one such story, Frank Yeager was flying a load of mail from Omaha, Nebraska, to Cheyenne, Wyoming, when dense fog knocked him off course. Left with little choice other than landing somewhere and waiting for the fog to lift, Yeager instead put his plane down on a prairie and taxied the last thirty miles. Each time he came to a fence line, Yeager turned his craft around, circled back, and picking up speed, hopped the fence.[7]

In 1925, Congress decided airmail service would be handled by private companies. After a bidding process with private operators, the first airmail contracts were awarded that October. Robertson Aircraft Corporation of St. Louis, owned by two wartime pilot brothers, William and Frank Robertson, received the contract to carry the mail between Chicago and St. Louis. Earlier they had promised the job of chief pilot, if they got the contract, to a 23-year–old, six-foot-two inch, 150-pound army pilot with a head of unruly hair named Charles Lindbergh.

Lindbergh, who would not undertake his famed solo flight to Paris for another two years, had spent the last few years "barnstorming" around the mid-west. A term derived from traveling troops of actors who often performed in local barns, airplane barnstormers frequently flew army surplus planes and traveled from town to town attracting crowds to a nearby field with their aerial stunts. They made their living, and supported what was often the first love of their lives—flying—by offering rides to paying customers, painting advertisements on the aircraft, and giving flight instructions to local men who also dreamed of soaring into the sky. Lindbergh's business card at the time explained it all: "We specialize in Fair and Carnival Exhibition Work, Offering Plane Changes in Midair, Wing Walking, Parachute Jumping, Breakaways, Night Fireworks, Smoke Trails, and Deaf Flights." Barnstormers were pushing the envelope on what pilots and airplanes could do in the sky.[8]

The Robertsons gave Lindbergh the good news and put him on the company payroll at $200 per month. Since the actual airmail flights were not scheduled to begin for several months, Lindbergh's first duties were to map out the flight plan for the run, arrange emergency landing sites along the 285-mile route, and hire two more pilots. Actually, the title of chief pilot was a bit overblown, considering that the Robertsons' airmail operation consisted of three pilots. "Slim," as Lindbergh was called by his friends, was thrilled to leave behind the barnstorming that had grown a bit wearisome and focus on something significant.

Lindbergh plunged into the potentially lifesaving task of finding fields—not airfields, but any fields where one of his company's airmail planes could safely land in an emergency. He needed nine of them spaced a little over thirty miles apart. He found places to store extra supplies of fuel, and nearby residents who would agree to lend a hand to a downed airmail pilot.

Robertson bought five Army surplus planes that wartime pilots called "flaming coffins," not without good reason. Their fabric wings were painted silver and their plywood fuselages painted maroon with "U.S. Air Mail" emblazoned in white letters.

When not working at developing the route and plans for carrying the mail, Lindbergh occupied himself flying Army airplanes. On March 14,

1925, he had graduated first in his class from the Army's Advanced Flying School at San Antonio's Kelly Field. The airfield was named in honor of Lieutenant George E. M. Kelly, who crashed while attempting to land an aircraft at Fort Sam Houston on May 1, 1911. Lindbergh was commissioned a second lieutenant in the Air Service Reserve Corps. He had accepted the job offer from the Robertsons after learning that few if any Army squadrons needed pilots, and therefore there was little chance of immediate active duty. After settling in near the Lambert Field base of the Robertson airmail operation, Lindbergh joined the 110th Observation Squadron of the Thirty-fifth Division Air Service of the Missouri National Guard. Commissioned a first lieutenant, Lindbergh gave lectures on the latest information on navigation, aerodynamics, and the proper care and use of parachutes, as well as flying the powerful Army planes almost every Sunday. The squadron comprised wartime Army pilots who had returned to civilian life.

Robertson Aircraft commenced its airmail service on April 15, 1926. Lindbergh piloted one of the company's planes from Lambert Field to Springfield, where he picked up fifteen thousand letters.

Civil aviation expanded rapidly over the next several years. This was partly due to the demand created by airmail service, including government stipulations in the McNary-Watres Act of 1930 that encouraged private mail carriers to buy newer, larger, and safer aircraft that could carry passengers as well as the mail. Single pilot planes with mailbags stuffed in every little space gave way to larger planes with multiple engines and passenger cabins.[9]

One could say this fledgling industry, for a time, became a casualty of the Hoover Derangement Syndrome that ran amok in Congress after Franklin Roosevelt defeated Herbert Hoover in the 1932 presidential election. Alleging widespread malfeasance by the Hoover administration, Democrats scoured government records for evidence, especially focusing on contracts issued by the War Department. Soon the nation's headlines were ablaze with lurid stories, some true some not, of scheming business executives making fortunes from contracts for Army supplies and services. Hardly a day went by without some senator or congressman pronouncing that he was on the verge of uncovering great skullduggery.

Cynical Washington watchers, however, attributed the furor to simple politicking in the run up to the 1934 mid-term elections.

Among the members of Congress who seemed determined to find some dirty linen on the Hoover administration was Democratic senator Hugo Black of Alabama, a former active member of the Ku Klux Klan notorious for defending a Klansman who had shot and killed a Catholic priest in 1921.[10] With a populist, anti-business streak, Senator Black had made a successful political career in Alabama by regularly attacking the twin evil bogeymen of Republicans and fat-cat business executives.[11]

In 1933, when newsman Fulton Lewis Jr. (who would later became one of America's most popular political commentators) compiled a long report alleging fraud, corruption, and collusion between the Post Office Department and the airlines in awarding airmail contracts, he took his findings to Black. If proven, such corruption would likely implicate Hoover who, before becoming president, had overseen the awarding of the initial airmail contracts when he was commerce secretary for President Calvin Coolidge. After reading Lewis's report, Senator Black, who was already leading an investigation into ocean mail, immediately refocused on airmail.[12] Organizing congressional committee hearings, the publicity-hungry Black sent word to reporters, "Tell the boys in the press to come in. The show is about to begin."[13]

Many of the allegations centered on former Postmaster General Walter Folger Brown, who had presided over the inception of the civil aviation industry. His central policy had been to force airmail contractors to fly passengers as well as mail, with the ultimate goal of developing a full-fledged passenger carrying air transportation system.[14] To this end, Brown had forced financially strapped companies out of the system or to merge to form more stable airlines. His heavy-handed methods had earned him many detractors within the aviation industry, particularly among poorly performing airlines, but in the end, he was responsible for creating a viable aviation industry and for the great airlines that survived—TWA, United, and American, as well as the creation of Eastern.

The poorly supported charges against Brown reflected political score-settling more than anything else. As well-known aviation historian and Smithsonian curator F. Robert van der Linden observes, "Every airmail contract with the exception of CAM-33 and CAM-34 and two irrelevant lines was awarded not by Brown but by his predecessor, and all of the contracts had been awarded through competitive bidding to the lowest responsible bidder and approved by an unsympathetic comptroller general."[15]

But Senator Black demagogued the issue, blaming the supposed corruption on an evil cabal of rich and powerful conspirators. Taking his message to the radio airwaves, Black charged in one grand speech, "The control of aviation had been ruthlessly taken away from men who could fly and bestowed upon bankers, brokers, promoters and politicians, sitting in their inner offices, allotting among themselves the taxpayers monies. Again fortunes were made overnight."[16] On January 26, 1934, at a lunch with President Roosevelt at the White House, Black updated the president on his investigation of what the press was now calling the "Air Mail Scandal." Black told Roosevelt, "The whole system of airmail contracts emanating from the 1930 split was fraudulent and completely illegal."[17]

At this point numerous administration officials, many of them with ties to smaller airlines who had failed to win airmail contracts, began lobbying Roosevelt's postmaster general, James Farley, to recommend to the president that he cancel the contracts.[18] Farley, who had repeatedly denounced alleged corruption in the contracts, made that suggestion to Roosevelt on February 9. Crucially, he also recommended allowing the current carriers to continue delivering the mail until June 1, giving the Post Office time to call for new bids. Attorney General Cummings agreed with him, but Roosevelt, who wanted the contracts cancelled immediately, overruled them.[19]

If Farley really believed the contracts were fraudulent, then his proposal was a prudent approach. But as one Roosevelt biographer noted, "Prudence … was outweighed in this instance by other considerations. Here was a golden opportunity for highly dramatic action whereby honesty in government was championed" and "the Hoover administration further discredited."[20]

Searching for an immediate replacement for the private airmail deliverers, the administration asked General Benjamin D. Foulois, chief of the Army Air Corps, if the Air Corps could fill the gap. Fatefully, Foulois viewed the Air Corps' *unsuitability* for this task as an advantage. The Air Corps, Foulois argued, was "in sad shape in the way of cargo equipment and none of our pilots had flown regular schedules on instruments or at night. However, we might use our bombers and observation ships and our pilots would get some badly needed training, which had been curtailed because of the shortage of funds to buy gasoline, equipment, and spare parts. The problems we might have [flying the mail] would focus national attention on the Air Corps and maybe we would then get the funds we needed for expansion."[21] General Foulois did not consider the possibility that allowing his pilots to fly the mail would entail a high cost in human life.

Having secured Foulois' commitment, Roosevelt announced he had canceled the airmail contracts and had issued an executive order directing the Army to carry the airmail. He directed the postmaster general, the secretary of war, and the secretary of commerce to work together to ensure uninterrupted airmail service. Roosevelt then told reporters it was his understanding that the companies whose contracts were annulled could not bid for five years on any government contract.[22]

Writing decades later, Dr. James P. Tate, a retired lieutenant colonel of the U.S. Air Force, evaluated the condition of the Army pilots and planes called on for this service. "The task required skills and equipment the Air Corps did not have," he wrote. "Army pilots had little experience in cross-country flying and only a few had done any actual weather flying. Except for a handful of test models, Army planes were not equipped for blind flying [i.e. flying in bad weather or at night]."[23] Likewise, Major Clifford A. Tinker, commander of the Seventeenth Pursuit Group, later reflected, "When the Army took over the mail flying there was no time to equip planes with instruments to meet fixed-route flying...no time to train the men for the work."[24]

There were numerous protests against Roosevelt's decision. Former postmaster general Brown denied there had been any collusion or other wrongdoing in issuing airmail contracts.[25] Transcontinental and Western Air also formally protested the cancellations.[26]

Airline holding companies, whose stock price commonly fell by 50 percent on Roosevelt's announcement, had particular cause for concern. When a rumor reached the Senate Banking and Currency Committee that there had been large sell orders of aviation stock in the days preceding the cancellation announcement, the committee requested the New York Stock Exchange to provide a list of those traders. High on the list were well-known Wall Street investments houses, including J. P. Morgan, Brandenburg, and Jacobson. Although none were found, many suspected that an administration insider had tipped the big houses off to what was coming. This left, as the *Chicago Daily Tribune* wrote, the small investor—the forgotten man—"alone to stand the loss. The 'new dealers' had forgotten to tell him what was going to happen."[27]

Two days after the airmail contracts' cancellation was announced, a thunderous protest was leveled from a surprising source—a pioneer of the airmail service. It came from, as Arthur Schlesinger described him, "the single American personality who might match Franklin Roosevelt in national popularity. This was the Lone Eagle, Colonel Charles A. Lindbergh, the one authentic American hero of the 1920's, still a young man of thirty-two."[28]

After completing his national tour that followed his renowned trans-Atlantic flight, Lindbergh had joined Transcontinental Air Transport (later to become part of TWA) as chair of its technical committee. He received an annual salary of $10,000 and a signing bonus of some 25,000 shares valued at $10 per share. (Lindbergh's name was so valuable that the company's stock price jumped 50 percent when the deal was announced.) He eventually gave the company permission to call itself "The Lindbergh Line." He also took a similar post with Pan American Airways for the same salary and a stock option. Lindbergh provided the same services to both airlines: technical consulting on aircraft manufacturing and engines, route selections, and flight-testing. Lindbergh had nothing to do with the management of either company, or with their airmail business. Therefore, it came as a surprise to some when he thrust himself into the center of the controversy.

The previous month Lindbergh had sent the Black Committee "a complete record of his financial transactions in aviation."[29] Senator Black had declined to call Lindbergh as a witness in his investigation of the airmail contracts, quite possibly because it was obvious he had nothing to do with the airline's airmail business, as he was neither a manager nor a director of the company, and his concerns were elsewhere.

On Saturday, the day after Roosevelt's announcement, Lindbergh and his wife Anne began preparing notes for a telegram to the president. Lindbergh was incensed that while no one had been found guilty of committing a crime, all the companies with airmail contracts and their thousands of employees were to be punished.

On Sunday, he worked up a final draft with his legal advisor, Colonel Henry Breckinridge, one time assistant secretary of war in the Wilson administration. According to Lindbergh, he did not discuss sending the telegram with anyone at the company until it was written and ready to mail.[30] On Sunday evening he and Breckinridge sent the telegram to the White House, and soon after released it to the press so it would make the Monday morning editions of the newspapers. The telegram read:

> Your action of yesterday affects fundamentally the industry to which I have devoted the last twelve years of my life. Therefore, I respectfully present to you the following considerations. The personal and business lives of American citizens have been built up around the right to just trial before conviction. Your order of cancellation of all air mail contracts condemns the largest portion of our commercial aviation without just trial. The officers of a number of the organizations affected have not been given the opportunity of a hearing and improper acts by many companies affected have not been established. No one can rightfully object to drastic action being taken provided the guilt implied is first established but it is the right of any American individual or organization to receive fair trial. Your present action does not discriminate

between innocence and guilt and places no premium on honest business. Americans have spent their lives in building in
this country the finest commercial air lines in the world. The
United States today is far in the lead in almost every branch
of commercial aviation. In America, we have commercial
aircraft, engines, equipment and air lines superior to those
of any other country. The greatest part of this progress has
been brought about through the air mail. Certainly most
individuals in the industry believe that this development has
been carried on in cooperation with existing government and
according to law, if this is not the case it seems the right of
the industry and in keeping with American tradition that
facts to the contrary be definitely established. Unless these
facts leave no alternative, the condemnation of commercial
aviation by cancellation of all air mail contracts and the use
of the army on commercial air lines will unnecessarily and
greatly damage all American aviation.

Charles A. Lindbergh[31]

When the telegram arrived at the White House Monday morning, the
president was in bed, meeting with Budget Director Lewis Douglas.
Roosevelt read the message and listened to his press secretary, Stephen
Early, describe how Lindbergh had already released it to the press.
Roosevelt told Early to tell the press it was in poor taste to release the
telegram before the president had a chance to read it. He also told Early
to acknowledge receipt of the telegram with his own signature, not the
president's. He then told Early, "Don't worry about Lindbergh. We will
get that fair-haired boy." When Douglas suggested the airlines were
entitled to an impartial hearing, Roosevelt responded that the evidence
against them was so overwhelming that such a hearing was a waste of
time.[32]

Writing to his father about the incident, which he called "an act
arbitrarily taken without thought or evidence," Douglas said Roosevelt's
threat to "get" Lindbergh made him "shudder—the brutal unscrupulous-
ness of it."[33]

On the morning of Monday, February 12, the *New York Times* carried the headline, "Action on Air Mail Unfair, Lindbergh Tells President."[34] Also that day, President Roosevelt's press secretary released his response to Lindbergh with, as instructed, his signature affixed, not that of the president:

> Except when the senders of telegrams or other communications act primarily for publicity purposes, the common practice is to allow the President, when he is addressed by them, the courtesy of receiving and reading their communications before they are read by others than the person addressed.
>
> In this instance the giving out of a telegram, which bears the name of Colonel Charles A. Lindbergh, by his attorney and legal advisor, Colonel Henry Breckenridge, would indicate the message obviously was sent for publicity purposes—at least it was published before it was received by the President.
>
> The President's Executive Order under date of February 9th was issued after the Postmaster General advised the President that "all domestic air mail contracts for carrying the mails have been annulled." The Postmaster General annulled these contracts. Colonel Lindbergh's telegram is in error in that it states the President ordered the cancellation of all air mail contracts.
>
> Colonel Lindbergh's telegram will be referred to the Postmaster General and to the Secretary of Commerce for consideration and action.
>
> Stephen Early[35]

Before Lindbergh sounded off, it appeared the public would side with the president in the cancellation dispute. After all, the story fit the prevailing narrative that greedy, corrupt Republicans had gotten the country into the mess it was in. However, Lindbergh was another story. He was the great American hero who had flown the Atlantic alone and was the subject of tremendous public sympathy stemming from his baby's recent kidnapping and murder. In the view of Lindbergh biographer Leonard Mosley, "The

entry of the popular hero into the arena immediately changed the controversy from a quarrel between the aviation companies and the Administration into a duel between Lindbergh and Roosevelt."[36]

Over the next week, the press was filled with charges and counter-
charges from both sides. Progressive Nebraska Republican senator
George W. Norris, who had openly supported Roosevelt's election and
would soon change parties, sneered, "Now Colonel Lindbergh is earning
his $250,000."[37]

Two congressmen almost came to blows when New York Republican
Hamilton Fish attempted to have Lindbergh's telegram entered into the
congressional record. This was not an unusual request, and the telegram
was already approved for entering in the Senate portion of the record.
But Democratic majority leader Joseph W. Byrnes refused Fish's request,
whereupon Fish brought the business of the House to a halt by voting
"no" on a series of measures that required unanimous consent. Fish and
Byrnes got into a screaming match that brought both men "to the verge
of a personal encounter." The House was forced to adjourn, and the
hard-hitting Fish issued a statement in which he called Lindbergh the
"greatest authority in the world on aviation." He said the colonel merely
wanted the airlines to be given a hearing before their contracts were
cancelled. He called Roosevelt's actions "autocratic and dictatorial."[38]

The following day Fish told reporters he had learned the Lindbergh
telegram had been given to a Western Union messenger at 8:15 Sunday
evening, and "should have reached the White House not later than 9:30
that same evening." He then pointed out that the "air-mail contractors
first learned of the cancellation of their contracts through the press." No
one from the administration or the Post Office Department made an
attempt to communicate directly with the airlines about their contracts
being cancelled.[39]

Hoping to smear Lindbergh's creditability among the cash-strapped
citizenry, administration supporters made much of the $250,000 pay-
ment he had received when he joined Transcontinental. In response,
Colonel Breckenridge released a statement to the press explaining the
$250,000 was not, as some had charged, "a gift," but was a signing
bonus. The arrangement was that Lindbergh would be given a check for

that amount from the airline; he would endorse the check and return it to purchase 25,000 shares of the company's stock. That was just what transpired. The attacks on Lindbergh's money temporarily abated when it was revealed he had voluntarily reduced his $10,000 annual salary by $3,000–$4,000 when the airline reduced pilot salaries.[40]

Another famous American aviator soon expressed his misgivings about the cancellation of the airmail contracts. Responding to questions from reporters, World War I flying ace Captain Eddie Rickenbacker, now associated with Eastern Air Transport, said he was concerned about replacing seasoned airline pilots with flyers who lacked the proper training for commercial flying. "What is going to happen to those young Army pilots on a [foggy] day like this?" he asked. "Either they are going to pile up ships all the way across the continent, or they are not going to be able to fly the mail on schedule."[41]

On the same day he received the Lindbergh telegram, President Roosevelt received one from another famous flyer, this one not associated with any commercial airline. Naval Reserve commander Frank M. Hawks was a world famous pilot who held numerous speed records. "With due respect to you as my Commander-in-Chief," Hawks's message began, "I believe it would be a terrible injustice to the existing airline organizations and a tremendous handicap to the development of the airmail system should your executive order canceling air-mail contracts become effective without granting operators a hearing. The United States has developed the finest air transport system in the world through the experience and pioneering of the present operators. To wreck an entire industry with an action so drastic as yours would be a national calamity."[42]

The president also received a telegram from Henry A. W. Wood, one of the original founders of the Aero Club some thirty years earlier. He urged Roosevelt, "I respectfully point out that no little part of the public's confidence in you comes of their belief that you are just and will unhesitatingly and promptly correct your errors. I suggest that you put the airmail carriers at once upon their trial before a properly constituted board and meanwhile that you suspend your order of cancellation."[43]

Presidential secretary Stephen Early claimed telegrams to the White House on the cancellations were about evenly divided.[44] It was becoming clear, however, that many people did not take to Early's charge that Lindbergh was a publicity hound. In fact, Lindbergh was well-known for trying his best to avoid a press corps that constantly hounded *him*. One typical correspondent called Early an "inconspicuous subordinate" who threw "mud at one whose modesty is universally recognized and for whom mere publicity has no charms." Early should have known "better than to expect success from a slimy innuendo about Colonel Lindbergh."[45]

Another correspondent to the White House, one with a strong talent for sarcasm, was Elmdorf Carr of New York City. Referring to Early's reply to Lindbergh as "an example of the insolence of office," he wrote,

> I had to read several columns down (in a news story) to find out who under the suffering heavens Stephen T. Early might be. Now I know, and can die happy. When the great silence settles over our generation, and the bones of the heroes of our times are dust, Lindbergh will be forgotten, along with Byrd and Scott and the Wrights and Peary and other seekers after publicity safely acquired, but the name Stephen T. Early will ring down the ages as an inspiration to our children's children unto the tenth generation—Stephen T. Early, the man who, from the White House roof's protection, told Lindbergh where to get off. Truly our descendants will sigh enviously; there were giants in those days.[46]

Then into the fray stepped America's leading humorist and commentator, and, according to *Time* magazine, America's number one airline passenger, Will Rogers. Rogers quipped, "What does it matter who carries the mail? There hasn't been an important letter written in years."[47] On a more serious note, Rogers wrote in the *New York Times* that what happened was "like finding a crooked railroad president, then stopping all the trains." He spelled out his primary concern: "You are going to lose some fine boys in these army flyers who are marvelously trained in their line but not in night cross-country flying, in rain and snow. I trust an airline, for I know that that pilot has flown that course hundreds of times. He knows it in the dark. Neither could the mail pilots do the army flyer's stunts and his close-formation flying."[48]

Rogers later attempted to act as a peacemaker between Roosevelt and Lindbergh. After meeting individually with the president, Farley, Brown, Lindbergh, and "dozens of air pilots, commercial and military," he told reporters,

> The President wanted to get the whole thing straightened out soon as he could, and yesterday morning I had a little chat with Colonel Lindbergh about it. Mr. Farley thought it was fraud and collusion, and Mr. Brown...said, "they have no case," and that the bill allowed him to do the things he did do.
>
> It would be a wonderful thing if the President and Colonel Lindbergh would get together, because Lindbergh is so well informed in such matters. The thing I was getting at was that people shouldn't get the idea that Colonel Lindbergh was acting as a shield for the company he represents and that he'd been paid for that.
>
> I talked with Colonel Lindbergh about ten minutes and I could tell he wouldn't do a thing like that. His knowledge of aviation and his value as a technical adviser was worth every nickel that he got.[49]

As criticism of Roosevelt's decision grew, the *Times* reported, "None of the criticisms or arguments thus far made against the cancellation of the airmail contracts have really disturbed the President."[50] Roosevelt continued to ignore pleas that he reverse his rush to judgment and allow the country's legal process to determine who, if anyone, was guilty of committing a crime.

————

Even before the first Air Corps airmail flights left the ground on February 20, there were disturbing indications that the Corps was ill-prepared for its new task. In a bit of irony, though perhaps unintended, the *New*

York Times of Friday, February 18, carried an article titled "Army Pilots as Postmen." Accompanying the piece were two photographs that starkly revealed the difference between a commercial airline and the Air Corps. The former was depicted by the new Transoceanic four-engine flying boat owned by Pan American Airways. With a range of 1,200 miles, it was equipped to carry thirty-two passengers, a crew of five, and 1,000 pounds of cargo. Below it was a photo of two Air Corps pilots practicing loading airmail bags in the rear seat of an open cockpit bi-plane not unlike the planes the Army had used to fly the mail in 1918.[51]

More important, two days earlier the first three pilots designated for the airmail service died in crashes. Two of them, 24-year-old Second Lieutenant Jean D. Grenier and Second Lieutenant Edwin D. White, 23, perished when their iced up Curtiss A-12 pursuit plane crashed and burned in a sheep pasture deep in the Utah mountains while exploring the route they were to fly. The other pilot, First Lieutenant James Y. Eastham, 22, was flying a two-engine Y1B-7 bomber in snow and fog when, according to witnesses, the plane suddenly nosed down, crashed, and burst into flames a mile short of the Jerome, Idaho airport. Four days later, on Sunday, Lieutenant H. L. Dietz was forced to make an emergency landing on a farm field in Dover, New Jersey, after going off course and running out of fuel. The same day, Lieutenant J. H. Gibson had to parachute from his airplane when he also ran out of gas after becoming lost.[52]

Late on February 18, in what many saw as a slap at the Roosevelt administration, Captain Eddie Rickenbacker, vice president of Eastern Air, and Jack Frye, vice president of TWA, shared piloting duties on a record-breaking cross-country flight that was billed as carrying the "last load of contract airmail." With a crowd of fifteen thousand looking on, the two men, along with a passenger list of mostly reporters, took off from Glendale, California, in TWA's newest passenger liner, the Douglas DC-1. Thirteen hours and four minutes later, they landed in a snowstorm at Newark airport. With three refueling stops across the country, they broke the previous record by five hours and nine minutes.

In his autobiography, Rickenbacker relates an incident that took place shortly before the flight. NBC headquarters in New York asked him to give a fifteen-minute radio talk before he took off. The network would broadcast it nationwide, probably assuming the famous war ace would discuss his impending flight.

But Rickenbacker was angry with Roosevelt on two fronts. One was the cancellation of the airmail contracts. The other was more personal. Unlike Lindbergh, Rickenbacker had voted for Roosevelt in the 1932 election. He believed the platform on which Roosevelt ran was "sound and conservative, was what the country needed." However, once in office, "he [had] made a complete 180-degree turn and taken off in the other direction toward liberalism and socialism."[53]

Intending to "blister" the radio airwaves with his attack, the World War I ace of aces enlisted the help of two newspaper editorial writers, one from the *Los Angeles Times*, the other from the *Los Angeles Examiner*, to help write his speech. After working on it for most of two days, the finished speech was as "vicious as I wanted it to be." Then, shortly before he was to broadcast it, Rickenbacker received a phone call from a New York NBC executive, William B. Miller, who told him that orders had come from Washington to cut him off the air if he said anything controversial. Rickenbacker thanked a somewhat embarrassed Miller, saying, "I'll keep it reasonable."

Rickenbacker writes that he tore up the original speech in a fit of anger, but that the speech he gave "went off fairly well. I could not help but inject one or two controversial remarks, but they were temperate under the circumstances." Nonetheless, when he arrived in Newark, where he was to give a post-flight radio address, Miller told him NBC was ordered to cancel the speech. "My remarks the night before, mild as they had been in comparison to what I had really wanted to say had proved to be too controversial for Washington."[54]

Who made the calls to NBC from Washington to muzzle the war hero? Unfortunately, no one ever stepped forward and admitted silencing Rickenbacker.

As Roosevelt's order to displace private airmail carriers was fulfilled, everything worked against the Air Corps. Its pilots were not trained for this kind of duty, its planes were not designed to carry the mail, and finally, the weather was among the worst recorded for a February. Once the Air Corps started flying the mail, crash landings became an almost daily occurrence. On February 22, two pilots died in crashes, one in Texas, the other in Ohio. The following day a forced landing in the Atlantic resulted in a pilot drowning. By March 9, the total fatalities reached ten, not counting numerous pilots injured in forced landings, and not counting the lost aircraft. The entire episode was turning into a colossal government blunder before the eyes of the whole nation.

Air Force general Henry "Hap" Arnold, who had been in charge of the western zone for the airmail operation, wrote in his memoirs, "Within two weeks we were forced to realize that although the 'will to do' might get the job done, the price of our doing it was equal to the sacrifice of a wartime combat operation. Courage alone could not substitute for years of cross-country experience; for properly equipped airplanes; and for suitable blind flying instruments, such as the regular air-line mail pilots were using."[55]

Distressed over the loss of these young lives, and holding himself partially responsible because he had been first to use the Army to fly the mail in 1918, Captain Benjamin Lipsner called the president and, in his words, "I begged him to stop those airmail deaths."[56]

Roosevelt ignored increasing pressure from members of Congress, the press, and the public to stop the Army airmail flights. Administration supporters deflected criticism by lashing out at Lindbergh, as if his telegram had caused the deaths. Minnesota congressman Francis H. Shoemaker remarked about Lindbergh, "I don't know why this whipper-snapper of a kid should take a bean shooter and aggravate the President."[57]

Day after day, newspapers carried headlines featuring Air Corps crashes and the deaths of young flyers, eventually amounting to twelve. At first, the public's anger was directed at the Air Corps. Then people began to realize that perhaps had the Army flyers been given the money and the planes they had requested over the years, they might have been better equipped for this job. If it was not the fault of the soldiers and the aviators, then who was at fault? Public condemnation turned toward the president and his administration. Roosevelt himself ran for cover, allowing Postmaster General Farley to take the blame. Typical of the treatment

Farley received was a cartoon showing him being chased by twelve skel-
etons representing dead Air Corps pilots.

Looking back on this period, a bitter Farley later wrote, "When I was
called a murderer, I began to look around frantically for help. I looked
to the White House. No help came. I was hurt that the President had not
seen fit to divert the wrath."[58]

The rotund and usually jovial Farley was a good team player and
longtime Roosevelt loyalist, so he took the hits for his president as he was
roundly condemned for making a decision he had not entirely supported—
Farley, recall, had wanted to cancel the contracts only after new commercial contracts were awarded. "Later, I realized it was part of my job to
take as many blows for him as I could," he said. "Nonetheless, a kind
word would have been a great help when the lashes were falling."[59]

Administration supporters continued to unload on Lindbergh. It was
a clear case of blame the messenger and ignore his message—a message
that was quickly proven correct by the Army airmail crashes. He was
accused of being a paid mouthpiece for the aviation industry, though the
charges rang hollow with a public that still viewed him as both a shy hero
and one of the world's leading aviation experts.

Several national publications attacked Lindbergh and sided with the
president, especially outlets with a liberal or anti-business slant. Shortly
after Roosevelt cancelled the contracts, the *New Republic* praised the
president's "prompt and decisive" actions, while denouncing Lindbergh
and Will Rogers as "allies, paid and unpaid" of the "big airline interests."[60] But a few weeks later, following the deaths of the first six Army
airmail pilots, the magazine conceded "it would have been wiser" if the
Army were given more time to prepare for the airmail duty. It went on
to advocate that the Post Office "own and operate the entire airmail
system of the United States." Then we could be sure it ran on a "cost
basis."[61] Three weeks later the magazine came directly to the point, suggesting "the government should own and operate all aerial services, of
every sort, in the United States." Presumably, this included passenger
airline service.[62]

The *Nation* thought it was "refreshing" that the country now had an
administration that "errs in the direction of too little instead of too much

tenderness toward business." Evidently not a proponent of airmail in general, the magazine said, "It is a question whether any but a few long-distance routes should be continued."[63] While not directly questioning the reason for Lindbergh's protest of the cancellations, the *Nation* did its utmost to remind readers that Lindbergh received $250,000 in stock of Transcontinental in 1928 as inducement to head its technical committee. It suggested people might recall this and "come to unflattering conclusions" about Lindbergh's motivation in opposing the cancellations, which included TWA's contract.[64]

A former naval officer even called for Lindbergh to face Army disciplinary action, though this was quickly turned down by the War Department. An official pointed out that although Lindbergh held a commission in the Army Air Corps Reserve, he sent the telegram to the White House as a civilian, and was subject to Army discipline only when on active duty.[65]

Some people were surprised when Lindbergh was attacked by what many thought should have been a friendly quarter, retired Air Corps general William "Billy" Mitchell, the maverick flyer. Lindbergh was, after all, an officer in the Air Corps Reserves and had long advocated increased funding for the Corps. However, Mitchell had his own agenda.

Mitchell retired from the Army Air Corps in 1926 rather than face the results of a well-publicized court martial for insubordination. A strong voice for an independent Air Force, Mitchell reasoned that if the Air Corps were paid for flying the mail, it could develop and build better airplanes. His "overriding concern was to unify all aviation, both civil and military, into a Department of the Air, under his control."[66] He was probably still hoping to accomplish his goal, including a presidential appointment, when he arrived in Washington on March 13, 1934. Summoned before a Senate committee over the airmail fiasco, Roosevelt invited Mitchell to have lunch at the White House before giving his testimony.[67]

It's hard to imagine Mitchell wasn't strongly influenced by Roosevelt in developing his vitriolic testimony, in which he lashed out at the airline executives as "aviation profiteers." But Mitchell aimed his harshest condemnations at Lindbergh, denouncing his fellow pilot as a "front man of the Air Trust" whose "motive is principally profit."[68]

As the attacks on Lindbergh escalated, the campaign against him became so "shocking" that liberal columnist Walter Lippmann condemned "overzealous partisans of the Administration" who attempted to discredit the colonel by investigating "his earnings, to make out that he was a vulgar profiteer who was disqualified and had no right to be heard."[69]

But as Lindbergh absorbed hit after hit, Roosevelt was also still under fire for the aircraft crashes and flyer deaths. Finally, he ordered Army chief of staff General Douglas MacArthur and Army Air Corps chief General Benjamin Foulois to the White House on the morning of Saturday, March 10, 1934, to discuss the situation.

The two generals drove in silence to the White House. MacArthur, who had faced the president's wrath over budget cuts the previous year, probably knew what to expect. Foulois, on the other hand, had never met Roosevelt and felt like a "condemned man must have when he is being taken for that last walk." Stephen Early escorted the pair to the president's second floor bedroom, where they found a scowling Roosevelt propped up in the famous Lincoln bed "looking like a high potentate ready to view the prisoners who had committed crimes against his kingdom."

MacArthur quickly introduced Foulois. "Without a word of greeting the voice everyone had come to know so well boomed, 'General, when are these airmail killings going to stop?'"

Foulois was thrown off balance by the question and the accusatory tone. Without thinking about his response, and realizing he was speaking to someone who knew nothing about the dangers of flying, the general responded, "Only when airplanes stop flying, Mr. President."

MacArthur, who remained stoically silent, and Foulois were subjected to a "tongue-lashing" for the next ten minutes. As Foulois later related,

> There was no doubt that what bothered Roosevelt the most was the severe criticism his administration was getting over the contract cancellation. He did not seem genuinely con-

cerned or even interested in the difficulties the Air Corps was having. It was the bitter editorials, the anti-administration slant of the news stories about the three accidents [the day before, three more pilots died in crashes] and the quotes from Capitol Hill opponents that had made him angry. The fact that three brave men had just died trying to do his bidding in the wrong equipment and under the worst possible weather conditions did not seem to concern him. That was my fault he said.[70]

Roosevelt brandished a piece of paper, which he told the two generals was a letter to their boss, Secretary of War George Dern, directing him to stop all Air Corps deaths immediately. The following day Foulois ordered a ten-day hiatus for all airmail flights. Lindbergh was about to win his first confrontation with Roosevelt—and the president would never forget it.

Chapter Two

✑

ROOSEVELT'S REVERSAL

The Roosevelt administration became desperate to extricate itself from the high-profile controversy over the cancelled airmail contracts. As historian Arthur Schlesinger Jr. wrote, "The national shock suddenly gave pent-up dissatisfaction with the New Deal a seemingly legitimate outlet."[1] Time magazine said Americans were asking "if President Roosevelt was not wrong on his airmail policy. Newspaper editors wailed loudly that the toll…was too high a price to pay for 'purging' commercial aviation of some wrongdoing that was not yet satisfactorily proved."[2]

The public was not only upset over the dead pilots and destroyed aircraft, but over the greatly reduced airmail service. By this time Americans had grown used to fast, efficient airmail, but the airplanes owned by the Air Corps were substantially smaller than the large commercial airliners and had less capacity. "It often took six or more Army flights to equal the normal load of one air liner. Service became so uncertain that many business firms, in violation of postal standards, began wrapping bundles of letters as parcels to be shipped by air express aboard commercial flights."[3]

General Foulois ordered a ten-day pause in airmail flights to examine the aircraft used to fly the mail and to check their instruments. The suspension also gave him time to meet with Post Office officials and decide on a reduced flight schedule. The air chief ordered two-way radios installed and tested in all aircraft, and he tapped experienced pilots to replace those who had been flying for less than two years.

For more than a week, the men of the Army Air Corps went about their business without having to endure near daily crashes. In nineteen days of flying the mail, they had suffered too many fatalities. The Air Corps was a small community, and it is likely that almost every member knew at least one flier who had perished carrying the mail.

The president, who remained publicly silent on the issue, found some solace from his supporters. One was close friend and adviser Felix Frankfurter, a future associate justice of the U.S. Supreme Court, who told Roosevelt, "The way in which you cancelled those air mail contracts must again have greatly heartened our people in proving to them that the government can act with courage and with concern solely for the public interest."[4] He later wrote the president from England, "The American papers have come, with the full details regarding airmail contract cancellation. I am glad to see Lindbergh's telegram dealt with, as it deserves. He is plainly the dupe of others."[5]

Air Corps operations were set to recommence on March 19, 1934, with a greatly reduced schedule depending on weather conditions. Two days before the flights were to restart, Lieutenant H. C. Richardson, a commercial pilot who had been called to active duty to fly the mail, died when his plane crashed near Cheyenne, Wyoming, while on a training flight. The last pilot to perish in this episode was Lieutenant Thurman A. Wood, whose plane went down on a farm in Iowa on the night of March 30.[6]

Public outrage spiked again with the latest casualties. Even some administration supporters began criticizing Roosevelt's decision to cancel the airmail contracts. In his biography of FDR, Pulitzer Prize winner Ted

Morgan recounts the following incident: "One of FDR's correspondents, W. R. Hutchinson, said he was lunching in a New York City downtown club with a prominent jurist, a staunch Democrat, who said, 'The President's actions in declaring air mail carriers guilty of misdoings without giving them the privilege of a hearing upsets the fundamentals of jurisprudence and smacks of Hitlerism; and the government, in hiding behind its prerogative of refusing permission to be sued, has placed itself in the position of being afraid to allow a just tribunal to decide.'"[7] The jurist was referring to a court's rejection of an airline suit against the cancellations on the grounds that the court had no jurisdiction. The court found the government could not be sued without giving its permission, and it was not about to do so.

Lost in all the furor over the crashes was any discussion of whether there had been wrongdoing by former postmaster general Walter Brown in doling out the airmail routes. The discussion turned to the impulsiveness of the president and Farley in canceling the contracts without having a practical contingency plan for delivering the airmail. The administration's response was to go to the House Post Office and Post Roads Committee and ask for a bill giving the postmaster general the authority to award temporary contracts without advertising for bids.

As public opinion turned against Roosevelt, the administration needed a scapegoat. The president himself pointed the finger at the Army General Staff. In a letter to the chairmen of both the House and Senate Post Office committees requesting immediate action on new legislation for awarding airmail contracts, Roosevelt mentioned that he had given the job to the Air Corps on a temporary basis because a member of the General Staff had given his assurance that the Army could do the job.

This claim aroused the interest of the highly respected former senator Hiram Bingham. At the time Bingham, who had been a lieutenant colonel in the Air Service during World War I, was president of the National Aeronautical Society. In an interview with the *Army and Navy Journal*, he said he'd like to know who on the General Staff had given the president such an assurance. Bingham was sure it was not General MacArthur. According to one report, the interview was shown to Roosevelt, who then called Secretary of War Dern about it. When Dern received the call, he happened to be in a meeting with MacArthur and Foulois. After Roosevelt told Dern that MacArthur had called him and given him the assurance before he issued the Executive Order, the secretary repeated the statement to MacArthur, who asked to speak to Roosevelt. MacArthur denied ever making such a call, adding, "I knew nothing about your plan to have the Air Corps carry the mail." The president responded, "But you are mistaken Douglas. You phoned me, as I have said."

MacArthur stood his ground, explaining that the first time he had discussed the subject with the president was when he and Foulois were called to the White House to be reprimanded over the crashes and fatalities. Sticking to his story, Roosevelt insisted that his appointment secretary Marvin McIntyre had put the call from the general through, and that he could substantiate that fact. When MacArthur asked to speak to McIntyre, Roosevelt hung up.[8]

Reportedly, McIntyre later visited the chief of staff at his office and attempted to get MacArthur to acknowledge he had called Roosevelt to say the Army could fly the mail before the contract cancellations. But an increasingly angry MacArthur finally forced McIntyre to admit there was no such call.[9]

Americans grew even more irate at the administration when Generals MacArthur, Drum, Westover, and Foulois appeared before a Senate appropriations subcommittee on March 12. Word quickly leaked out of the ostensibly secret hearing that the four generals had all testified that the first they knew of the airmail being transferred to the Air Corps was when reporters told them shortly after the president announced his Executive Order. General Foulois acknowledged speaking to Second Assistant Postmaster General Harllee Branch about the issue, but he had no idea the decision would be made right away.

One committee member asked MacArthur directly if he had expressed an opinion about the Air Corps flying the mail. The general responded, "I knew nothing about carrying the mails until I was told of it by Mr. Leverts, of the Associated Press. I had not been called into any conference by anyone with reference to that."[10]

As Norman E. Borden Jr. wrote, "The disclosure that the decision for the Army to carry the mail appeared to have been based on only one man's opinion served to increase the intensity of the controversy....To lessen the attacks on Roosevelt and Farley, Democratic leaders in both houses of Congress and Post Office officials placed the blame for all that had gone wrong on the shoulders of Foulois."[11]

Several congressional Republicans defended Foulois, noting that soldiers do not usually say no to the commander in chief. But two questions were left unanswered. First, why had no one in the White House, especially the president, asked MacArthur's opinion? After all, these were his pilots and his airplanes being enlisted in what had otherwise been a civilian enterprise. Second, why had Harllee Branch been so vague in asking Foulois about the Army's ability to take over airmail service? It appears as if the question was asked in the course of a more general conversation, and Foulois answered rather informally. If Branch had asked Foulois directly, "Can you take over flying the mail next week?" his answer, while it may have been the same, might have included a request for time to discuss the issue with his superior and with his own staff. One can easily suspect the administration got the answer it sought. If the Air Corps did not immediately agree to take over flying the mail, there could be no flourish of self-righteous cancellations. They would have to wait for Farley to advertise for new bids.

The following day the *New York Herald Tribune* went after Farley for acting impulsively without inquiring further concerning the Air Corps' ability to perform the service he asked them to do:

> The political blunders of Postmaster Farley are the primary concern of his political chief, President Roosevelt. The appalling air mail blunder ranks high on the list. It is not the end yet. A brave and loyal arm of the national defense was asked to fly the air mail with inferior equipment and inadequate training. Every expert in the country, from Colonel Lindbergh down, understood the risks involved. Mr. Farley could have known for the asking. Yet, because politics called for a sweeping gesture, a great American industry was wrecked, a vital service of business was halted and ten Army fliers were ordered to their deaths.[12]

Roosevelt's letter to Secretary of War Dern "demanding the airmail killings stop" prompted Dern to establish a board of review to examine the
performance of the Air Corps. Perhaps as a conciliatory gesture or perhaps as a way to co-opt an outspoken critic, Lindbergh was invited to
join the board. Suspecting the latter motive, Lindbergh declined the invitation. He sent Dern a telegram explaining why:

> I believe the use of the Army Air Corps to carry the airmail
> was unwarranted and contrary to American principle. This
> action was unjust to the airlines whose contracts were can-
> celled without trial. It was unfair to the personnel of the Army
> Air Corps who had neither equipment designed for the pur-
> pose nor adequate time for training in a new field. I do not
> feel that I can serve on a committee whose function is to assist
> in following out an executive order to the Army to take over
> the commercial air mail system of the United States.[13]

———

With the public outcry over the pilot deaths showing no signs of
abating, Roosevelt was finally forced to ask Congress to pass a bill turning the airmail back over to private carriers. But the draft bill included
restrictions that many found distasteful. The worst of these was the provision that no company that was suing the government for cancelling a
previous contract could bid on a new contract—an obvious ploy to force
these airlines to withdraw their lawsuits. When a committee member
asked Post Office Solicitor Crowley about this provision, he testified that
it "was included in the bill at the request of President Roosevelt."[14]

At the invitation of the Democrat-controlled senate, Lindbergh
appeared on March 16 before a committee holding hearings on the bill.
Broadcast nationwide, the proceedings were the first time a radio audience had heard Charles' voice since 1931.

Lindbergh's appearance was expected to draw an overflow crowd,
so the hearings were moved into the Senate caucus room, the largest room
available in the Senate office building. Seated in a large red leather witness

chair, Lindbergh responded to questions "courteously, but firmly" for two and a half hours, the *New York Times* reported. He told the senators, on whom he made "an unmistakable impression," that he still opposed the cancellations, which he claimed had delivered a "serious blow" to commercial aviation and were "as contrary to American liberty as any action I have ever seen." He called the exclusion from the new bidding of companies that were suing the government "one of the most unjust acts I have ever seen in American legislation."

When Senator McKellar asked him if he had read the bill, Lindbergh replied that he had. "I believe the bill leaves untouched the most fundamental question—whether or not the air lines have a right to trial before they are convicted."

Speaking without notes, Lindbergh transfixed the crowd, which "hung eagerly on the lanky Colonel's words and watched his every move.... Whenever his face flashed into the familiar, winsome smile, a murmur of approval ran through the hall," according to the *New York Times*. It added, "He seemed still to be one of the world's most fascinating figures."[15]

Lindbergh frankly discussed his financial arrangements with various airlines, as well as his investments in airline stock. He told the committee he had invested more in Pan American (a company not involved in the cancellations) than he had received from the airline. Still on the subject of his personal finances, something the senators argued among themselves over the propriety of asking, he told them, "When I returned from Europe there was a question of what I wanted to do. From a financial standpoint, it [earning millions from endorsements and personal appearances] was not the desirable thing to do, but I wanted to stay in aviation." When asked about some warrants he had received from Pan American, he "did not show any expert knowledge of finance," prompting one senator to smile and remark, "You're an aviator and not a stock speculator."[16]

The hearings were more belligerent the following day, when the star witness was Captain Eddie Rickenbacker. Perhaps still angry over the administration's muzzling of his radio broadcasts, Rickenbacker read his prepared statement to the committee, then stood up, thrust his hands into his pants pockets, and looked directly at the committee chairman, Democratic senator Kenneth McKellar, a close ally of Senator Black. "Mr. McKellar," he declared, "with due respect to you all, I think I have earned my heritage to citizenship in this country. I have a fundamental interest in the country's welfare far and beyond my interest in air transport or the science of aeronautics. To that end, I believe in fairness to our Chief Executive.... [H]e should, in purging this industry of so-called undesirable elements which have as yet not been proven, purge his official family of those traitorous elements who have misadvised, or advised without giving full facts, and have caused him to act contrary to American justice."[17]

Following his appearance before the committee, Carl L. Ristine, special assistant to the attorney general, and the man investigating the airmail cancellation affair for the Justice Department, asked Lindbergh to meet with him privately "about some matters pertaining to airmail contracts and controversial subjects." When the colonel arrived at Ristine's office, he found there Andrew Patterson, the former Alabama sheriff and chief investigator for Senator Black's committee, along with a stenographer. That was when Charles, who often appeared to act somewhat naïve in such situations, realized that Ristine planned something more serious than a "private conversation." Lindbergh called his attorney back in New York, Henry Breckenridge, who told him not to make any statement or even have a conversation with anyone from Black's committee without first being served a subpoena and having a lawyer and witnesses present.

Breckenridge also told his client that if he was questioned by an accredited representative of the attorney general he should "give freely any facts in his possession that had to do with any offense against the laws of the United States." Breckenridge then spoke to Ristine, who claimed Patterson had only stopped by for a visit, and that the stenographer worked for the attorney general directly. Breckenridge agreed to allow Lindbergh to answer Ristine's questions, provided the Justice Department investigator promise to send him a copy of the transcript promptly. Ristine agreed. Lindbergh then answered questions for three and a half hours, until he felt the atmosphere grew too hostile, at which point he got up and left. It was more than a month before the transcript was sent to Breckenridge.[18]

As the reinstatement of airmail contracts to civilian carriers moved forward, the administration adamantly refused to investigate the corruption allegations that had sparked the entire episode. As Post Office Department Solicitor Crowley insisted, "The evidence in the possession of the Department having been sufficient to demonstrate the illegality of the contracts referred to, the conduct of a hearing would serve no useful purpose and been only the means of unnecessary delay."[19]

This is a rather startling comment from a government lawyer, considering he is referring to the fundamental constitutional right of trial by jury. Crowley was essentially declaring the airlines were guilty simply because he said they were. Especially guilty was United Air Lines, which lost its Chicago-to-Dallas airmail route. Meanwhile American, which was controlled by Errett Lobban Cord, the great auto and transportation tycoon, was granted a new route between New York and Chicago. What explains American's good fortune compared to United? *Time* reported Cord was believed to have been a "substantial contributor to the 1932 Democratic campaign." Additionally, one of his former vice presidents was conveniently serving as an assistant postmaster general.[20] With this affair proving his political adroitness, Cord went on to develop a long-lasting political machine that "dominated the (Nevada) state Democratic convention" years later.[21]

Senator McKellar's hearings continued while Farley called a meeting of airline operators to temporarily assign routes. Some critics charged he was presiding over a rigged process just as Brown had allegedly done. New bids were opened for the routes from a variety of airlines, some that had previously flown the mail and many that had no mail experience at all. At the president's urging, Farley excluded from the bidding process any airline that had participated in Brown's so-called "spoils conference." This was a series of meetings Brown had convened with airline representatives in 1930 to discuss reforming airmail routes to improve efficiency.

Although critics later denounced Brown's meetings as a "secret" conference for connected insiders, the *New York Times* debunked the charge. "There was nothing secret about it," the *Times* reported. "The press carried reports of the meetings in the Post Office Department in 1930, when representatives of the various airlines met with postal officials, in order to devise consolidations and extensions for the more efficient service of both the post office and the public."[22] Nevertheless, the supposed corruption of the "spoils conference" became an article of faith among Roosevelt's supporters, who were delighted with Farley's populist move to exclude the conference's corporate participants from the new round of bidding.

Farley even banned from the new bidding process individual executives who had attended Brown's conference. This forced several key players in the development of commercial aviation to leave their companies, including men described by *Time* as "famed pioneers"—Thomas B. Doe (Eastern), Richard W. Robbins (TWA), and Harris M. Hanshue (Western Air).[23] Another pioneer, Philip G. Johnson, left United and looked north, where he helped create Trans-Canada Airlines. In eighteen months, Johnson helped build that airline into a national force to rival any in the United States. During the Second World War he oversaw the huge expansion and production of Boeing, included the development of the B-29.[24]

Disgusted that politics had driven aviation leaders from the industry, especially his close friend Richard Robbins, Lindbergh wrote a letter of resignation to TWA. He said he did not want to be part of a company "based on injustice, and which necessitates the resignation of officers who have contributed so greatly to its development." TWA managers eventually talked him into rescinding his resignation.[25]

Despite all the administration's chest thumping, in the end the same airlines that had been carrying the mail when the contracts were cancelled continued to carry most of the mail under the new contracts. Since the companies that had attended Brown's conference were the operators with the most experience and the most modern fleets, they could not really be excluded. To do so would have set the airmail system back at least a full decade. Therefore, the simple solution was to have the airlines slightly change their names when they submitted their bids. American Airways became American Airlines; United Aircraft became United Airlines; Eastern Air Transport became Eastern Airlines; Northwest Airways became

Northwest Airlines; and Transcontinental and Western Air became Trans World Airlines.

This subterfuge, while it fooled no one in the public or the press, and least of all Lindbergh, satisfied the administration that it not only found a way out of this terrible mess, but it could claim it had punished the wrongdoers by banning them from the airmail business. But even liberals were unhappy with the results. In his Washington Side Shows column in the *Nation*, Paul Y. Anderson wrote, "Alas, the air-mail thieves are to be permitted to resume operations at the same old stand, provided they conform to custom by wearing masks. Surely that will cause them no embarrassment."[26]

Ironically, TWA showed what it could accomplish. Remember that on the last day the airlines flew the mail, TWA vice president Jack Frye and Eddie Rickenbacker made the final cross-country airmail flight in record time. Now Frye was back on the first day civilian airmail resumed, May 8, 1934, for another cross-country flight from Los Angeles to Newark. This time he completed the flight in eleven hours and thirty-one minutes, cutting about an hour and a half off the earlier flight. The airlines were definitely back, though it would take several years before they recovered their financial stability.[27]

Meanwhile, the battle over the permanent future of civilian aviation and the airmail continued in the Senate. The bill Lindbergh had testified against—the Air Mail Act of 1934, often called the Black-McKellar Act after its cosponsors—drew fierce condemnation from some Senate committee members for excluding from the new contracts airlines that had sued the government. Senator Marvel M. Logan, Democrat of Kentucky, for example, called that provision "the most obnoxious thing I ever saw in a legislative bill. It is entirely autocratic and unfair."

Post Office Solicitor Crowley, however, argued, "It would have a salutary effect on some of these people who have secured illegal contracts to say to them that they have secured a contract in this way and if they are asserting a claim against the government we are not going to have anything to do with them."

Senator Logan shot back, "It might have a salutary effect on them, but I am wondering what it would do to the Constitution." He then reminded Crowley, "We are living under the Constitution. If we are going to have a government of men and not laws, that is probably all right."[28]

In fact, McKellar appears to be the only committee member who supported the provision, which was eventually dropped from the bill. In the end, hardly anyone was happy with the resulting legislation, which ultimately passed Congress and was signed into law by the president. The airlines were unhappy about new regulations included in the act, and the independent operators were disappointed because it gave them no advantage over the large airlines.

The administration soon received a severe rebuke for its handling of the airmail fiasco from the D.C. Court of Appeals. On February 4, 1935, the court ruled that "cancellation of the air mail contracts in February amounted to a breach of contract." The court then gave five airline companies the right to sue the government in the U.S. Court of Claims. Likening the contracts to property, the court said the action "amounted to the taking of their property without due process."[29]

Over the next few years, several members of Congress attempted to address the shortcomings of the Black-McKellar Act. It was not until 1938 that they achieved success. "In 1938, Congress repudiated the Black-McKellar approach and passed the Civil Aeronautics Act, which restructured the industry according to the assumptions of the once discredited Hoover-Brown policy. The new law emphasized government-corporate linkages, limited competition, and restricted entry to the industry."[30]

As for the much maligned Walter Brown, he remained "unrepentant and dignified amidst the righteous alarms of Black and other politicians who sought to capitalize at the expense of his reputation."[31] Justice was finally served to the former postmaster general on July 14, 1941, when Commissioner Richard H. Akers of the U. S. Court of Claims issued a definitive report on the airmail contract cancellations. "Akers found that there was no fraud in the airmail contracts canceled in 1934," reported *Time* magazine. Moreover, Akers "almost charged the President with a mistake (something he has only once publicly admitted), but he backed delicately away. But one fact seemed clear: the Army need not have taken over the airmail routes; the deaths of twelve Army pilots were needless."[32]

———

When Charles Lindbergh sent his fateful telegram to President Roosevelt condemning the cancellation of the airmail contracts, it was the second time he had thrust himself into the public limelight in the political arena. The first time was a telegram he sent to Secretary of Commerce Herbert Hoover, who was then running for president against Democrat Al Smith. Dated October 3, 1928, Lindbergh's brief telegram read in part, "I have recently flown to St. Louis to register. The more I see of this campaign the more strongly I feel that your election is of supreme importance to the country."[33]

Lindbergh's support probably had little, if any, influence on the ensuing landslide victory for Hoover, who won 444 electoral votes to Smith's 87. Lindbergh's decision to back Hoover, which was really a *public* show of support since Lindbergh must have known the Hoover campaign would release the telegram to the press, was likely influenced by his relationship with Harry Guggenheim of the Guggenheim Fund, who was a Hoover supporter. However, Hoover's tireless campaigning for the development of American aviation also likely played a large role.

What the aviator may not have realized at the time was that such a public position often comes with a price, sometimes to be paid in the future. Writing two days later, Will Rogers expressed this truth in his inimitable way: "Charles Lindbergh holds the world's record for length of time he remained a hero from the time he landed in Paris until yesterday, when he declared his preference for President. That took more nerve for a man with his standing to do than his flight did, for with these people that take politics serious they don't believe there is any way in the world where if you belong to the opposite party, that you could possibly be any good."[34]

Was Lindbergh really a member of the "opposite party," or did Democrats henceforth simply seek to define him as one? It's hard to say at that early date; aside from endorsing Hoover, Lindbergh did not express an interest in politics at the time. His full entry into the political arena really occurred with the airmail controversy. And Roosevelt and his backers would not forget the political damage Lindbergh helped inflict on the administration. As Arthur Schlesinger observed, "The fight (over the airmail contracts) dented the myth of Roosevelt's invulnerability and strengthened the business community's dislike of what it considered personal and arbitrary actions by the New Deal." It also "uncovered in Charles Lindbergh a man who perhaps appealed to more American hearts than anyone save Franklin Roosevelt."[35]

Thus, regardless of whatever political inclinations he may have previously had, Lindbergh emerged from the airmail contracts dispute as the face of the opposition. And the fact that he proved correct about the folly of the president's actions earned him Roosevelt's intense personal animosity. Over time, the issue was personalized into a contest between Lindbergh and Roosevelt. When discussing the affair, Americans asked, "Whom are you for, Lindbergh or Roosevelt?"[36] Lindbergh biographer Walter S. Ross wrote that Roosevelt "did not like to be wrong or seem to be wrong." Humiliated by the weight of public opinion that rallied behind Lindbergh, the president "hated Lindbergh, and never forgot his hatred or forgave Lindbergh, as later events proved."[37]

Roosevelt was particularly incensed because this was the first event that damaged his tremendous popularity as president. As *New York Times* columnist Arthur Krock wrote on February 25, 1934, because of the airmail fiasco, "[f]or the first time since the President was inaugurated, a year ago next Sunday, his administration seems really on the defensive." Krock continued, "Feet of clay have been revealed, if behind a veil. An impression has gone more widely abroad that even Mr. Roosevelt cannot always be right...a degree of distrust of his methods and judgment pervades groups where it did not exist before....Congressional mail is revealing a growing public consciousness that perhaps the administration may be a trifle precipitate in grave matters. The charge will be made, and it will have weight, that the President and the Postmaster General moved too fast, made too brusque a gesture."[38]

In his biography of Lindbergh, Leonard Mosley discussed what he saw as the long-term effect of the airmail dispute on its two leading players. "In a sense, though they did not know it yet, they were shaping up as rivals, rivals who did not respect each other. Roosevelt considered that Lindbergh had unfairly used his fame to plead the cause of big business. Lindbergh (as he told Harold Nicholson shortly afterward) 'loathes Roosevelt because of the latter's treatment of the airmail companies.'"[39]

Likewise, historian Kenneth S. Davis emphasized that Lindbergh had inflicted a rare political defeat on Roosevelt:

> [T]here was no blinking the fact that the entire affair, which had attracted a concentrated popular attention, constituted a personal defeat for Roosevelt in the court of public opinion—not a grave or permanently damaging defeat, certainly, but the first since his taking office that affected in any way his popularity with the great mass of Americans. And there was significance for the future in the fact that the defeat had been in part administered by Charles Augustus Lindbergh, a personality and mind and temperament as antithetical to Roosevelt's as can easily be imagined. The aviator hero and Franklin Roosevelt had apparently come together in head-on collision, and it was Roosevelt who had been forced to back down.[40]

As for Lindbergh, Davis wrote, "[T]he shining heroism of the Lone Eagle remained untarnished in the eyes of the vast majority of Americans. His repeated charge of 'condemnation without trial' was not only plausible but persuasive."[41]

Another Roosevelt biographer wrote, "Roosevelt had kept his distance from the issue publicly while Farley and Dern loyally took the heat for him, but it was a setback and an embarrassment. There would be a rematch between Roosevelt and Lindbergh in a few years, on a much larger issue and with a very different result; in the meantime the President looked uneasily upon the popular aviator."[42]

Looking at one effect of the cancellations, *Business Week* commented, "Most disquieting of all was the impression created in some quarters that the President had here shown an impetuosity that might, if it cropped out again elsewhere, be highly dangerous."[43]

Historian Albert Fried believes President Roosevelt took at least one lesson away from his battle with Lindbergh. It was "a fundamental truism in politics: the best professional is no match against a smart, popular amateur."[44]

Chapter Three

❧

EXILE

In his history of the early years of the New Deal, Arthur Schlesinger wrote, "The air mail fight flared up in January 1934, died down by April, and was largely forgotten by summer. Yet its significance far outweighed its brevity."[1] Indeed, the episode significantly impacted the careers of many of the main participants.

Senator Hugo Black succeeded in raising his public profile and cementing his relationship with President Roosevelt. This effort led to Black's appointment as an associate justice of the U.S. Supreme Court three and a half years later.

Budget Director Lewis W. Douglas, the only close presidential confidant to advise Roosevelt that he did not have the authority to cancel the contracts, resigned his position on August 30, 1934.

Postmaster James Farley, the genial, loyal Roosevelt man who had managed FDR's first presidential campaign, became disillusioned about being hung out to dry by a president who virtually went into hiding until the storm blew over. Although Farley reprised his role as FDR's campaign manager in the 1936 election, he broke with his patron over FDR's coy strategy to have Democrats "draft" him as their presidential candidate in 1940, without announcing his candidacy. After seeking the Democratic presidential nomination himself in 1940 and losing to Roosevelt, Farley resigned from the administration and was later instrumental in creating the 22nd Amendment, limiting a president's tenure to two terms.

Major General Benjamin Foulois came under continuing fire from many quarters, especially Congress. One congressional subcommittee, headed by New Hampshire's William N. Rogers, caught the general in the same predicament that had confronted Walter Brown—the awarding of contracts, in Foulois' case, for the procurement of aircraft. The 1926 Air Corps Act authorized the secretary of war to purchase aircraft "with or without competition, by contract or otherwise." Another section, reminiscent of the McNary-Watres Act of 1930 regarding awarding airmail contracts, required that contracts for the construction of aircraft be awarded to the "lowest responsible bidder." As far as General Foulois was concerned, a "responsible bidder" was a company that had experience building airplanes, was fiscally sound, and had the plant facilities needed for the work. But Rogers and many of his colleagues believed government contracts should be awarded only to the lowest bidder. "The plain truth," wrote the general, "is that if the Air Corps had attempted to buy its aircraft on this basis, there would have been no Air Corps. Low bid does not mean competence."[2]

Perhaps the differing views of Foulois and his Air Corps officers on the one hand, and Rogers and his congressional allies on the other, stemmed from the fact that Foulois and his officers would have to fly the aircraft purchased by the Air Corps and the politicians would not. For the aviators, it was a matter of life and death.

The Rogers subcommittee report blamed Foulois for "mismanagement" and "inefficiency" in the Air Corps handling of the airmail, completely overlooking the fact that Congress had underfunded the Air Corps since its inception. It also charged that in order to improve the morale and material well-being of the Corps, "Major General Benjamin D. Foulois must be relieved from his position as chief of the Air Corps. We unanimously recommend that the Secretary of War take such action without delay."[3]

The committee had failed to apprise Foulois "of accusations contained in the report, nor was he confronted by the witnesses against him and given an opportunity to hear their testimony and cross-examine them, and then offer evidence in his defense." Angered by the shoddy treatment of the Air Corps chief, Secretary of War Dern refused to remove him. He complained that the committee had violated Foulois' rights that "are sacred to every American citizen and are guaranteed by the Constitution."[4]

One has to wonder if Dern saw the irony of using the same line of defense for Foulois that the defenders of the airlines, including Lindbergh, had employed in arguing against the cancellation of the airmail contracts—cancellations, incidentally, that Dern had strongly endorsed.

A *Washington Post* editorial supported Dern by claiming he "has taken a proper stand in refusing to remove Foulois as chief of the Army Air Corps.... [T]he committee had exceeded its power."[5] Despite such support, General Foulois retired at the end of the following year.

The airlines carrying the mail lost hundreds of thousands of dollars due to the greatly reduced rates imposed on them. They managed over time to move to a profitable position by doing exactly what Walter Brown had coaxed them to do—increase their passenger service. They did this by purchasing larger, more comfortable and efficient aircraft. They were forced to shed their relationships with companies manufacturing airplanes, and holding companies were banned from owning an airline carrying the mail. These mostly positive changes greatly contributed to the future growth of the industry.

Despite its terrible loss of killed and injured pilots and destroyed aircraft, the Air Corps managed to reap some benefits from the airmail affair. As it turned out, the affair played out much the way Foulois had predicted. Though Foulois surely didn't anticipate crashes and deaths, the controversy made an otherwise complacent public aware of the miserable condition of the Air Corps. President Roosevelt was forced "to release Air Corps research and development funds that he had impounded and he even authorized $7 million in PWA (Public Works Administration) funds to be used for new aircraft and other badly needed equipment."[6]

This was a crucial step. The politicians had ignored the Air Corps' pleas for financial support for years, and had roundly defeated several attempts to set up a separate headquarters for the Corps under the Army General Staff. Despite the increasing awareness of the importance of aircraft in any future war, it remained just another part of the Army, like the Signal Corps. For its part, the General Staff had for years looked on the Air Corps as something to support ground troops, not as an independent force for engaging the enemy. General MacArthur had agreed with that view, but by 1934 he had begun to change his attitude. With his backing, Secretary of War Dern called for a five-year program in which the Air Corps would purchase 800 combat aircraft each year.

Dern finally created an Air Force General Headquarters reporting to MacArthur—a first step toward developing an independent air force. Notably, this drew the vociferous opposition of Congressman Rogers, who proclaimed that Dern's action was illegal. There was no need, Rogers insisted, to build an air force "that could fly beyond the coast to repel enemy planes and ships."[7]

Finally, having suffered a humiliating defeat over the airmail contract cancellations, President Roosevelt quickly began castigating a new group of villains—one he was sure he could attack with public support: so-called Wall Street stock manipulators. He sent word to Democratic congressional leaders to hurry up a proposed bill to regulate the stock exchanges and establish the Securities and Exchange Commission. When the bill passed, the president selected Joseph P. Kennedy, who had made a fortune on Wall Street, to be its first chairman.[8] The choice of Kennedy to head the Securities and Exchange Commission did not sit well with Interior Secretary Harold Ickes, who referred to Kennedy in his diary as a "former stock market plunger."[9]

———

For Charles Lindbergh, the airmail controversy brought renewed public attention. Having surely foreseen this result, his decision to speak his mind on the issue could not have been an easy one. Since his landing in Paris, he had been, as *Time* magazine would later write, the reluctant subject of hysterical and uncritical hero-worship. "The press succumbed to mob psychology, augmenting it beyond belief. In Lindbergh's mind, however, the press became something far worse: a personification of malice, which deliberately urged on the crazy mob and printed lying stories about him."[10]

Indeed, Lindbergh deeply resented the media's determination to reveal and photograph every detail of his life. He and Anne were trailed everywhere they went by reporters and photographers. Following the kidnapping and murder of their son, a photographer broke into the county morgue and "snapped a picture of the dead baby, copies of which were peddled for five dollars each."[11]

The Lindberghs could not go out to dinner or a show unless they were disguised and used rear entrances. Reporters paid cash to people who often invented stories of listening in on Lindbergh dinner conversations that never took place in restaurants the couple had never entered. Police had to be called to a nursery school that the Lindbergh's second son Jon was attending because of a mysterious, canvas-covered truck parked nearby that turned out to contain photographers snapping pictures of the little boy at play. In another incident, photographers ran a car carrying Jon off the road and photographed the terrified, sobbing child.[12]

The public glare on Charles eased somewhat as he returned to his duties after the airlines resumed carrying the airmail. One of his tasks was to pilot a brand new Pan American "Brazilian Clipper" seaplane down the Atlantic seaboard and back to the harbor at Bridgeport, Connecticut. The record-breaking flight lasted eight hours, covered 1,242.8 miles, with an average speed of 157.5 miles per hour.

In January 1935, however, the trial of Bruno Richard Hauptmann for the kidnapping and murder of Lindbergh's son dragged Charles and Anne back into the spotlight they had worked so assiduously to avoid. Hundreds of reporters, radio commentators, photographers, and columnists descended on the courthouse in Flemington, New Jersey, for what many dubbed, with justification, "the trial of the century." All the big names in the news business were there, including Walter Winchell, Damon Runyon, Dorothy Kilgallen, and Adela Rogers St. Johns. H. L. Mencken called the trial the biggest story "since the Resurrection."[13]

After a six-week trial, Hauptmann was convicted and sentenced to death. With that ordeal behind them, the Lindberghs searched for normalcy away from prying reporters. Between the omnipresent press, regular threats against young Jon, and fanatical autograph seekers, Charles said life had become "close to intolerable for my wife and son, and consequentially for me."

Too anguished to return to the East Amwell, New Jersey home from which Charles Jr. had been kidnapped, the Lindberghs moved in with Anne's family. They lived behind a gated entrance with twenty-four hour guards, and they had to be escorted everywhere. Charles was in a quandary about his work. He had planned several visits to Robert Goddard's New Mexico experimental rocket station, but feared leaving his family at home, even within the well-protected cocoon offered by the Morrow estate in Englewood, New Jersey.[14]

Lindbergh considered moving elsewhere within the country, but feared his family's security would be inadequate. So he decided on a different course. The Lindbergh family slipped out of New York's harbor as the only passengers aboard a freighter named *American Importer* on the morning of December 22, 1935. Before leaving the Morrow home, Charles told his old friend and *New York Times* aviation editor Lauren D. "Deac" Lyman of their plans to move to England. Lyman promised not to reveal what he considered "one hell of a news story" until twenty-four hours after the ship had sailed.

Charles explained to Lyman that his enormous fame had resulted in myriad threats against his family, including threats of further kidnappings, and these were forcing them to move abroad. They had no plans to change their citizenship, simply their home. Both Charles and Anne were anxious to find a place where Jon would be safe, and where both his parents could work in peace—Charles was interested in numerous aviation projects, while Anne was preparing to work on her next book. Her first book, *North to the Orient,* which tells of the Lindberghs' 1931 flight across the Great Circle Route to Asia, was the number one non-fiction book for 1935.

The day before they left, Anne wrote her mother-in-law, "I do feel that we are doing the right thing and will find safety where we go and security during a difficult time, for Jon and for us all."[15]

As promised, Lyman broke the story after the *American Importer* was well out to sea. The press responded with an outpouring of compassion for the Lindberghs. The *New York Times* editorialized that the Lindberghs' decision was "as if America had decreed exile for her own sons." The *New York Herald Tribune* called their plight "a national disgrace." The *Baltimore Sun* decried a condition "that literally drives a famous man to exile himself from his homeland." The *St. Paul Pioneer Press* said it was "understandable and provocative of sympathy" that "two such highly intelligent individuals, who have every reason for wishing to remain in their own country, feel compelled to look for safety elsewhere."

The *San Francisco Chronicle* proclaimed, "It is a national disgrace that Colonel Lindbergh should have to smuggle his wife and baby out of America." And the *Chattanooga Times* railed that it was a "sinister shame...that the United States must lose, even temporarily, one of its first citizens, the man who brought greater honors to American aviation and who has spread more good-will on his numerous flights than any other individual."[16]

Perhaps most notably, the staid *Christian Science Monitor* published a stirring indictment of the press:

> Unless one has been besieged in his home, has had his life endangered on scores of landing fields, has had every move even on his wedding trip watched by news spies, has been forced to his wits' end to circumvent photographers who honor no plea for a second son after one feels the first has had "the finger" put on him by undue publicity—unless one has had just a taste of Colonel Lindbergh's experience with the press that respects no law and knows no decency—it may not be possible to understand that this is a retreat after repeated

defeats by unfair odds. Newspapers more than kidnappers have exiled the Lindberghs.[17]

Leaving their homeland was another difficult decision for the Lindberghs. Anne had to leave behind her closely knit family, and her husband was forced to abandon some promising aviation projects.[18] Charles would later explain to a reporter why he left America: "It was impossible for me or my family to lead a normal life.... We couldn't go to a theater, a store, or even for a stroll without being surrounded, stared at and harassed." Despite the move abroad, he insisted, "America always was and always will be my country."[19]

Not everyone was sympathetic to the plight of the Lindbergh family, however. A Democratic Party official, Kansas City manager Henry F. McElroy, who was a member of the notorious Pendergast political machine, called Lindbergh's move "an act of cowardice."[20] A more prominent critic was Chicago mayor Edward J. Kelly, boss of that city's Democrat political machine. Kelly was a close political advisor to President Roosevelt, and would later be instrumental in winning FDR an unprecedented third term. According to the *Encyclopedia of Chicago*, Kelly's terms as mayor "were bathed in controversy. Gambling and organized crime ran rampant with little mayoral concern."[21]

The day after the *American Importer* sailed, Kelly told reporters he thought the Lindberghs' decision to leave the country was "ridiculous" and "un-American." His comments drew sustained criticism, reflecting the overwhelming public sympathy for the Lindberghs. Kelly was even widely denounced in the Lindberghs' adopted home country; in a dispatch filed from London, the *New York Times* reported, "The Chicago Mayor's remark was bitterly assailed in London, especially where women assembled."[22]

As the American press reflected on its shabby treatment of the Lindberghs, Charles, Anne, and little Jon arrived in Liverpool, England, on December 31, having celebrated a small, private Christmas while at sea. The scene at the Liverpool dock was sadly reminiscent of their lives in America. A mob of reporters, photographers, and curious onlookers followed them from the dock to the Adelphi Hotel, where they spent their first night in England.

The following day Anne's brother-in-law, Aubrey Morgan, took them to the Morgan family estate in Wales, where they spent the next few weeks adjusting to a new, quiet lifestyle. While they found the peace and quiet of the Morgan estate a comforting change, Charles and especially Anne began to feel isolated from the rest of the world. But this was only a temporary impression. On several trips to London, they were happy to discover they could walk the streets of the old city, dine at nice restaurants, and shop without being harassed.

On one trip, they dined with the author and diplomat Harold Nicolson. Charles and Anne had first met Nicolson and his equally well-known wife, the author and poet Vita Sackville-West, at a dinner party at New York's Waldorf Astoria in January 1933. At the time, Nicolson recorded his first impressions of Charles: "He has a fine intellectual forehead, a shy engaging smile, wind-blown hair, a way of tossing his head unhappily, a transparent complexion, thin nervous capable fingers, a loose-jointed shy manner." Anne, he thought was "tiny, shy, timid, retreating, rather interested in books, a tragedy at the corner of her mouth."[23]

At the London dinner, Charles told Nicolson they would like to live closer to London. Nicolson, as it turned out, had the answer. It was, he said, a "tumbled-down cottage" near the tiny fourteenth-century village of Sevenoaks in the western part of Kent. Nicolson, Sackville-West, and their two sons had moved from the cottage to a dilapidated castle nearby called Sissinghurst that they were busy restoring. The cottage, called Long Barn, had periodically played host to other literary luminaries as well, including members of the Bloomsbury Group. Visitors to the fourteenth-century hall house and the sixteenth-century L-shaped cottage and barn included Virginia Woolf, E. M. Forster, Lytton Strachey, Charlie Chaplin, and Douglas Fairbanks. Just an hour from London, the cottage had a garden, a pool, and tennis courts.

Upon their first visit to the cottage, Anne noted in her diary that the rambling old house gave her "an incredible feeling of peace and security—the low house backed up to a hill, its arms around you." The cottage looked upon "that great sweep of freedom—complete country, fields and hills, escape."[24] Once the lease was done, Nicolson asked the village postmistress to use her influence with the locals to see that the Lindberghs were left in peace. "No sir," she replied, "we shall not stare at the poor people."[25]

Settling down in Long Barn, Anne began work on her next book, *Listen! The Wind*. Cut off from his former business associates and isolated from the aviation R&D taking place in the United States, Charles spent most of his time corresponding with international luminaries whose work interested him. Foremost among these were Robert Goddard, who was developing liquid propellant rockets in Roswell, New Mexico; Harry Guggenheim; and the Nobel Prize winning surgeon and biologist Dr. Alexis Carrel. Lindbergh had worked the previous year with Carrel at the Rockefeller Institute for Medical Research to develop a "perfusion pump" that would allow a surgeon to remove a living organ from a body and keep it infection-free until returned to the body or transplanted in another. They would also write a book together, *The Culture of Organs*.

———

As the Lindberghs settled in to their new life in England, the situation across the channel was deteriorating fast. On Saturday, March 7, 1936, German forces marched into the demilitarized Rhineland in a brazen violation of both the Treaty of Versailles and the Locarno Pact of 1925. Hitler's generals feared that the larger and better-equipped French Army would repel the invaders. In an effective subterfuge, German soldiers marched across half a dozen bridges with music blaring and banners flying as foreign journalists watched. That night they quietly retraced their steps so they could cross the same bridges again the following day, giving the impression of a much larger force.

Italy and Britain were responsible for ensuring the Rhineland remained demilitarized, but they did nothing to stop the Germans. France asked the British for at least moral support to oppose the Germans, but nothing was forthcoming from London. Italy, meanwhile, was fully occupied with its own invasion of Ethiopia. The Poles offered to invade Germany from the east if the French Army would strike, but the French refused.

If the French had blocked the invasion, it's possible that a cadre of German officers who feared another war would have driven Hitler from power. Hitler later described the gamble he took:

> We had no army worth mentioning; at that time it would not even have had the fighting strength to maintain itself against the Poles. If the French had taken any action, we would have been easily defeated; our resistance would have been over in a few days. And what air force we had then was ridiculous. A few Junker 25s from Lufthansa and not enough bombs for them.[26]

Two days after the German troops entered the Rhineland, Charles and Anne had what Anne described as a "long argument" over the event. Anne recorded in her diary that Charles argued that the Allies, especially France, had made a "big mistake" at the close of World War I by not crushing Germany "completely." His position was that "Germany, for France's own good, should have been completely incapacitated for a century or else not humiliated at all." By humiliating the Germans but failing to prevent them from rebuilding their forces, the Allies brought the world to the current situation, he claimed. Many Germans wanted revenge for their humiliation and for the heavy financial burdens placed on them by the victors, and Hitler offered them that revenge.

While Anne took a more pacifist position, Charles argued that France should attack the German forces and crush them while Germany was still comparatively weak. According to Anne, Charles believed "the war would have been fought for nothing if they permit Germany again to build the military machine she had in 1914."[27]

Charles' insistence on the need to quickly "crush" the Germans is notable in light of his enduring image as a Nazi sympathizer. One should also consider the Roosevelt administration's reaction to this initial Nazi provocation. While U.S. Ambassador to Germany William E. Dodd filed a formal protest with the Nazi government over the invasion of the Rhineland, "the White House remained deafeningly silent amid French pleas for condemnation. Mrs. Roosevelt went so far as to write an editorial condoning the occupation."[28]

Roosevelt biographer Ted Morgan reports that the president was "concerned" by Germany's move into the Rhineland, and he wrote Ambassador Dodd, "Everything seems to have broken loose again in your part of the world." But in truth, even if Roosevelt had more strenuously opposed Hitler's gamble, he could do little because "the mood in Congress, which had extended the Neutrality Act for another year in February, was deeply isolationist. So was the mood of the country."[29]

The growing international tension did not at first affect Lindbergh's day-to-day activities. As the U.S. aviation industry rebounded with the return of the airmail revenue and technological improvements in aircraft construction, both of Lindbergh's primary former employers, Pan American Airways and Trans World Airways, urged him to return to his previous position as technical adviser. He reluctantly declined because he still feared for his son's safety and the family's security and saw no possibility of "maintaining a home in the United States to which I am willing to take my family."[30]

Unemployed, Charles kept occupied with his many avocations, including scientific and medical interests, but also primarily his first love, aviation. He continued intensive correspondence with officers of Pan American and Trans World concerning aircraft development and air routes. At one point, he succeeded in getting both companies to join forces to solve the problem of pressurized cabins. He also reviewed bids from eight manufacturers for the construction of an airplane capable of carrying one hundred passengers at a cruising speed of two hundred miles per hour with a range of five thousand miles. As A. Scott Berg pointed out, just ten years after his trans-Atlantic solo flight, the Lone Eagle was looking at plans for aircraft that could make the same flight with a cabin full of passengers.[31]

Charles was invited to visit various British aircraft manufacturing facilities and airfields. Except for a few isolated places, he was shocked to find that British aviation had fallen into decay. Over the next few months, the Lindberghs visited friends in France several times. Charles once again accepted invitations to visit aircraft facilities, and was appalled by the condition in which he found French aviation as well.

It was here that the gathering clouds of war over Europe began to involve Lindbergh. It has since been reported that "the French Air Ministry had deliberately invited Lindbergh to see just how badly off they were with the hope that he would say so publicly and perhaps galvanize other branches of [the French] government to act before it was too late." With the Germans engaged in more saber rattling after their victory in the Rhineland, the French remained complacent behind the much-heralded protection of their Maginot Line.[32] Lindbergh, however, was hardly complacent, and he would soon become even more unnerved after getting a close-up glimpse of the rapidly expanding power of the German war machine.

Chapter Four

❦

THE LONE EAGLE'S ALBATROSS

Life took a dramatic turn for Charles and Anne one day in early June 1936. On that day they received a letter from a U.S. Army officer they had never met, Major Truman Smith, then serving as the senior military attaché at the U.S. Embassy in Berlin.

Born at West Point in 1893, Smith was the grandson of a U.S. senator and the son of a U.S. Army captain who was killed in action in the Philippines in 1900. General Albert Wedemeyer described the six-foot-four-inch Smith as cutting "a dashing military figure, towering over most of his associates." The famed author of the *Wedemeyer Report* also said of Smith, "Of the many officers I met before and during World War II, few impressed me as being more destined for challenging responsibilities and signal success" as the man now reaching out to Lindbergh for help.[1]

In part because he could read and speak German, Smith was posted as an assistant military observer to the U.S. diplomatic mission in Germany in June 1920. In November 1922, U.S. Ambassador to Germany

Alanson B. Houghton sent Smith to Munich to interview various political figures. Among these was a little-known political agitator named Adolf Hitler. Smith interviewed Hitler in a private residence in Munich on November 20. In his brief notes on the interview, he described Hitler as a "marvelous demagogue" and a "fanatical man. His power over the mob must be immense." This is the first known interview of Hitler by a U.S. official.[2]

After various assignments within the United States, Major and Mrs. Smith were transferred in August 1935 to Berlin, where the responsibilities of the senior military attaché included tracking and reporting back to Washington about expansion in the German Army—issues such as manpower growth, weapons development, and battlefield tactics used in training. Smith's thorough reports were filled with valuable information about artillery enhancements, the creation of antitank regiments and infantry tactics, and also included evaluations of various senior officers.

The one area in which Smith lacked hard information was the huge expansion of the Luftwaffe—a topic that concerned U.S. experts due to the lack of reliable information. Primarily because he was an infantry officer, Smith had few contacts within the emerging German Air Force. As a result, he had to make educated guesses based on fragmentary information. Smith did have an assistant who was a U.S. Air Corps pilot, but as good as the man was, he had no real technical or engineering background to make useful evaluations of the German aircraft then under construction or in the planning stage. He needed to find someone who was knowledgeable about aircraft to assess the planes the Luftwaffe was having built and determine how many and what types they were. He also needed a way to get into the aviation facilities from which most foreigners were blocked. To make his job more difficult, he had no funds to pay for spies.

Smith was in a bind, for he needed to assess the accuracy of an alarming report about the Luftwaffe's development. The report was relayed by Henry "Hap" Arnold, a lieutenant colonel who would later become a five-star general of the U.S. Air Force. Arnold came across the information in 1934, after General Foulois ordered him to lead ten of the Air

Corps' newest high tech bombers, the B-10, on a flight from Dayton, Ohio, across the United States and Canada and across Alaska, where they would take aerial photographs for future mapping of that territory. While staying at a hotel in Fairbanks, Arnold received a phone call from a man with a foreign accent. He said he was in the hotel lobby and would like to come to Arnold's room to speak to him. Arnold agreed.

Arnold's visitor explained that he was a German, had been a pilot in the Great War, and was in the process of becoming an American citizen. Since the war, he had studied aviation in Russia, England, France, and most recently, Germany. He was in Fairbanks because he was establishing a freight and passenger airline in Alaska.

He asked Arnold if he thought the B-10 was a good aircraft, to which the American officer replied he thought it the "best bomber in the world." The visitor then asked what Arnold would say if he told him the Germans had a bomber that was "far better." Arnold was incredulous. The man insisted it was true. When Arnold objected that Allied commissioners were all over Germany making sure the Germans were not building war planes, the visitor smiled and responded, "Just have your Military Attaché go to the Junkers plant, the Heinkel plant, or the Dornier plant, and take a good look at the ships they are calling 'high altitude transport planes.' They are making pursuit planes as well." Arnold's German visitor then described how Germany had dispersed its component factories around the country to prevent the Allied commissioners from linking them to the aircraft assembly plants.

When he returned to Washington, Arnold discussed the matter with the Intelligence Division of the War Department. They knew nothing about Germany building transports or pursuit planes, so he asked that the military attachés in Berlin look into it. He was not optimistic though, because he realized "the set up in Nazi Germany made it especially difficult for regular attachés to get such information." Within a few months, Arnold learned that General Hermann Goring had announced that Germany was rebuilding its air force. The following March Goring "boasted that the Luftwaffe would be the strongest air force in the world."[3]

In Berlin, Smith weighed his options. He thought up an intriguing, though somewhat unlikely, solution during breakfast one morning in

May 1936, after his wife showed him a front page article from the *Paris Herald* describing a visit Charles Lindbergh had made to a French aircraft factory. The article got Smith thinking about the possibility of Lindbergh gaining access to German facilities and reporting on what he saw. He knew Lindbergh only by reputation, one that assured him the famous pilot was extremely qualified to judge technical developments in aircraft design and construction.

What Smith did not know at the time, but would learn later through his close association with Lindbergh, was that the Lone Eagle was much more than a pilot. He had an incredible ability to analyze the design and performance of an aircraft and make suggestions for its improvement. Aircraft designer and builder Igor Sikorsky reportedly declared, "The extraordinary thing about Lindbergh was not that he could fly a plane, but he could come down and correct its mistakes on the drawing board."[4]

Smith met with his contact at the attaché section of the Air Ministry to see if the Germans were interested in inviting Lindbergh. He had his answer that same day—a resounding yes. Smith even obtained a list of the research facilities, factories, and combat units Lindbergh would be invited to inspect. He discussed his plans with Ferdinand Mayer, acting as *charge d'affaires* in the absence of the ambassador, who approved the plan.

On May 25, Smith wrote to Lindbergh conveying General Goring's invitation to visit a number of civilian and military air establishments in Germany. Smith emphasized that the trip would be made without any public announcement to keep the press away, and he listed several of the facilities Lindbergh would see. Knowing Lindbergh lived in England, but lacking his address, Smith mailed the letter to the U.S. air attaché in London, asking him to locate Lindbergh and forward it to him, which he did.

In the letter, Smith intimated that Lindbergh's role would be far more than that of a mere tourist. For obvious reasons, he could not put in writing that he was effectively asking Lindbergh to spy on German aviation sites. He did write Lindbergh, "I consider that your visit here would be of a high patriotic benefit. I am certain that they will go out of their way to show you even more than they will show us."[5]

On June 5, Lindbergh responded that he was interested in inspecting the progress being made in both civilian and military aviation by Germany.[6] He also asked for, and was granted, a change of dates that made the visit coincide with the August 1 opening of the Olympic Games in Berlin.

Following a family breakfast on July 22, Charles and Anne took off in a rented low-wing monoplane from a grass field at Penshurst and headed to the continent.[7] In Berlin, they were treated to lunch at the Air Club and were introduced to numerous German aviation figures, including the World War I ace Ernst Udet; Germany's first post-war female pilot, Thea Rasche; and General Erhard Milch, inspector general of the Luftwaffe. Anne was somewhat annoyed by all the *Heil Hitler* salutes, noting in her diary, "This raising of the arms business adds to the complications of life. It is done so often and takes so much room."[8]

Following lunch, Charles gave a prepared speech in which he warned that due to the huge changes aviation had wrought in the world, aviators must be careful "we do not destroy the very things we wish to protect." Although General Milch told her it was a very good speech, Anne wrote privately that she thought it rebuked Hitler's expansionist policies.[9]

Lindbergh biographer A. Scott Berg penned a succinct account of Lindbergh's ensuing inspection tour:

> Accompanied by an assistant air attaché, (Captain) Theodore Koenig, Lindbergh visited the Tempelhof civil airport, where he was permitted to pilot a Junkers (JU) 52, the Luftwaffe's standard bombardment plane, and the Hindenburg, a large four-motored experimental passenger plane. He spent a day with the Richthofen Wing, the elite fighter group of the Luftwaffe. One day he visited two Heinkel factories and saw their latest dive-bomber, medium bomber, fighter, and observation planes—all, Lindbergh found, of superb design. He spent another day at the Junkers works at Dessau, where he saw their new JU 210 engine, a liquid-cooled engine far more advanced than he or Koenig had expected, and a JU 86, a low-wing, all metal medium bomber already in mass production. Lindbergh

spent another day at the German air research institute of Adler-shof, where the scientists spoke freely of their work until he steered the conversation to the subject of rockets.[10]

The tour was a real revelation for Lindbergh. "Within days," he later recounted, "I realized that Nazi Germany intended to become the greatest air power in the world." In part from conversations German leaders were having about the need to acquire more space for their growing population, Lindbergh "gained the impression that Germany was looking eastward, militarily, yet it was obvious that bombing planes would not find the Maginot Line a formidable obstacle should they wish to cross it. The Germans knew that France was deficient in both defensive and retaliatory power."[11]

Following lunch one day, Goring showed Lindbergh a photo album he called "our first seventy." Inside were pictures of seventy different military airfields around the country. Lindbergh noted, "From the inspection trips I made through German factories, I knew warplanes were being built to fill those fields. Obviously Germany was preparing for war on a major scale with the most modern equipment."[12]

On August 1, Charles and Anne attended the opening ceremonies of the now-infamous Berlin Olympics after Goring insisted they attend as his guests. The following day, they left Germany and flew to Copenhagen, where Charles was scheduled to attend a scientific conference before returning to England.

After the trip, Anne wrote her mother of her impressions of the German people: "There are great big blurred uncomfortable patches of dislike in my mind about them; their treatment of the Jews, their brute-force manner, their stupidity, their rudeness, their regimentation. Things which I hate so much that I hardly know whether the efficiency, unity, spirit that comes out of it can be worth it."[13]

Although he was not yet keeping a diary, Charles later described how the visit filled him with a sense of foreboding:

I knew theoretically what modern bombs could do to cities. At the same time, experiences in war games had convinced me that claims for the effectiveness of both ground and air defense were tremendously exaggerated. In Nazi Germany, for the first time, war became real to me. The officers I met were not preparing for a game. Their discussions gave a sense of blood and bullets, and I realized how destructive my profession of aviation might become.[14]

Back home in England, Charles and Anne dined at the Nicholson's castle, Sissinghurst, on September 8, 1936. Harold recorded Charles' impressions of Nazi Germany in his diary:

> He considers that they [the Germans] possess the most powerful air force in the world, with which they could do terrible damage to any other country, and could destroy our food supplies by sinking even convoyed ships. He admits that they are a great menace but he denies that they are a great menace to us. He contends that the future will see a complete separation between fascism and communism.[15]

Charles apparently still believed the Germans' war aims were confined to the east. He also thought the Germans were "especially anxious to maintain a friendly relationship with England."[16] But he could see the Germans were intent on war, and the potential destructive power of their war machine filled him dread.

———

The Lindberghs made three trips to Germany—in 1936, 1937, and 1938—at the request of Major Smith on behalf of U.S. Military Intelligence. In 1938 and 1939, Charles also visited Berlin twice at the request of the French government, whose Air Ministry was trying to arrange to buy German engines for use in French planes. Despite later accusations, Charles never met Hitler. He encountered Goring three or four times, always at large formal occasions. The two never met alone.

Charles largely refrained from commenting on the Nazis' anti-Jewish policies until after the deadly Kristallnact riots of November 1938, as discussed below. Until that point, though he may have encountered signs of these policies on his tours of Germany, Lindbergh remained directly focused on his mission of collecting intelligence on the Luftwaffe. He did not receive any special briefings or other classified information on the Nazis' ominous plans for the Jews.

The same could not be said for Roosevelt. We now know that FDR, whose attitude to Jewish issues is unjustly remembered much more charitably than Lindbergh's, was warned of the Nazis' horrific anti-Semitic policies as early as 1933, though he refused to condemn the Nazi government over it. In November of that year, Roosevelt's close friend and advisor Felix Frankfurter, whom FDR would later appoint to the U.S. Supreme Court, forwarded him a letter he had received from James Grover McDonald, high commissioner for German refugees at the League of Nations. Recounting a meeting he held with Hitler in April 1933, McDonald reported that Hitler told him, "I will do the thing that the rest of the world would like to do. It doesn't know how to get rid of the Jews. I will show them."[17]

In the letter, McDonald asked Frankfurter's help in dealing with a developing "tragedy" in Germany. "The German government is contemplating the issuance in the near future of a decree or decrees establishing formally a second-class citizenship for German Jews," he asserted. "Such action once taken would not only further humiliate and degrade hundreds of thousands of men and women; it would make much more difficult any softening in the German Government's attitude later. Such retrogression to the inhumane and unchristian practices of an earlier age should, I think, be forestalled if there is any conceivable way of doing so."[18]

There is no record of Roosevelt responding to McDonald's letter.

Furthermore, McDonald reported in his diaries that he met with Roosevelt in 1933, at which time the president expressed deep concern over the fate of Jews in Germany. The president, however, did nothing about it. He explained his attitude in June of that same year to his ambassador-designate to Germany, William E. Dodd: "The German authorities are treating the Jews shamefully and the Jews in this country are greatly excited. But this is not a government affair. We can do nothing except for American citizens who happen to be made victims." There was no thought of sending any kind of warning to either the German government or the German people over their actions.[19] In other words, as far as Roosevelt was concerned, Germany's Jews were on their own.

———

Lindbergh's tours of Germany yielded a bonanza of much-needed intelligence on the Luftwaffe. During his first tour, Lindbergh and the U.S. air attaché, Captain Koenig, who accompanied Lindbergh during the entire visit, met each morning, usually accompanied by a stenographer, to discuss what they had seen the day before. Captain Smith wrote, "Perhaps the most interesting feature of these informal morning meetings was the comparisons which Lindbergh frequently drew between the airplanes he had observed (and sometimes flew) the day before in Germany, and the comparable planes being built in France, Britain, and America."[20]

That tour also opened a great many doors for Captain Koenig. Where he had previously had no access to Luftwaffe facilities, his association with Lindbergh gained him *entrée* to factories and airfields second only to the Swedes and Italians. Yet another result, according to Smith, who was Koenig's superior, was that Koenig's reports transmitted to Washington henceforth were "to be rated as first-class intelligence reports."[21]

Before departing Berlin after that first tour, Charles and Major Smith prepared an intelligence report for the U.S. government. Smith noted the importance of Lindbergh's participation by explaining that Washington had been largely discounting reports from the Berlin military attaché's office of a "fantastic German air buildup." With U.S. press reports making it clear "the American aviator shared" the view that a big build-up was occurring, it was taken more seriously.[22]

Still, Lindbergh's intelligence was not flawless. It is important to keep in mind that Charles, despite his commission as a colonel, was by experience primarily a civilian aviator who had never actually engaged in or witnessed combat. He could examine the planes in Germany, Britain, France, and the United States and make excellent judgments on their potential performance and flaws. But he could not always understand what a particular aircraft was to be used for in wartime. This was made clear by his surprise at seeing the virtually obsolete JU-52, which the Germans were still building in large numbers. Lindbergh, as well as most Western military leaders, did not realize the Luftwaffe was planning to use these planes as platforms from which to drop German troops behind enemy lines in parachute battalions.[23]

Another thing Lindbergh, Koenig, and Smith failed to detect, as did most Western observers, was that Goring and Hitler were building a huge air force not primarily for long-range bombing missions, but as air support for ground combat operations. This would have explained the emphasis the Germans placed on the JU-87, later known as the "Stuka," a plane that lacked retractable landing gear and "appeared slow and clumsy." This dive-bomber would prove its value over the skies of Polish and French cities in coming years.[24]

———

In June 1936, the National Democratic Convention took place in Philadelphia. The results were a foregone conclusion—the delegates nominated Franklin D. Roosevelt to run for a second term as president, and he was later swept back into office in an historic landslide. Also in June, the president debated making a campaign issue of the Supreme Court, which had come into Roosevelt's crosshairs after it struck down a number of key New Deal programs. The president was confident he could win popular support for altering the court itself, but Jim Farley, the postmaster general who also managed Roosevelt's first two presidential campaigns, warned him it would play poorly as a campaign issue.[25]

Roosevelt decided to keep the Supreme Court out of the campaign, and only referred to it obliquely in his inaugural address. Sixteen days into his second term, however, the president made his plan public. Roosevelt knew there was nothing he could do about the court's current nine members, who enjoyed life tenure and often voted five to four against him. Therefore, under the guise that slow-working, older justices were causing a backup of their workload (a claim disproved by a Justice Department report), Roosevelt devised a scheme to add six new justices to the court. If Roosevelt were to select the new members, and the Democrat-dominated Senate approved them, the court could be expected to take a sharp turn to the left and support FDR's social programs.

The bill for "judicial reform" was "drawn in total secrecy by a handful of New Deal insiders."[26] Several Democratic members of Congress were shocked that the president sent them a bill for which they had no advance notice and no opportunity to provide input. Hatton Summers, chair of the House Judiciary Committee, told fellow Democrats, "Boys, here's where I cash in my chips." House speaker William Bankhead told another member that the president had not informed his own party leaders about the bill "because he knew all hell would break loose."[27]

The "court-packing scheme," as critics called Roosevelt's plan, earned the opposition of all sixteen Republicans in the Senate as well as a good many Democrats. Historian Thomas Fleming describes the Republicans' strategy: "In a move that revealed for the first time a glimmer of intelligence in the Republicans' opposition to Roosevelt, the GOP decided to say nothing. They even banned a radio address by former president Herbert Hoover attacking the president's lust for power. The GOP sat on the sidelines while the Democratic Party tore itself into chaotic shreds over the court-packing bill."[28]

Despite opposition from within his own party, the president persisted. But the whole scheme finally fell apart when the Democrat-dominated Senate Judiciary Committee voted ten to eight to reject the bill. The committee's report called the proposal "a measure that should be so emphatically rejected that its parallel will never again be presented to the free representatives of the free people of America."[29]

It was a shocking defeat for a powerful president whose party controlled both houses of the Congress. But Roosevelt had gone too far in his quest for political control over the only branch of government designed by the Founders to be above politics. Roosevelt biographer Ted Morgan called the court-packing scheme "the worst blunder of Roosevelt's peacetime presidency. He had a bad case of post-election hubris."[30] Likewise, in his biography of Roosevelt, Frank Freidel writes, "Roosevelt had suffered a staggering setback from a Congress top-heavy with Democrats. He had expended a large part of his political capital on a failed enterprise." The whole affair, he reports, left Roosevelt depressed for months.[31]

Coming so close to controlling all three branches of the federal government, Roosevelt was angry over his loss. That bitterness spilled out when his successor as New York governor, Herbert Lehman, a close friend and reliable supporter of Roosevelt's, wrote an open letter urging New York Democratic senator Robert F. Wagner to oppose the court-packing scheme. According to *Chicago Tribune* correspondent and the ghostwriter of Jim Farley's autobiography, Walter Trohan, Roosevelt had a shocking reaction to Lehman's letter. Trohan reports that he and several other reporters were at the president's Hyde Park estate accompanying Roosevelt on a tour of his Christmas tree crop when he was asked to comment on Lehman's letter. Losing his famous smile, Roosevelt responded, "What I have to say will have to be off the record."

Trohan writes, "We had no choice, so we had to agree, knowing that whatever we got would serve as a guideline. However, we were taken aback when he thrust out his chin and sneered, 'What else could you expect from a Jew?'"[32]

During the 1938 mid-term elections, Roosevelt sought revenge on the opponents of his court-packing plan, especially southern and western Democrats who had led the fight against it. When his vindictive attitude toward fellow Democrats became public, some in the press accused him of seeking to "purge" his opponents[33]—and that certainly seems to be the case. In Georgia, the president attacked a sitting Democrat senator up for re-election, Walter F. George, which drew boos from Roosevelt's audience as the senator sat in the front row. George was renominated and reelected despite Roosevelt's meddling. In Iowa, Roosevelt confidant Harry Hopkins attacked Senator Guy Gillette, who likewise was reelected. In South Carolina, the president showed his displeasure with Senator Cotton Ed Smith, who was also reelected. Roosevelt's attack on Millard Tydings in Maryland may have actually rescued the senator's failing campaign.

In fact, while working on his enemies list, Roosevelt's only success was New York congressman John O'Connor, who lost his bid for reelection. Meanwhile, many of Roosevelt's congressional supporters were in trouble. By the time the president was finished attacking members of his own party, the Republicans picked up eight seats in the Senate and went from 88 seats in the House to 170. They were still a minority, but when combined with southern and western Democrats whom Roosevelt had alienated, they became a meaningful voice for moderation.[34]

Following the defeat of his court-packing bill, Roosevelt faced more bad news. Depression conditions resurfaced in the fall of 1937, making New Deal anti-depression programs look hollow. Between September 15 and December 15, 1.8 million people lost their jobs. The *New York Times* reported on October 19 that corporate bond prices had taken their worst fall in three years, and the price of a seat on the New York Stock Exchange had dropped to its lowest level since 1919. The *New York Times* Index of fifteen stocks saw its largest decline since September 24, 1931.[35]

Further complicating Roosevelt's job, labor leader John L. Lewis, a financial and organizational backer of the president, made 1937 the year of the sit-down strike. Hardest hit were automakers and steel mills, crippling further a badly shaken economy. Vice President Jack Garner lashed out at Roosevelt's inability to stop the megalomaniac Lewis. When Roosevelt admitted he could not end the strikes, Garner angrily told him, "Then John L. Lewis is a bigger man than you are if you can't find some way to cope with this."[36]

Roosevelt was convinced he was the victim of conspirators determined to drive him from office. At one cabinet meeting he declared, "I know that the present situation is the result of a concerted effort by big business and concentrated wealth to drive the market down just to create a situation unfavorable to me. The whole situation is being manufactured by Wall Street."[37]

Despite a massive government spending program, economic conditions failed to improve, and by some measurements deteriorated further. Unemployment in November 1937 had climbed to 11 million people, with another 3 million working part-time. Several widely ballyhooed programs appeared to be falling flat. The Resettlement Administration had claimed it would relocate one million urban families to small farms, but the latest report showed only 11,000 had been relocated, and the communities thus formed were reliant on charity.

The imploding economy was particularly problematic for Roosevelt in light of the progress being made by other countries. In Britain, national income had soared to 124 percent of the 1929 high-water mark, while in the United States income was at 86 percent of the 1929 level. Japanese employment was 75 percent above the 1929 figure. The growth rate of the U.S. economy was a dismal negative 7 percent, while countries like Sweden, Chile, and Australia were in the plus 20 percent range. Even Hitler had succeeded in raising national income.[38]

Seeking to divert attention from the failing economy and his faltering political fortunes, Roosevelt needed enemies who would unite the country behind him. Hitler obviously fit the bill. But the president also found that tying one of his own chief opponents—and America's most popular aviator—to Hitler could turn a beloved American hero into a despised but useful public villain.

———

Returning from Germany, Charles and Anne settled back in at Long Barn. Anne resumed writing her book and caring for Jon. In November 1936, Charles took advantage of an invitation from Pan American to inspect a landing field in Ireland. While there, he took Irish prime minister Eamon De Valera for his first flight.

On December 9, Lindbergh had lunch at the House of Commons with British parliamentarian Harold Nicolson, former British prime minister Ramsey MacDonald, and Thomas Inskip, then serving as Britain's first minister for coordinated defense. MacDonald's mental faculties were rapidly failing, which had caused him to resign as prime minister in June of the previous year in favor of Stanley Baldwin. During the luncheon, he kept confusing Lindbergh with Professor Frederick A. Lindemann, scientific advisor to Winston Churchill and a future advocate of carpet-bombing German cities. The more important guest was Inskip, whose position was created by Baldwin in response to complaints from numerous quarters, especially Winston Churchill, that Britain's armed forces were lagging behind those of Germany.

Discussing German air power developments, Charles said he knew of no real defense against air attacks and that "all fortifications are useless." He believed the best defense was deterrence, such as the development of night bombers that can reach an altitude of 30,000 feet. The idea was to strike the enemy before he strikes you, and cripple his ability to attack. Nicolson noted in his diary, "He [Lindbergh] and Inskip get off into technicalities, and I observe that Inskip ceases to regard L. as an interesting person to meet at luncheon, and regards him (as he is) as a person whom he wants to talk to again. It is a successful luncheon and for once I feel that I have done some good."[39]

In his autobiography, Lindbergh explained the evolution of his thinking on air power. He and Anne were flying from Copenhagen back to England after their first trip to Germany when he "began to think about the vulnerability of men to aircraft carrying high-explosive bombs. As we started across the Channel, I realized how concepts of military geography must change. What contrast between my viewpoint from the sky then and the earth perspective of Napoleon as he looked across the Channel!" He noted that only a quarter-hour of water lay between the mainland and England. "England was no longer a wide-moated fortress protected by majestic ships of war. Aviation had transformed her into a target for continental bombing squadrons."[40]

In February, Charles set off with Anne, now pregnant with her third child, on a flying tour that included Europe, Africa, and Asia. Their route took them to Rome, Sicily, Tripoli, and through the Middle East to India. They spent over two weeks touring India mostly by train as they awaited delivery of a replacement rod for their airplane. The return flight included a stopover in Greece to visit the Athenian acropolis. Worried about the future of Western civilization, Charles compared the situation of England facing off against Germany with Athens battling Sparta two thousand years earlier. The outcome of that contest, he noted, "brought the downfall of Greece. War! War! What useless conflicts there had been through those intervening centuries! Yet one could see no end."[41]

Back in England, Anne gave birth to another son, Land. The baby was born on May 12, 1937, at the London Clinic as the streets below resounded with the celebrations of the coronation of Britain's new king, George VI.

Later in the year Charles and Anne were invited to attend the Lilienthal Aeronautical Society's annual congress in Munich from October 12 to October 16. The invitation for his second German visit came from Goring himself via a Colonel Hanesse of the Air Ministry. Major Smith was "particularly pleased" by the timing of the invitation, as Captain Koenig's replacement as assistant air attaché, Major Albert C. Vanaman, had recently arrived and would be able to accompany Charles on any aviation tours that could be arranged.

During the congress, Charles and Anne, along with Smith, Vanaman, and their wives, stayed at the thirteenth-century castle home of Baron and Baroness Kramer-Klett. The Baron, an outspoken opponent of Nazism, had many friends in the government and especially the Luftwaffe. Arranging for the Americans to be their guest, these Luftwaffe friends hoped to neutralize some of the Nazis' attacks on the Baron.

Lindbergh and Vanaman toured several aviation sites, including a Bavarian Motor Works plant that was manufacturing aircraft engines. In a break from normal tradition, General Udet took Lindbergh to the highly secret Rechlin air testing facility in Pomerania, a location off limits to all foreign air attachés. Here Charles closely examined over a half dozen Luftwaffe aircraft, including the Messerschmidt (ME) 109, which was the air service's premier single-engine fighter, and the Dornier (DO) 17, a new light bomber-reconnaissance plane just beginning to be issued to light bomber squadrons. As far as is known, this is the first time an American got a look at these two aircraft. In addition, Charles made two solo flights on another new aircraft, the Fiesler FI 156 Storch. This was an infantry and artillery support plane that the Luftwaffe would use throughout the war to great effect. One had the distinction of being the last German aircraft shot down on the Western front in a dogfight immortalized in Cornelius Ryan's *The Last Battle*.[42]

Before leaving Germany, Charles spent three days with Smith preparing an intelligence report for the Intelligence Division of the General

Staff. Titled "General Estimate of November 1, 1937," the detailed report contained some startling revelations about Germany's secret progress in military aviation. Smith and Lindbergh "believed that it was high time that America should awaken to a realization of the German air potential, to the ever-growing, ever-improving Luftwaffe. Both felt that the United States could not rest much longer on its air laurels and that its Air Corps and air industry must be expanded."[43]

Believing the report to be vital, Smith hoped it would be read by the highest U.S. authorities, including the Army chief of staff, the secretaries of war and state, and maybe even the president himself. And indeed, the report was widely distributed in military circles. On a trip to Washington, Smith was questioned about it by the Army chief of staff, General Malin Craig. Smith also reported that General George Marshall told him that in 1942, as the Roosevelt administration was criticizing the Army for allegedly overlooking the Luftwaffe build-up, Marshall gave a copy of the report to Clarence Cannon, Democratic chairman of the House Appropriations Committee, to refute the charges.

In 1944 the report, which Smith admits largely comprised Lindbergh's thoughts and observations, was made public by Republican congressman Albert J. Engel of Michigan. Engel charged, "When our military attaché in Berlin reported that 'Germany is once more a world power in the air,' just what did President Roosevelt do? He reduced the War Department's requested appropriation by $40,000,000 for the following year." Referring to the report, Engel declared, "President Roosevelt withheld vital information from Congress with respect to Germany's air rearmament during the pre-war years."[44]

Major Vanaman proved to be an imaginative, prescient officer who made the most of his tours with Lindbergh and his resulting contacts within the Luftwaffe. Smith tells us that the air attaché's reports on German air power soon recognized that the Germans were not building an air force for long-range bombing missions. He discovered that despite several four-engine bombers being built, they were all just prototypes. None was in production, and no Luftwaffe combat unit was equipped with them. This indicated Hitler and Goring were preparing for a war close to the German borders, most likely against their immediate neighbors. Vanaman also became convinced that the JU-52 bombers everyone considered obsolete were actually to be used to transport troops and paratroopers into combat. This was exactly how they were used in Rotterdam in 1940 and Crete in 1941.[45]

Less than a year after their second trip to Germany, on August 16, 1938, the Lindberghs flew out of England, made an overnight stop in Warsaw, and landed in Moscow the next evening. Tension over Hitler's designs was mounting—Germany had already annexed Austria, and would gain a large slice of Czechoslovakia the following month when the French and British prime ministers offered up the Sudetenland to Hitler in the Munich Accord.

Charles was anxious to evaluate the status of Soviet aircraft development and manufacturing plants. Such a trip was arranged through the U.S. air attaché in London, Colonel Raymond L. Lee. Over the course of two weeks, they visited aircraft factories, motor works, and even an ice cream plant. Lindbergh found poor conditions prevailed in our future wartime ally. Soviet factories had little of their own modern machinery, with most of it originating in America or Germany. Furthermore, the plants were generally unorganized, the workers were poorly trained, and plant production was typically low. (Charles was, however, impressed by the ice cream plant: "Unlike the products of the aviation factories I had inspected, this factory's products were first-class."[46])

But his overall evaluation of Soviet aviation was stymied by the limited access he received. Charles later wrote he was shown "so little of the Soviet aviation industry that I could make no estimate of its production capacity. Clearly, Stalin's Russia did not wish to expose her Air Force to foreign eyes."[47] Nevertheless, Lindbergh saw enough to conclude, in a view he shared with British and French officials, that the Soviet Air Force "probably consisted of several thousand planes which would be effective in a modern war but were no match for the Luftwaffe in either quality or quantity."[48]

Arriving in Paris on the way home, the Lindberghs found a request from U.S. ambassador William Bullitt to have dinner and spend the night at his residence. Bullitt also invited French air minister Guy la

Chambre. They spent the evening discussing the condition of French aviation and the general European situation. Ten days later, after receiving an urgent telegram from Joseph Kennedy, the U.S. ambassador to Britain, Charles and Anne had lunch with Kennedy and his wife in London. The ambassador told Lindbergh German troops were massing along the Czech border and could invade at any moment. He said he had discussed the situation with Prime Minister Chamberlain and was worried such an invasion would drag an ill-prepared England into war.

Lindbergh described their conversation: "We discussed the military strength of European countries, the attitudes of various governments, and the part military aviation was likely to play in event of war." Kennedy also arranged for Charles to meet a number of people both in and out of the British government to discuss military aviation issues.

At Kennedy's request, Lindbergh drafted a short letter summarizing his thinking on military aviation. Encapsulating what he had learned about the Luftwaffe, he told Kennedy he was sure the German Air Force was now larger than all other European air forces combined. He believed the United States was the only country in the world with the capacity to compete with Germany in the field of aviation. He estimated that the Germans were building between 500 and 800 warplanes per month, while France was producing a mere 50 and England 200. Every month Germany extended its lead over them.

He went on to discuss the Czech reliance on Russian military aircraft and the poor organization of the Soviet Air Force, though he noted the Soviets had enough serviceable aircraft to make their presence known in a war situation. He explained to Kennedy that he believed a general war in Europe would leave all the participating nations prostrate and could result in Communism sweeping through Europe.

That was a relatively common belief at the time, held even by some of Roosevelt's top officials, for example, by the president's close friend, campaign speechwriter, and foreign policy advisor, William Bullitt. And Bullitt was no anti-Communist hardliner; to the contrary, he had been a longtime advocate of establishing formal diplomatic relations with the Soviet Union. He personally negotiated the Soviets' terms of recognition in 1933, after which he became America's first ambassador to the Soviet Union.[49]

In December 1936, then serving as ambassador to France, Bullitt wrote a letter to Roosevelt arguing, "I am more convinced every day that the only chance of preserving peace in Europe lies in the possibility that the French and the Germans may reach some basis of understanding." Referring to the "efficiency" of bombers and their ability to destroy a rival's cities, he concluded, "There is beginning to be a general realization, therefore, that war will mean such horrible suffering that it will end in general revolution, and that the only winners will be Stalin and Company."[50]

History proved Lindbergh right on all counts, except for Communism sweeping all of Europe. With U.S. power largely beating back Communism in post-war Western Europe, the Soviets merely swept up half the continent, keeping the nations of Eastern and Central Europe under Communist domination for the next forty years.

The same day Lindbergh wrote to Kennedy, Kennedy sent a cable to the secretary of state in which he quoted most of Lindbergh's letter. He also recommended that the letter be passed on to the president and to the Navy and War Departments. There is no record that the cable was distributed as Kennedy suggested.[51]

It is possible that the president read Kennedy's cable, however, for shortly after Kennedy sent it, Roosevelt sent his friend Bernard Baruch on a secret mission to Europe to "verify the intelligence received from Army sources and from Ambassador Joseph P. Kennedy." Among other things, Baruch "verified the extent of the head-start Germany had won in the race for control of the air. A few months later, the Military Intelligence Division of the General Staff revealed how close Germany was to winning by default. For the Luftwaffe commanded five bombers to Britain's one, and eleven to our one." When the General Staff reviewed military preparedness around the world, they concluded that Germany's medium and heavy bomber force totaled 3,353; Russia's between 1,300 and 1,900; France had 956; Italy 916; Britain 715; Japan 660; and the United States 301.[52]

While in France, Baruch found little faith in the ability of the French Army to defend the nation. In Britain, he also found little faith in the French. He cabled his assessment to the president, warning that "France and England would not be able to fight."[53]

———

In October 1938, Charles and Anne made their third and most fateful trip to Germany. This time it was at the request of Ambassador Hugh R. Wilson, who had replaced Ambassador Dodd in the Berlin embassy in March. There was also a second invitation, this one to attend another congress of the Lilienthal Aeronautical Society. Ambassador Wilson hoped that Lindbergh would help him establish contacts with Goring, whom many foreigners believed was the most reasonable of the Nazi leaders with whom to deal. Wilson was evidently trying to get the German government to stop forcing Jewish émigrés to leave their money and possessions behind in Germany.[54]

The Lindberghs arrived in Berlin on October 11. That evening Charles, Wilson, military attaché in Berlin Truman Smith, and Major Vanaman, along with American aircraft designer Dr. Igor Sikorsky, attended the opening ceremonies of the congress. During the congress, Sikorsky gave a talk on the development of helicopters. Goring, obviously anxious to show the world what a first class air force he had built, gave instructions that Lindbergh could go anywhere he wished and see whatever he wanted. This allowed Lindbergh to collect extremely valuable, high-grade intelligence. As Smith explained, "Lindbergh's third visit actually resulted in more inspections of German air installations than had ever occurred previously in any equivalent period of time. Indeed, as far as positive air intelligence was concerned, it was probably the high point in the four years."[55]

But just as Lindbergh's effective espionage against Germany was bearing the most fruit, he became involved in an incident that his critics seized upon to paint him as a German sympathizer. On October 18, Ambassador Wilson, as part of his plan to draw closer to Goring, planned a dinner in the Luftwaffe chief's honor at the U.S. Embassy. In addition to Goring, the attendees were to include German generals Milch and Udet, German aircraft designers Dr. Ernst Heinkel and Dr. Wily Messerschmitt, Dr. Sikorsky, the ambassadors from Belgian and Italy, several U.S. embassy officials, and a few officers from Goring's personal entourage. It was a small enough gathering hopefully to allow Ambassador Wilson to take Goring aside for a private conversation.

Unknown to any of the American attendees at the time, at about 4:00 p.m. an officer from the German Air Ministry had called Colonel Smith's office. There being no officer present at the time, the German left a message with a secretary saying that Goring intended to confer a German decoration on Lindbergh at the dinner that evening. Smith did not see the message until the following morning.

Goring and his aides were the last to arrive. After shaking hands and exchanging greetings with Ambassador Wilson and several others, Goring spotted Lindbergh and walked over to him. He immediately began making what appeared to be a formal speech, which caught all the Americans off guard. Realizing that Lindbergh, who spoke no German, had no idea what Goring was saying, U.S. Embassy consul-general Raymond Geist quickly stepped forward to translate for him. As the German general spoke, one of his aides handed him a small red box, which he gave to Lindbergh. Charles listened to the translation and was surprised to learn he was being awarded the Service Cross of the German Eagle, Germany's highest civilian decoration. Geist translated that the award was being given to Lindbergh for his services to world aviation and particularly for his 1927 solo flight across the Atlantic. Germany was one of the few European countries that had not made such an award to Charles soon after the historic flight.[56]

So, what does a guest of the U.S. ambassador do at the U.S. Embassy when he is unexpectedly handed a medal by the second highest-ranking German official "in the name of the Fuhrer"? It was easy for some people to say at the time, and for years to come, that Lindbergh should have rejected the medal or in some other way returned it. But remember, the United States was not at war with Germany; in point of fact no one was at war at the time. By refusing the medal, Lindbergh would probably have caused a well-publicized diplomatic incident that would have killed Ambassador Wilson's attempts to negotiate with Goring while failing to improve one iota the plight of German Jews or have any other positive effect. Most important, and something unknown to Lindbergh's critics at the time, publicly humiliating Goring would have undoubtedly cost Lindbergh his unique access to Luftwaffe facilities—access that was yielding a trove of intelligence for the U.S. government and U.S. military.

Lindbergh accepted the medal, and Ambassador Wilson certainly appreciated his tact. He later wrote Lindbergh, "Neither you, nor I, nor any other American present had any previous hint that the presentation would be made. I have always felt that if you refused the decoration, presented under those circumstances, you would have been guilty of a breach of good taste. It would have been an act offensive to a guest of the Ambassador of your country, in the house of the Ambassador."[57]

Following the dinner, Goring took Lindbergh aside for a private conversation, with Geist translating again. The Nazi leader was curious about Lindbergh's trip to the Soviet Union, and his impressions of the people and cities there. He then boasted to Charles about the performance of the JU 88, a brand new bomber that no one outside German military aviation circles knew existed.

Smith and Lindbergh returned to the military attaché's apartment, where Charles and Anne were once again staying as guests of Colonel and Mrs. Smith. Neither Charles nor the colonel thought much of the award, and neither could have dreamed of the trouble it would cause him. The same could not be said of their wives. As the two men entered the apartment, Lindbergh casually handed the box to his wife. Anne opened it, glanced at the medal, and commented impassively, "The Albatross"— foreseeing that the medal, while not actually around her husband's neck, would hang there nonetheless. Mrs. Smith told her husband later that evening, "This medal will surely do Lindbergh much harm."[58]

Indeed, the vituperative campaign against Lindbergh recommenced almost immediately with an erroneous report in the *New York Times*. While the newspaper admitted the award surprised Lindbergh, it inaccurately described Goring as placing a ribbon accompanying the medal around Lindbergh's neck and pinning the medal on his chest. Lindbergh, the article wrongly reported, "thanked Marshal Goring but proudly wore the decoration during the evening."[59] Other papers and magazines piled on, probably, as Scott Berg reports, because they "had grown to resent Lindbergh's uncooperative attitude" with the American press that had hounded him and his family and forced them to flee the country.[60]

The Roosevelt administration saw this as a golden opportunity to marginalize one of its prominent detractors. Speaking before the Cleveland Zionist Society, Interior Secretary Harold Ickes launched a scathing attack against Charles, implying America's most renowned aviator was a traitor and claiming that any American who accepted a decoration from a dictator "automatically forswears his American birthright."[61]

A few months later, in his diary entry for January 7, 1939, Ickes complained that some newspapers criticized his attack on Lindbergh when word began to leak out that "while Lindbergh was accepting this decoration he was getting valuable and confidential information for his own government." Refusing to give Lindbergh any credit, Ickes insisted that accepting the decoration while he "was serving as a super-spy for his own country" was "a contemptible thing." After accepting the medal, Ickes wrote, Lindbergh did not even deserve to be an American citizen.[62]

Despite the reflexive criticism from the U.S. media and from Roosevelt's mouthpieces, Lindbergh's handling of the medal ceremony quickly paid off when Charles and Vanaman gained access to several more aviation sites. On October 21, they were shown the top-secret JU 88, the new ME 109, and the twin engine ME 110. Lindbergh and Vanaman were allowed to take all the time they wanted to minutely examine each aircraft, and Charles was permitted to take the ME 109 fighter for a forty-five minute solo flight. The twin engine JU 88 was introduced the following year, and became the most versatile combat aircraft the Germans had during the war. Fifteen thousand JU 88s were built, and its variants served as bombers, dive-bombers, night fighters, torpedo bombers, reconnaissance aircraft, and heavy fighters. "Major Vanaman recognized that this visit to Rochlin had produced unusual intelligence. The following day he submitted a special airplane report to Washington on the JU 88." He also sent a separate report on the ME 109

Charles Lindbergh as a second lieutenant,
March 1925.

Lindbergh with the *Spirit of St. Louis*,
May 31, 1927.

Raymond Orteig presenting Charles with the $25,000 Orteig Prize for his New York–Paris solo flight, June 14, 1927. (Photo subject to the GNU Free Documentation License)

President Herbert Hoover, a longtime proponent of American aviation.

As postmaster general, Walter Brown was instrumental in building the nationwide airmail system.

Franklin Roosevelt and Herbert Hoover on their way to the U.S. Capitol for Roosevelt's inauguration, March 4, 1933.

Senator Hugo Black, the man behind the investigation that led to the cancellation of private airmail contracts.

Major General Benjamin Foulois. He did not foresee the tragic cost when the Air Corps took over the airmail.

Lindbergh speaking at an America First Committee rally in Fort Wayne, Indiana, October 3, 1941.

Secretary of the Interior Harold L. Ickes, the Roosevelt administration's most ferocious critic of Lindbergh.

Lindbergh's supposed Nazi sympathies were a favorite theme of the aviator's critics, as shown in this *Shreveport Times* cartoon. (Image courtesy of the *Shreveport Times*)

Returning from a combat mission, Charles (right) speaks with Major Thomas
McGuire on the island of Biak in 1944. McGuire, the second highest scoring
American ace in the war, died in combat on January 7, 1945.

President Franklin Roosevelt signing the declaration of war against Japan, December 8, 1941.

The Apollo 7 and 8 crews (seated) sign a commemorative document to be hung in the Treaty Room of the White House, December 3, 1968. Standing behind them (left to right) are Lindbergh, Lady Bird Johnson, President Lyndon Johnson, NASA administrator James Webb, and Vice President Hubert Humphrey. Lindbergh also signed the document at the astronauts' request.

flight characteristics as Lindbergh explained them to him. This was important data if the U.S. Air Corps ever had to face these two highly developed aircraft in combat.[63]

During this time, Lindbergh contemplated moving his family to Berlin. It's unclear what motivated Charles, but Anne speculated on his reasons in her diaries:

> His viewpoint was primarily technical. He was interested in the facts and he saw them clearly. In the field of technical aviation in which he was put to work, he was not naïve. By nature and by training he was fitted for the job he was asked to do and that he willingly accepted without thought of personal loss or gain. He was astonished and impressed by the rapid growth of German air power, but also saw its danger. True to his nature, wherever there was danger he wanted to get closer to it, to face it, measure it, and if possible, prepare to combat it. It was as a "trouble-shooter" that he became of such value to the airlines, which he served all his life. His role was to detect the danger points and try to circumvent them. Even in early air pioneering, this was his method in approaching storms. If we got a bad weather report, his response was invariably, "We'll go and see what it looks like—we can always turn back." I am sure it was this characteristic attitude that led him to consider spending the winter of 1938/39 in Germany. He knew without a doubt that Germany was the danger point in Europe. He wanted to get as close as possible to the danger, to assess it accurately, and to warn others of its potential.[64]

On November 10, 1938, reports reached Charles and Anne about Kristallnacht—Nazi-instigated, anti-Jewish riots that broke out across Germany the previous evening, marked by the burning of synagogues and Jewish-owned stores. Using the killing of a German Embassy official in Paris as a pretext, the Nazis murdered hundreds of Jews and dragged off thousands more to concentration camps. Amidst worldwide condemnation of Germany, Ambassador Wilson was recalled to Washington, never to return.

This was probably the first time that Charles, with his tunnel vision focused on aviation issues, truly realized the depths of Germany's anti-Jewish barbarity. He was not alone. A great many people across Europe and the world were shocked out of their stupor concerning the Nazis by the savagery of Kristallnacht. Charles wrote in his diary, "My admiration for the Germans is constantly being dashed against some rock such as this."[65] Cancelling their tentative plans to move to Berlin, Anne reports that Charles called Smith in Berlin and told him they would not take a house "in a country that committed such outrages—he was vehement."[66]

Charles made two more trips to Berlin, in December 1938 and January 1939, both at the behest of the French, who were trying to arrange the purchase of German aircraft engines for use in French warplanes. The negotiations, however, ultimately failed to produce the desired results.

In November, Major-General Henry H. "Hap" Arnold, who had been promoted to Chief of the Army Air Corps, began a series of communications with Lindbergh, based in part on a suggestion by Major Vanaman to Arnold "to get in touch with Lindbergh soon, because he knows more about the German Air Force than anybody." General Arnold immediately began writing to Charles, who replied to his every query. "His letters were full of striking information, and I wrote him that as soon as he returned to the States, I was most anxious to talk with him."[67]

Unfortunately, much of the information Charles and Smith sent to Washington sat on shelves until the United States was drawn into the war, and only then was its importance more widely recognized. Still, a significant circle of people had either read the reports or knew their contents, and these people understood the value of the service Charles had performed for his country. These figures included U.S. military officials (General Arnold and Colonel Smith), U.S. ambassadors (Kennedy and Wilson), European political leaders (French premier Edouard Daladier), and British and French Air Ministry officials. After the war, reading through the reports written by Smith and Lindbergh from Berlin,

U.S. Army Intelligence specialist Colonel Ivan D. Yeaton called them "the finest example of intelligence reporting that I have seen."[68]

But the American press saw an opportunity to strike down the hero who had spurned their attention and provoked public criticism of their actions. With the misreporting over Goring's medal, the media had created the incipient image of Charles as a disloyal American. Now, they enhanced this theme by viciously attacking Charles for his tentative plans to move to Berlin. With characteristic bile the *New Yorker* sneered, "With confused emotions, we say goodbye to Colonel Charles A. Lindbergh, who wants to go and live in Berlin, presumably occupying a house that once belonged to Jews....If he wants to experiment further with the artificial heart [a reference to the perfusion pump he had co-invented], his surroundings there should be ideal."[69]

Thus, as he was providing the U.S. military with top-rate intelligence reports on the Luftwaffe, the American press pilloried Charles as, of all things, a Nazi stooge.

———

In March 1939, Germany reneged on the Munich Accord and dismembered Czechoslovakia. The autonomous governments of Slovakia and Ruthenia, under German prompting, declared their independence using documents prepared in Berlin. Britain and France cited these declarations as an excuse to disavow the pledge they made at Munich to guarantee Czechoslovakia's new borders. Meeting no resistance, Hitler sent German troops to take over Bohemia and Moravia, comprising the bulk of the Czech lands. Soon after, Hitler turned his attention toward Poland.[70]

After reading the accounts of Czechoslovakia's downfall, Anne wrote morosely,

> German soldiers are at Prague. Hitler is in that castle on the hill we looked at so often and the swastika floats on top of the city. I am glad there is no war and Prague has not been

destroyed, but there is something terrifically sad about the accounts of those German soldiers filing grimly into the streets of Prague with the snow falling. The silent crowds of Czechs, and that heartbreaking and spontaneous last singing of the Czech national anthem bursting from the crowd in the square.[71]

On March 31, British prime minister Neville Chamberlain announced his country would "lend the Polish government all support in their power" if Polish independence were threatened. To many it seemed an empty promise, and in fact when Hitler attacked Poland in September of that year, there was so little action to back up the Brits' declaration of war that the conflict was popularly dubbed "the phony war."

On April 7, Charles wrote in his diary, "Italian troops entered Albania this morning. Germany and Italy undoubtedly plan on dominating all of Eastern Europe (and what of the Russian Ukraine?). What will France and England do? And America? Are we on the verge of the world's greatest and most catastrophic war?"[72]

Recognizing war could be imminent, Charles wanted to get some idea of the conditions his family would face back home. If matters were acceptable, he would send Anne a cable to pack up the boys and join him. So Charles said farewell to his family, boarded the *SS Aquitania*, and set sail for America.

Chapter Five

❦

PREPARING
FOR WAR

C harles was heading home to a frosty reception from the American press. Many reporters continued to begrudge his reluctance to grant interviews and have his family photographed. Others, including the famed columnist and gossip purveyor Walter Winchell, blamed Charles for the Munich Accord, claiming erroneously that his alarming statements about the Luftwaffe's development had frightened Chamberlain into giving in to Hitler's demands.[1] Portraying Charles as a gullible dupe of the Germans, some reporters fabricated stories of Goring moving planes around so that Lindbergh repeatedly saw the same aircraft.

However, while the media may have cavalierly dismissed Lindbergh's warnings about the Luftwaffe, the military brass who read Charles' secret reports or were briefed by him were more appreciative. General "Hap" Arnold, now Chief of the Air Corps, wrote in his autobiography, "Nobody gave us much useful information about Hitler's air force until

Lindbergh came home in 1939."[2] Of course, once the war began, Charles' accounts of the growing might of the German Air Force proved tragically correct.

Lindbergh did have a few supporters in the press. For example, the "Dean of the Washington Newsmen," Arthur Krock, who was chief of the *New York Times* Washington bureau, defended Lindbergh in his January 31, 1939 column. "When the new flying fleet of the United States begins to take the air," Krock wrote, "among those who will have been responsible for its size, its modernness, and its efficiency is Colonel Charles A. Lindbergh. Informed officials here, in touch with what Colonel Lindbergh has been doing for his country abroad, are authority for this statement, and for the further observation that criticism of any of his activities—in Germany or elsewhere—is as ignorant as it is unfair."

Describing Charles' visits to Germany, Krock added significantly to the trickle of public information about Lindbergh's real mission. Krock revealed, "During his stay in Europe the Colonel has sent back reports to the War Department which have been read in conjunction with dispatches from the air attachés at the various diplomatic posts." He continued, "Because Colonel Lindbergh is who he is European governments have permitted him to see and do things no other airman would be allowed to see and do. He has even been able to take air attachés into factories and laboratories otherwise barred to them." Of the medal given Charles by Marshal Goring, Krock seemed to agree that "under the circumstances, he felt constrained to accept."

Krock ended the column with this observation: "Colonel Lindbergh is no usual man, and that applies to his temperament and methods. This individualism has earned him some personal unpopularity. But any founded on belief he has not been a patriot, and most valuable one, is ill-founded indeed."[3]

As Charles quickly discovered, whether reporters loved him or hated him, few had forgotten him during his stay abroad. As the *Aquitania* entered New York Harbor on April 14, 1939, some friends came aboard via a tugboat to welcome Charles home. Once docked with the gangway down and the other passengers departed, the press poured onto the ship. Two police officers arrived at Charles's cabin and offered to escort him through the mob, but he decided "to go out alone if possible." The offi-cers did not think that was a good idea, and explained they would be nearby to lend assistance. The small group talked as reporters and pho-tographers banged on the cabin door. One photographer broke into the cabin next door, pushed open the door between the cabins, and managed to snap the first photograph of Colonel Lindbergh returning home.

Charles described the scene as he and his friends left the cabin. "Both sides of the corridor and stairs were lined with cameramen and flashing, blinding lights. They started shoving and blocking the way in front of us. The police immediately formed a wedge and pushed them out of the way. There were dozens of uniformed police in addition to many plain-clothes men. All the way along the deck the photographers ran in front of us and behind us, jamming the way, being pushed aside by the police, yelling, falling over each other on the deck." Lindbergh thought there were at least a hundred photographers, and described the deck as covered with broken glass from their flash bulbs. He later called the scene "a barbaric entry to a civilized country."[4]

The Morrow family driver hustled Charles into a car and drove him to the family's home in Englewood, New Jersey. Once there, he phoned General "Hap" Arnold, who had sent Charles a message aboard the *Aquitania* requesting that Charles call him after he arrived in New York. They arranged to meet for lunch the following day at West Point.

The next morning, Saturday, April 15 was clear and sunny, and Charles borrowed the Morrows' De Soto and drove himself north to the military academy. General Arnold, who was traveling there with his wife to visit their cadet son, thought the security offered by the facility would make it easier to talk with Lindbergh. Along with Mrs. Arnold, the two Army officers spent three hours in the main dining room of the Hotel Thayer discussing the German aviation situation. The three later moved to the upper grandstand of the baseball stadium, where they sat unno-ticed by the cheering cadets who were absorbed in a game between Army and Syracuse.

Arnold later wrote, "Lindbergh gave me the most accurate picture of the Luftwaffe, its equipment, leaders, apparent plans, training meth-ods, and present defects that I had so far received." Chief among those defects was a shortage of trained personnel; aircraft production was outstripping the Germans' ability to train pilots to fly the new planes. But Lindbergh, like Arnold, Smith, Vanaman, and French and British spies, still did not understand another significant defect—that the Luftwaffe remained a force for use primarily in support of ground operations and not for strategic long-range bombing missions, although they were building bombers with extended range.[5]

Arnold asked Lindbergh if he would serve on a board along with General Walter Kilner and three other officers to develop a five-year plan for revising and updating the development of U.S. military aircraft. Charles agreed. Arnold later called the findings of that board "inestimable." Three days later Charles accepted the general's offer to be reinstated on the Army's active duty list as a colonel in the Air Corps. He cabled the news to Anne, with a request that she plan to bring the family home as soon as possible.

Suddenly, everyone from Army officers to naval intelligence experts wanted to meet with Colonel Lindbergh, possibly because War Department personnel had read Ambassador Kennedy's cable about Lindbergh's report on German aviation. It is possible Roosevelt himself read the cable, because the president issued a surprising invitation for Lindbergh to meet him privately at the White House on April 20.

The meeting began at 12:45 and lasted just fifteen minutes. It was the first and last time Lindbergh and Roosevelt met face-to-face. Lindbergh wrote of the president, "He was seated at his desk at one end of a large room. There were several models of ships around the walls. He leaned forward from his chair to meet me as I entered, and it is only now that I stop to think that he is crippled. I did not notice it and had no thought of it during our meeting."

The meeting appears to have been relatively cordial in light of the bad blood between the two. The president asked about Anne, and told Lindbergh that his daughter had known Anne in school. There is no record of what the two discussed, but Lindbergh did note that he liked the president, and found him an interesting conversationalist and a suave man. He thought he could get along well with him, although "there was something about him I did not trust, something a little too suave, too pleasant, too easy." Noting Roosevelt had the tired, gray look of an overworked businessman, Lindbergh said he thought they might be able to work together, but suspected it would not be for long.[6] Later that evening, Roosevelt used some of the figures on German aircraft production he had gotten from Lindbergh to drive home an argument he'd begun making—that the U.S. needed to bolster its aircraft production.[7]

Roosevelt biographer Ted Morgan wrote of this meeting, "And so on April 20 the two men who would become the chief isolationist and the chief interventionist met privately for the first and last time. FDR already saw Lindbergh as a potential danger who had to be neutralized, but charm couldn't do it."[8]

Historian Walter L. Hixson described the two men at that meeting in this way:

> Roosevelt and Lindbergh were opposites that did not attract. The former loved politics, which the latter hated; FDR often acted precipitously and liked to "play it by the ear," whereas Lindbergh rarely acted without careful and meticulous planning. Both were phenomenally successful men who had grown accustomed to achieving their aims while overcoming opposition. These differences, coupled with lingering resentment over the air mail controversy, formed the basis for a bitter rivalry between two of the most prominent Americans of their time.[9]

There is some irony in the fact that the two rivals by this time were both determined to build up America's military aviation. However, there the similarity ended. Whereas President Roosevelt was primarily interested in building large quantities of warplanes to assist Britain and France, Lindbergh emphasized the need to develop bigger, faster, more efficient aircraft on par with the best being built in Europe.[10] For Charles, this meant building fighters equal to or better than the British Spitfire and the Germen Messerschmidt 109. He pursued this goal as a member of the Kilner Committee, where he headed up efforts to revise the Corps research and development program, and he fought for it when he was given responsibility to examine existing aeronautical facilities and make recommendations for their improvement, expansion, and future use. He also advocated for better fighters in his work with the National Advisory Committee for Aeronautics (NACA), a military aviation body and forerunner of NASA, to which Charles had first been appointed in 1928.

The Air Corps assigned him a Curtiss P-36, its most modern fighter, to use as he spent the next few weeks examining aviation facilities across the country. He toured engine and aircraft design labs, educational facilities, and production plants, as well as military and civilian airfields. He met and spent time speaking with virtually everyone whose work related to aviation issues, especially military aviation.

Lindbergh's whirlwind tour of the country's aviation facilities can be seen in one day's entry in his diary:

> May 8, 1939: Drove with Kindelberger [an aeronautical engineer and president of North American Aviation] to the North American factory. We went through the factory together and discussed plans for future designs, production, and development. It is a very efficient establishment—in many ways the most efficient I have yet seen. They are now producing planes for England and France in addition to those for the United States.
>
> We had lunch in Kindelberger's office. Then I went through the El Segundo Douglas factory, which is just a few yards away. From there I took the Army car and driver assigned to me to the Douglas factory at Santa Monica. After a fifteen-minute talk with Douglas [the president of Douglas Aircraft] and some of his officers, we went through the factory and the experimental department. From the Douglas factory, I flew to Mines Field in the DC-5 (as a passenger). The DC-5 is the latest Douglas attempt at a bi-motored passenger transport—high wing and tricycle gear.
>
> At Mines Field I borrowed a single-engine plane from the Douglas Company and flew to the Vultee factory, where I spent an hour with Dick Miller, going through the factory and talking over plans. Then flew back to Mines and took Army car

to Douglas-home for dinner and night. Douglas had invited a dozen or so of his officers and military "attachés" for dinner. Discussion again about various phases of aviation. I spent half an hour talking to Douglas alone after they left.[11]

At all his stops, Charles expressed interest not only in what the aviators were doing today, but in their long-term plans as well. He urged everyone with whom he spoke to focus on developing better engines and aircraft. Other than airplane expenses, Lindbergh paid for everything himself, including his assigned Army driver, and he was drawing no pay during this time.

Meanwhile, the president was pursuing a different strategy. Shortly after the Munich Pact was signed, Roosevelt called a meeting at the White House to discuss, among other things, air power. He emphasized the need for "mass production" of military aircraft. General Arnold pointed out that "mass production" must include many essential elements such as R&D and pilot and mechanic recruiting and training. Arnold later noted that Roosevelt "seemed to understand," but that he was "still primarily engrossed with the problem of sending planes and material to Britain and France."[12]

Even before war broke out on the continent, Roosevelt clearly anticipated an armed conflict and wanted America to become involved in it, at least indirectly. At a secret meeting at the White House on September 20, 1938, ten days before the Munich Accord was signed, Roosevelt revealed to the British ambassador to Washington, Sir Ronald Lindsay, his determination to find a way to circumvent the Neutrality Acts— popular legislation Roosevelt himself had signed that prohibited Americans from providing war materials to warring nations. In the event of a European war, the president explained to Lindsay, the United States might be able to continue supplying arms to Britain and France if those nations refrained from formally declaring war against Germany. Lindsay then related the president's position in a telegram to British foreign minister Lord Halifax.[13]

Roosevelt convened another secret meeting about a month later, on October 19. Meeting at his Hyde Park estate with the influential French economist Jean Monnet, who was sent to see FDR by the French premier, the president again discussed how he could exploit loopholes in the Neutrality Acts, this time by having U.S. companies ship aircraft parts to Canada, where planes could be assembled in new plants and then shipped to Europe. He recommended that two plants with a total capacity of 5,000 planes per year be built, one of which, he suggested, could be erected across from Detroit and the other near Niagara Falls.[14]

In January 1939, the public got a peek into Roosevelt's secret dealings with the French and the British. Despite objections from the War Department, including Secretary Woodring and General Arnold, a secret French mission headed by Monnet was given access to a highly classified airplane, the Douglas twin-engine light bomber, then undergoing testing in California. On the 23rd of that month, one of the bombers crashed and burned. The pilot died, but his passenger, who was at first identified as "Mr. Schmidt," was pulled from the wreckage with minor injuries.

The Associated Press soon revealed that "Mr. Schmidt" was actually Paul Chemidelin, a technical advisor to the French Air Ministry. Within days the Senate Committee on Military Affairs, which contained numerous members passionately opposed to America's involvement in another European war, launched an investigation. During his testimony, General Arnold explained that the order to allow the Frenchman "full access" to the secret warplane had come from Treasury Secretary Robert Morgenthau Jr. through Secretary Woodring to him. Morgenthau told Woodring the president had ordered such access be granted. It was soon discovered that "FDR had handed this hot potato to Henry Morgenthau, Jr., because the War Department was in open rebellion, refusing to show the French anything."[15]

This incident helped bring to a head a long, simmering disagreement between Roosevelt and some of America's most powerful senators, including Edgar Borah, Burton Wheeler, Arthur Vandenberg, Hiram Johnson, and Gerald Nye. These men had participated in the Senate Munitions Committee investigation in 1934–35 and concluded that weapons makers had reaped huge profits from World War I. Many suspected, but could not prove, that the munitions makers and big investment houses, especially J. P. Morgan, planned to make millions of dollars off a new war and were privately pressing for U.S. participation. At least partially based on what their investigations had uncovered, for these men "isolationism was not a political position but an article of faith."[16]

The president met with the senators on January 31, 1939, in the Oval Office. Turning up his well-known charm, he asked that his remarks be kept confidential. He then explained he did not want to frighten the American people about the growing danger of war. Speaking about America's first line of defense, he declared that in Europe "the safety of the Rhine frontier does necessarily interest us." When asked if he meant the Rhine River was our frontier, he replied, "No not that, but practically speaking if the Rhine frontiers are threatened the rest of the world is too." Someone at the meeting leaked the details to a reporter, resulting in a deluge of articles reporting that the president had said America's frontier was on the Rhine.[17]

Throughout 1939, Roosevelt continued his efforts to sidestep the Neutrality Acts and find ways to aid Britain and France, even while both countries were still at peace. But his endeavors had to be kept secret, as polls showed widespread public opposition to anything that smacked of military involvement with Europe. Meanwhile, Lindbergh moved inexorably toward another open confrontation with a president who was, wittingly or unwittingly, putting the U.S. on the path to war.

Chapter Six

❦

A RELUCTANT CRUSADER

On May 17, 1939, Lindbergh fulfilled a request from General Arnold to appear before the House Military Appropriations Subcommittee to discuss increased funding for the Army Air Corps, especially for aviation research projects. The *New York Times* reported on Lindbergh's appearance with the headline, "Lindbergh Favors Swift War Planes."

Lindbergh told the committee that although he believed the Germans had already outstripped the United States in aviation advancement, we faced no danger of a German attack in the near future, since the Luftwaffe had not yet developed a plane with the long-range capability of the U.S. "flying fortress" bombers. Still, Lindbergh emphasized the need to spend more money and more effort on developing the next generation of warplanes.

He did not, as many later charged, attempt to frighten the congressmen about the Luftwaffe's abilities. One congressman later told the press that Lindbergh testified with a "lack of hysteria. He emphasized quality in aircraft, not quantity. He gave us a calm dispassionate picture of affairs abroad." Charles' key advice was not to attempt to match the number of warplanes being built by Germany, Italy, and Russia, but to focus their efforts on building better, faster, and more powerful aircraft capable of defending America.[1]

One of the first to attack Lindbergh after his testimony was made public was former British prime minister David Lloyd George, who called Lindbergh a "tool of much more astute and sinister men than himself." He belittled Lindbergh's negative opinion of the Soviets' air force and their aviation facilities, claiming implausibly that they actually had "the finest air force in the world."[2] George's charges, however, were somewhat compromised by his increasingly erratic behavior. At age seventy-three, he had become a somewhat confused politician. In 1936 he visited Hitler in Germany and wrote that the Nazi dictator was "the George Washington of Germany."[3] It's hard to justify that it's Lindbergh, not George, whom history has recorded as a Nazi sympathizer.

At any rate, George's claims were disproved and Lindbergh's evaluations were validated yet again on June 22, 1941, when in a matter of hours "the German Air Force had destroyed more than a thousand Soviet aircraft on the ground or in combat: a quarter of Russia's whole air strength."[4]

But in mid-1939, Lindbergh's vindication still lay two years in the future. At the time, he was coming under increasing fire for supposedly exaggerating the Luftwaffe's strength in order to scare Germany's potential enemies into appeasing Hitler. It was a ludicrous charge, in that Lindbergh's primary goal in shuttling between Paris and London in 1938, then sharing his conclusions with U.S. military and civilian aviation people, was to convince all three nations to strengthen their air power as a deterrent against German war plans.[5]

Both Britain and France needed to buy time with the Germans while they rebuilt their aviation infrastructure. Charles worried that they had neither the time nor the will, especially the French. Writing later about his views at the time, Lindbergh observed:

Tensions, especially in eastern Europe, had increased to a point
where the outbreak of war seemed probable. My greatest hope
lay in the possibility that a war would be confined to fighting
between Hitler and Stalin. It seemed probable that Germany
would be victorious in such a conflict; and by that time France
and England would be stronger. Under the circumstances, I
believed that a victory by Germany's European peoples would
be preferable to one by Russia's semi-Asiatic Soviet Union.
Hitler would not live forever, and I felt sure the Germans would
eventually moderate the excesses of his Nazi regime.[6]

Although Lindbergh's hope that the war would be limited to Germany
and the Soviet Union was unfulfilled, he was far from the only American
to wish for that outcome. Especially after Germany invaded Russia in
June 1941, a good many people hoped the two dictatorships would crush
one another and leave Western Europe alone. Among these was Missouri
senator and future U.S. vice president and president Harry Truman, who
told reporters, "If we see that Germany is winning we ought to help
Russia, and if Russia is winning we ought to help Germany, and that
way we let them kill as many as possible."[7]

Truman biographer David McCullough explains the future president's thinking on the topic: "[L]ike many Americans, and many in
Congress, Truman saw little difference between the totalitarianism of
Fascist Germany and Communist Russia, and particularly since the Nazi-
Soviet Pact of 1939 and Russia's invasion of tiny Finland. Stalin was only
getting what he had coming to him was the feeling and one shared by a
very large segment of the American people."[8]

Back home in the United States, Lindbergh sought support from all
quarters for strengthening the Air Corps. He advocated developing new
aircraft that could outperform any enemy air force, as opposed to Roosevelt's
strategy of simply building a great number of warplanes (which would
soon be obsolete) and transferring them to the French and British. In the
end, Roosevelt's strategy won out—to predictable effect. As the official
U.S. Army history of World War II notes, this policy of "diverting abroad

much of the flow of new equipment…temporarily retarded the equipping and hence the training of the new United States Army units whose performance in battle would one day prove a requisite of Allied victory."[9]

In June 1939, Anne and Charles rented a home in the semi-secluded section of Lloyd's Neck on the north shore of Long Island. Charles spent very little time there as he continued his trips to Air Corps facilities and manufacturing plants. His work for NACA focused primarily on research and development of all aviation. Having predicted the year before that war would probably break out in 1939, he was racing to improve the Air Corps' ability to defend the U.S. homeland before Germany could develop a transoceanic bomber capable of attacking U.S. cities.

———

Meanwhile, Europe continued the march to war. After seizing rump Czechoslovakia in March, Hitler pressured Lithuania to surrender to Germany the port city of Memel and surrounding territory. This was the last bloodless reoccupation of former German territory. His next target was the city of Danzig.

Part of present day Poland and now known as Gdansk, Danzig had a bewildering history destined to lead to trouble. When an independent Poland was created in the aftermath of World War I, the Poles hoped they would be granted control of Danzig, a great port on the Baltic Sea. But with Germans comprising nearly 98 percent of Danzig's population, the Treaty of Versailles instead created the Free City of Danzig, a quasi-independent state with its own constitution, parliament, postage stamps, currency, and even national anthem. The city was put under the protection of the League of Nations, with its external affairs to be controlled by Poland.

Further complicating matters, a large slice of former German territory was given to Poland to ensure the Poles access to the Baltic Sea. Known as the Polish Corridor, it cut off both Danzig and East Prussia from the main part of Germany. William Bullitt, a member of the U.S. delegation to the 1919 Paris peace talks, wrote to President Wilson that the decisions concerning Danzig and East Prussia were "unjust" judgments that, along with other stipulations in the Treaty of Versailles, made "new international conflict certain."[10] Later denouncing the treaty as "one of the stupidest documents ever penned by the hand of man," Bullitt claimed that the entire mess confronting Europe in the 1930s stemmed from the "criminal errors" French premier Clemenceau had written into the treaty.[11]

In her history of the 1919 Paris Peace Conference that produced the Versailles Treaty, Margaret Macmillan points out, "Germany never really accepted its loss of territory, and virtually all Germans, good liberals or right-wing nationalists, regarded Poland with contempt."[12] As many observers noted at the time, these and other conditions stemming from the Versailles Treaty made another war highly likely. Even British prime minister David Lloyd George, one of the architects of the treaty, recognized its weaknesses would lead to another war. He warned, "The proposal of the Polish commission that we should place 2,100,000 Germans under the control of a people (the Poles) which is of a different religion and which has never proved its capacity for stable self-government throughout its history must, in my judgment, lead sooner or later to a new war in the East of Europe."[13]

Most of the Danzig population resented Polish control of their foreign affairs and favored reunification with Germany. Capitalizing on this sentiment, the city's Nazi Party won half the parliamentary vote in 1933 and began demanding that the League of Nations high commissioner return the city to German control.

For a time, the Poles appeared amenable to such an arrangement. Perhaps they understood that earlier French and British guarantees of support against a potential German invasion were not as valuable as they first appeared. After all, the military clique that ruled Poland could not have mistaken the meaning of France's huge undertaking, beginning in 1929, to build the Maginot Line—a long series of complex defensive positions along the German border consisting of fortifications, artillery, anti-tank emplacements, infantry shelters, and communications centers, all connected with electrical and telephone lines, and served by a specially built narrow gauge railroad to deliver supplies and reinforcements. The Poles had to wonder if the French would actually come out of their fortifications and attack Germany if Poland were invaded, or if they would wait for the Germans in the relative safety of their Maginot Line. Of course, we now know they opted for the latter course.

The Poles put relations with Germany on a relatively good footing with the German-Polish Non-Aggression Pact of 1934. The agreement recognized borders and ended a customs war between the two countries, while both sides pledged to deal with any outstanding issues between them, which included Danzig, through bilateral negotiations. However, relations soured in September 1938 with the signing of the Munich Agreement. The Poles felt that Hitler had double-crossed them by expanding German influence into Slovakia, a region the Poles "regarded as within their sphere of influence." As a result, the Poles' "resentment turned to mistrust."[14]

Polish-German relations deteriorated further the following month, when the German foreign minister, Joachim Ribbentrop, haughtily proposed that the non-aggression pact be renewed and extended, but only in return for German annexation of Danzig and the right to build and control a highway and rail line between Germany and the port city. The Poles then broke off talks over Danzig and looked to their Western allies for advice. They received renewed pledges from Britain and France to go to war against Germany if the Fuhrer invaded Poland. On March 31, 1939, British prime minister Neville Chamberlain declared the British and French commitment to Poland before the House of Commons:

> [I]n the event of any action which clearly threatened Polish independence, and which the Polish Government accordingly considered it vital to resist with their national forces, His Majesty's Government would feel themselves bound at once to lend the Polish Government all support in their power. They have given the Polish Government an assurance to this effect. I may add that the French Government have authorized me to make it plain that they stand in the same position in this matter as do His Majesty's Government.[15]

Thirteen days later, this guarantee was extended to Romania and Greece.

Britain's guarantee was dangerous. British military historian B. H. Liddell Hart noted that the pledge "placed Britain's destiny in the hands of Poland's rulers, men of very dubious and unstable judgment."[16] British Ambassador to Berlin Sir Neville Henderson pointed out another fundamental problem: "From the outset, however, it was quite obvious that, in spite of the Anglo-Polish Agreement and whatever might be the outcome of war, neither Britain nor France was in a position to render any effective immediate aid to Poland if she were attacked."[17] Note that Henderson was simply expressing Charles Lindbergh's long-held viewpoint that Britain and France were unprepared for war with Germany.

Convinced that the guarantee to Poland would soon lead to war, Lindbergh wondered, "Why in heaven's name did not England move in 1934 if she intended to stop Germany" instead of waiting as Germany grew increasingly powerful? "These last five years of indecision may well bring the end of her empire, if not all Europe," he warned. He bemoaned Britain's incoherent policymaking, noting that Britain "took part in Versailles. She stood by and watched Germany rearm and march into the Rhineland. She advised a Czech mobilization last spring. She advised them to surrender to Germany last fall. And now she wants to guarantee Polish integrity. England," he lamented, was "again on the verge of war and not well prepared to enter it."[18]

Lindbergh had been warning about Britain and France's military unpreparedness since his first visit to Germany. He had talked endlessly to British and French officials, describing the advances of the Luftwaffe and urging them to improve their military positions. Few heeded his words, however, and soon it would be too late for France, while Britain would suffer horrendous wartime losses.

Meanwhile, Hitler prepared for what almost everyone considered the inevitable invasion of Poland. Hitler was furious with the Poles over the Danzig issue, and besides, he wanted Polish territory for resettling Germans. The Fuhrer thought very little of the British and French guarantee to Poland, since he correctly expected his forces to defeat Poland in a few weeks at most, leaving no time for her Western allies to render any meaningful help. The only potential problem was the Soviet Union, which might back Poland, although the latter feared Russia as much as it did Germany. Hitler settled this issue in August by signing a non-aggression pact with the Soviets that included a secret protocol dividing up Eastern Europe, including Poland, between the two dictatorships.

With all issues now settled, German forces swept across the Polish frontier on September 1, 1939, triggering World War II. Seventeen days later Soviet troops attacked the Poles from the east, erasing the independent state of Poland.

On September 3, Britain and France declared war on Germany. Lindbergh and Henderson were proven right—Anglo-French actions did not amount to much, since they were not about to launch a frontal attack against Hitler's much heralded Western Wall. Remaining inside the fortifications of the Maginot Line, over a hundred French divisions refrained from attacking across the border, where they would have faced just twenty-three German divisions constituting little more than a "military screen, not a real defense."[19] Thus began "the phony war," which lasted until Germany attacked France and the Low Countries in May 1940.

———

The week before Germany invaded Poland, Lindbergh had dinner with William R. Castle, who had served in a variety of State Department positions during the Harding, Coolidge, and Hoover administrations. Joining them was Fulton Lewis Jr., the journalist who had alerted Senator Hugo Black to the so-called "spoils conference" that began the airmail investigation. Lewis was now a well-known radio personality whose commentary was carried nationwide over the Mutual Broadcasting System.

Knowing Lindbergh's feelings about the coming war, Castle suggested that Charles declare on the Mutual Broadcasting System his opposition to U.S. involvement. But perhaps recalling the abuse his father suffered when he opposed American entry into World War I, Lindbergh expressed reluctance to become another anti-war spokesman.

In his diary entry for September 1, Lindbergh wrote, "The war has begun. What will England and France do? If they try to break the German Western Wall, I think they will lose unless America enters the war. In that case, if we go in, Europe will be still more prostrated after the war is over." He wondered why the French and British had allowed themselves to get into such a "hopeless position" and asked, "Why now?" Why fight over Poland and Danzig, both unreachable by the Western allies? He did not think that Poland, Danzig, and the Polish Corridor were adequate causes to rally Allied troops to attack Germany. For the English, it was "The Charge of the Light Brigade" all over again. As far as Lindbergh was concerned, it was the wrong reason and the wrong time to attack Germany, and neither France nor Britain was prepared for it. As it turned out, once again, he was correct on all counts.[20]

In light of widespread public concern that America could get sucked into the war, on the evening of September 3, the president broadcasted a "fireside chat" radio address about events in Europe. His statement included this commitment to the American people: "This nation will remain a neutral nation. I hope the United States will keep out of this war. I believe that it will. And I give you assurances that every effort of your government will be directed toward that end."[21] Despite FDR's assurances, Charles feared the United States would be drawn into the war. Charles thought Roosevelt had sounded better than in most of his radio talks but lamented, "I wish I trusted him more."[22]

Lindbergh was right to suspect Roosevelt's sincerity. Seven days later the president wrote a personal letter to British prime minister Neville Chamberlain revealing that his policy was less "neutral" than he had told the American people. Referring to the arms embargo stipulation of the Neutrality Acts, Roosevelt told Chamberlain, "I hope and believe that we shall repeal the embargo within the next month and this is definitely a part of the Administration policy."[23] FDR had clearly lied to the public about his intentions.

On that same day, Roosevelt began a secret correspondence with Britain's new Lord of the Admiralty, Winston Churchill. Since Churchill was, from the first, committed to getting the United States into the war, these communications were bound to help. He would later all but welcome the Japanese attack on Pearl Harbor, saying it was "a blessing that Japan attacked the United States and thus brought America wholeheartedly and unitedly into the war."[24]

Roosevelt, of course, had been maneuvering for at least a year to assist the British and French to prepare for war with Germany. This went well beyond his secret talks about exploiting loopholes in the Neutrality Acts. For example, in January 1939 William Bullitt, then ambassador to France, returned to Paris after consultations with Roosevelt in Washington. Bullitt immediately met with the Polish ambassador, Juliusz Lukasiewicz, and assured him that if war broke out, the United States would be involved. According to Lukasiewicz, Bullitt's exact words, which the Pole assumed were in accord with Roosevelt's plan, were, "Should war break out, likely we shall not take part in it at the beginning, but we shall finish it."[25]

As 1939 wore on, Roosevelt became more open about his plans for the U.S. to join the coming war. At a press conference on April 11, according to the *New York Times*, the president "strongly implied that he believed the involvement of the United States in any general European war was inevitable."[26] Three days later, *Times* columnist Arthur Krock wrote, "The President...ended all pretense that this nation, so far as he can act for and influence it, will attempt to maintain neutrality in a European war."[27] Roosevelt's intentions were further exposed the following month, when his administration began pressing Congress to water down the Neutrality Acts, as described in chapter seven.

The president also continued privately to commit to the war. In June 1939, King George VI and Queen Mary visited the World's Fair in New York City and made a stop at the Roosevelt estate in Hyde Park on their way to Canada. The king and the president had several discussions either alone or in the company of Canadian prime minister William Mackenzie King. The international situation was a primary topic, especially the inevitability of war. King George, known for being a meticulous note taker, wrote the following about their talks: "[Roosevelt] showed me his naval patrols in greater detail about which he is terribly keen. If he saw a U-boat, he would sink her at once & wait for the consequences. If London was bombed U.S.A. would come in."[28]

Thus Lindbergh, even knowing nothing of Roosevelt's secret dealings, did not trust the commitment to neutrality declared by the president following the outbreak of war in Europe. Despite his initial reluctance to speak out on the topic, Charles quickly felt compelled to do so. On

September 7, Lindbergh wrote in his diary, "I do not intend to stand by and see this country pushed into war if it is not absolutely essential to the future welfare of the nation. Much as I dislike taking part in politics and public life, I intend to do so if necessary to stop the trend which is now going on in this country."[29]

Three days later, on Sunday, September 10, he accepted Fulton Lewis's offer to use the Mutual Broadcasting System's facilities to make a radio address on the war. This was a major decision for a man who treasured his privacy and assiduously tried to avoid the public spotlight. The broadcast was scheduled for Friday evening.

That week, Lindbergh prepared his address and exchanged ideas with officials responsible for aviation issues, both civilian and military, including Air Corps chief General Arnold. Lindbergh showed a copy of his speech to Arnold, who said he saw nothing unethical or damaging to the Air Corps in his remarks, and suggested that Lindbergh might give Secretary of War Henry Woodring an opportunity to read them. Lindbergh declined, saying that Woodring, who ironically would be forced out by Roosevelt the following year over his own non-interventionist views, was too close to the president. Arnold also suggested they change Charles' status with the Air Corps, which was "inactive-active." This came as a surprise to Charles, since he had received no pay since the first two weeks when he became temporarily "active." The general and the colonel agreed that Lindbergh would request a move to the "inactive" list to avoid any embarrassment to the Air Corps.

Arnold told Woodring later that day about Lindbergh's planned radio address. He reported to Lindbergh that Woodring was "very much displeased," and had asked if there was any way to stop Charles from making the speech. Arnold had responded that he did not think there was.[30]

Woodring then informed a cabinet meeting of Lindbergh's upcoming address. He incorrectly reported that the colonel had refused to allow anyone to read the text of his talk, although it is possible General Arnold did not tell Woodring he had read it. He was sure, the secretary of war told the gathering, that Lindbergh was "going to take a stand against" further revisions to the Neutrality Acts. He also told them that he "sent word to Lindbergh that there was a likelihood of his losing his position and rank in the office of Reserve Corps" if he took such a stand.[31]

On September 15, the very day of his first radio address against U.S. intervention in the European war, Lindbergh was busy helping to lay the groundwork for the defense of the United States with superior air power. He spent most of the day meeting with the other members of the National Advisory Committee for Aeronautics. On Lindbergh's recommendation, NACA voted to recommend to Congress that the nation's second military aircraft research center be built at Moffett Field near Sunnyvale, California. The $10 million facility was approved after Army and Navy officials explained to Congress "that European nations had taken the lead from the United States in caliber of warplanes as a result of numerous research centers."[32]

Presiding over the NACA meeting was Dr. Vannevar Bush, who had a long professional relationship with Lindbergh in both NACA and the Carnegie Institution, of which he had been president. Bush had evidently taken to heart Charles' warnings about German advances in modern weaponry. As a result, he gathered a group of scientists to form the National Defense Research Committee, which in May 1941 became the Office of Scientific Research and Development—bodies that would preside over military research that led to the development of radar, sonar, and eventually, the atomic bomb.[33]

Following the NACA meeting, Lindbergh went to the small apartment he used while in Washington. Having arrived from New York the prior evening, Anne awaited him there. They were soon joined by Truman Smith and Fulton Lewis. Smith took Charles aside and relayed a message delivered to him verbally by General Arnold, who indicated it came from Secretary Woodring: if Charles would cancel his address that evening and refrain from actively opposing U.S. intervention in the war, Roosevelt would create a cabinet level position of secretary of the air and appoint Lindbergh to the post.[34]

Refusing the offer outright, Lindbergh did not reveal this bribe attempt for a year. Although the offer did not come as a surprise to Charles, he had not expected the president would use General Arnold to relay such an unseemly message. He noted in his diary for that day that he thought it "a great mistake for [Roosevelt] to let the Army know he deals in such a way."[35]

The attempted bribe was a particularly cynical move in FDR's struggle to neutralize his long-time nemesis. One Roosevelt biographer described the offer as a "startling attempt...to win over Lindbergh, a formidable opponent."[36] Noting rumors that FDR threatened Lindbergh with a tax audit, another claims, "Roosevelt apparently considered muzzling Lindbergh [by exploiting his authority over Lindbergh stemming from Charles' position in the Air Corps]...but he rejected that as politically dangerous."[37] Conrad Black reports, "Roosevelt had been eyeing [Lindbergh] warily since the fiasco over airmail routes in 1933," adding that "he had long considered [Lindbergh] a Fascist sympathizer."[38]

The Roosevelt administration was looking for a pretext to make this accusation publicly. Politically naïve, Charles promptly provided it to them.

———

Lindbergh broadcasted his radio address from a room in Washington's Carlton Hotel. There were around twenty people present, including Anne, Fulton and Mrs. Lewis, and numerous technicians. Six microphones were placed on a desk. Charles asked that they be faced upwards, so he could stand at the desk while he spoke. A commercial photographer took several pictures of Lindbergh standing at the microphones, and then everyone waited for the broadcast to begin. Charles had written the speech himself, and had allowed only a few people to read it, including General Arnold, Anne, Fulton Lewis, and Truman Smith.

At 9:45 p.m. an announcer made a ten-second introduction, and Colonel Charles Lindbergh began his address. Despite Roosevelt's alarm at the prospect that Lindbergh would attack either the administration or its proposed revisions to the Neutrality Acts, Charles did neither. Instead, his talk focused on what the *Washington Post* described as "America and European Wars." The *Post*, the *New York Times*, and numerous other newspapers nationwide published the full text of the speech. The *Times* called it "Lindbergh's Appeal for Isolation," while the *Post* better described it as his "Neutrality Talk."

Lindbergh began his address by commenting, "In times of great emergency, men of the same belief must gather together for mutual council and action. If they fail to do so, all that they stand for will be lost. I speak tonight to those people in the United States of America who feel that the destiny of this country does not call for our involvement in European wars." He called on his listeners to "band together" to avoid American deaths for the sake of Europe's internal struggles. He also warned against allowing "foreign propaganda" to push the United States into war, declaring, "We should never enter a war unless it is absolutely essential to the future of our Nation."

Invoking President George Washington's warning "against becoming entangled in European alliances," Charles observed that Americans whose ancestors came from the very nations now at war lived peacefully together in America. He then spoke of the massive loss of life in World War I, and how we had fortuitously avoided greater loss of American lives because the war ended before we became fully engaged. He also mentioned that the same countries now at war were "unable or unwilling to pay their debts to us" from the last war.

Considering U.S. troops remain stationed in Europe today, sixty-five years after the war ended, Charles' next statement was prophetic. "If we enter the quarrels of Europe during war," he said, "we must stay in them in time of peace as well. We must either keep out of European wars entirely or stay in European affairs permanently."

Then Charles made a fateful comment: "There is no Genghis Kahn or Xerxes marching against our Western nations. This is not a question of banding together to defend the white race against foreign invasion. This is simply one more of those age-old quarrels within our own family of nations—a quarrel arising from the errors of the last war—from the failure of the victors of that war to follow a consistent policy either of fairness or of force."

Critics frequently cite this passage to tar Lindbergh as a racist, but the accusation is profoundly unfair. The phrase "white race," while jarring to our ears today, was a common term in the twenties and thirties used to describe Europeans. Charles was simply placing America alongside Europe as part of Western civilization. He believed if some foreign enemy threatened all of Western civilization, America might have to go to war. But since this was a conflict among European nations and posed no threat to America, our best course was to avoid war. It was hardly a racist argument.

Charles then discussed the failures of the Treaty of Versailles and the additional treaties that followed it, how they failed to set fair and equitable boundaries between nations, and the refusal of England and France to keep Germany weak by force. He then made another accurate prediction. "If we take part successfully," he said, "we must throw the resources of our entire Nation into the conflict. Munitions alone will not be enough. We cannot count on victory merely by shipping abroad several thousand airplanes and cannon."

He warned once more against propaganda aimed at sucking the United States into the war, and called on people to question the motives of writers, speakers, and the owners of media outlets that promoted intervention. He ended by declaring, "This is the test before America now. This is the challenge—to carry on Western civilization."[39]

Although unsatisfied with his high-pitched and flat delivery, Lindbergh accepted the congratulations of the people in the room on a fine speech. He and Anne, along with the Lewises, slipped past the reporters in the hotel lobby and returned to the Lewis home, where they listened to a rebroadcast of the speech. Charles and Anne boarded a 2:00 a.m. train and headed home to New York. There, they received thousands of letters and telegrams, mostly favorable, about Charles' address.

However, the speech provoked scathing attacks from Roosevelt backers. One of the worst was from leftwing columnist Dorothy Thompson, who had gone from being an early critic of the New Deal to a worshipful believer in the power of Franklin Roosevelt—such a believer that she wrote that the "greatest thing" the Republican Party could do for the nation was "to announce, and as quickly as possible, that if the President will accept a third term it will offer no candidate in opposition to him, but will offer instead, only a Vice Presidential candidate." She went on to propose that Roosevelt replace the current vice president, "Cactus

Jack" Garner, who had opposed the court-packing scheme and opposed intervention in the war, with Republican interventionist Wendell Willkie. Willkie, who had been a Roosevelt delegate to the 1932 Democratic convention, switched parties in 1939 over the government's takeover of private utilities through the Tennessee Valley Authority. He later earned the Republican Party nomination for president in 1940.[40]

Within a week of Lindbergh's speech, Thompson launched her first attack. She questioned the sincerity of Charles' desire for America to stay out of European affairs by claiming he himself had lived in Europe and "exercised a certain influence over European policies." Portraying Charles as unpatriotic, she conveniently ignored the fact that the Lindberghs did not want to live in Europe, but had been forced to flee there for security reasons in light of the rabid U.S. press corps and innumerable threats following the abduction and murder of their baby. Without even a hint of proof, Thompson wrote that when he left this country, Lindbergh "did not believe that the United States or its institutions were the hope of the world." She then claimed that while in England, Lindbergh discussed with "English friends the possibility of relinquishing his American citizenship," which was a complete fabrication.

Thompson also attacked Lindbergh for his friendship with Lady Nancy Astor, the American-born member of the British Parliament whose vociferous and sometimes outrageous anti-Communist, anti-Catholic ideology led some to suspect she was a Nazi sympathizer, an accusation she repeatedly denied. Regardless of her views, the mere fact that she was a friend of Lindbergh's does not mean her political beliefs can lazily be attributed to him. It was a textbook case of guilt by association.

In her column, Thompson also drew a picture of Goring hanging the now infamous medal around Lindbergh's neck—a total fallacy. She followed this with the comment, "Colonel Lindbergh's inclination toward fascism is well known to his friends"—but failed to name any such friends.[41]

The vicious attack, which fell only slightly short of calling Lindbergh a Nazi, kicked off an entire series of columns by Thompson assaulting Lindbergh's character, political views, and patriotism. With her hysterical insistence that Lindbergh "has a notion to be the American Fuehrer,"[42] she became the poster child of the anti-Lindbergh movement. That movement certainly included the mouthpiece of the Roosevelt administration, Interior Secretary Ickes, who declared that he "heartily approved" of Thompson's "smashing attack" on Lindbergh. For good measure he added, "I have never cared for Lindbergh and the last two or three years I have come to distrust his good sense, if not his motives."[43] On another occasion Ickes proclaimed that Thompson would make a "perfect Minister of Propaganda."[44]

Another *Washington Post* columnist took Thompson to task for her blatant misrepresentation of Lindbergh. Ernest K. Lindley, who was also the *Newsweek* Washington bureau chief, was an unlikely defender of Charles. Considered a reliable liberal, Lindley was a friend and early supporter of the president, and was even described as Roosevelt's "reporter/confidant."[45] But Lindley could not abide the outright falsehoods Thompson had proffered about Lindbergh. He wrote that although he did not know Lindbergh personally, he knew "a few people who know him moderately well but have not noticed that 'inclination toward Fascism' which Miss Thompson says is well known to his friends. Miss Thompson's case is built largely on circumstantial evidence."

Lindley then discussed Thompson's charge that Lindbergh had expressed a "high opinion of the German air force" to which he responded that if this were true, Lindbergh "was in substantial agreement with other military observers." On the issue of the German medal, he was quite clear. "The fact seems to have been that it was given him as a kind of surprise under circumstances which prevented his declining it without creating an ugly situation. Besides, it probably would have meant cutting himself off from further information about German aviation—information which was of great interest, perhaps value, to our own War and State departments."

Comparing Charles to the senior Lindbergh, Lindley recounted the abuse C. A. had endured for his opposition to U.S. involvement in World War I, including charges he was "pro-German. During the hysteria of World War I that was the obnoxious label plastered on everybody in this country who had the courage to say that we had no vital concern in the outcome of that war."

Charles' father "saw through the beguiling arguments and slogans of the same kind that are being used today, and by nobody more persistently

than Dorothy Thompson," Lindley wrote. On Lindbergh's insistence that
we wouldn't be able to achieve victory by simply sending planes and
cannons to Europe, he commented, "Possibly Colonel Lindbergh meant
only that once you commit yourself to a course of action, it becomes
almost impossible to back out on the ground that the cost is becoming
too great."

He closed the column with the following comment: "Whatever the
facts, Colonel Lindbergh arrived at a conclusion which seems abhorrent
to Miss Thompson: the conclusion that the United States is not a colony
or in any other form an adjunct of Europe."[46]

After his radio address, Lindbergh suffered attacks from numerous
other quarters, but perhaps the most puzzling was American Communist
Party chief Earl Browder's denunciation of Charles for being, of all things,
a "warmonger." Browder charged Lindbergh with being part of a
"monopoly" that harbored a "special plan to get America into the war
through retaining the neutrality act," though Browder never quite
explained how they were going to do this. At any rate, it should be noted
that as soon as Germany invaded the Soviet Union, the American Communists instantly transformed into "warmongers" themselves.[47]

Charles Lindbergh had waded into the debate over intervention with
his eyes wide open, but also a bit naively if he did not anticipate similar
treatment to that which was meted out to his father. He was not a politician, but instead saw himself as a mere citizen speaking his mind. Anne
wrote that she often thought, "If he had been more of a politician, he
would not have made the mistakes that trapped him in his prewar
speeches. But, if he was not a politician, why did he draw such crowds?
Certainly not by his oratory. I have to agree with one of his critics, who
ridiculed the cold 'schoolmarm tone' of his wartime address. The Lindbergh speeches for the most part were logical and technical."[48] Looking
back on this time, Anne later wrote that her husband

> was not by nature a political leader. As a public figure, his
> appeal was emotional, but he always resented and denied that
> aspect of his personality. He bent over backwards to be ratio-
> nal and to persuade people to use their minds and not their
> emotions. He never wanted to be regarded as either a hero or

a leader. Never did he wish to, or in fact did he, lead a movement—not America First, not any of the aviation organizations with which he worked, not the conservation groups
among which he ended his career.[49]

Lindbergh later described his role in the emerging "great debate" over
intervention as that of "an independent citizen, co-operating with anti-
war groups, meeting with Congressmen and Senators, testifying before
committees, writing articles, making addresses."[50] He perhaps best
described his own driving force in one of his last speeches, given in Ft.
Wayne on October 3, 1941, two months before the Japanese attacked
Pearl Harbor:

> In making these addresses, I have had no motive in mind other
> than the welfare of my country and my civilization. This is
> not a life I enjoy. Speaking is not my vocation and political
> life is not my ambition. I have done this because I believe my
> country is in mortal danger and because I could not stand by
> and see her going to destruction without pitting everything I
> had against that trend.[51]

Once he decided to speak out, Charles quickly realized that the fight over
intervention was one of the most divisive issues in American history. Just
as the coming of the Civil War divided families and friendships, the coming of World War II ruptured even the most devoted relationships. The
Lindberghs' family and circle of friends were certainly not immune to
the sometimes bitter feelings among people who had previously been
close but now differed over the great debate on intervention. Anne's
mother joined an interventionist group in opposition to her son-in-law's
position, and Anne sadly noted that most of her former classmates were
interventionists who avoided all contact with her. As she wrote in her
diary, the "arguments on both sides are becoming more and more vehement, the language increasingly bitter."

Charles had his own falling out with two close friends. The first,
Henry Breckenridge, was Charles' attorney and legal advisor since 1927,
who had advised Charles during both the airmail cancellation episode

and the kidnapping case. In June 1940 their friendship ended after Breckenridge became an outspoken interventionist. The second, Harry Guggenheim, had been even closer to Lindbergh, as the two worked on a variety of aviation and rocketry issues over the years. As Charles became increasingly active in the non-intervention movement, Guggenheim quietly withdrew from Lindbergh's circle of friends, though their friendship resumed late in the war.

Despite the personal friction, Charles had made the irrevocable decision to lead the charge against intervention. And though he was not politically astute, he had well-supported views on foreign affairs buttressed by his unique knowledge of American and European military aviation. As one writer observed shortly after Lindbergh's first radio speech,

> [T]he blitzkrieg in Poland was over, and all Charles Lindbergh's predictions about the might of the German Luftwaffe had been fulfilled. The air arm had won the war against Poland, and Britain and France had stood helplessly by while their ally was bombed and strafed into defeat, its troops panicked and put to flight by screaming Stukas, its ancient cities rubbled by Goring's bomber fleets.[52]

Being proved right, however, merely confirmed the threat Charles posed to Roosevelt and his ill-disguised war plans. Instead of being recognized for his foresight, Charles came under savage assault by FDR's partisans. Lindbergh had made enormous contributions to his country, including his aviation achievements as well as medical advances like his co-development of several versions of a perfusion pump—innovations that laid the groundwork for the invention of heart surgery. But his stellar accomplishments became irrelevant as he came under furious attack as an unpatriotic and perhaps treasonous Nazi sympathizer. These charges would largely destroy his good name for decades to come.

Chapter Seven

❧

DRAGGING AMERICA INTO WAR

The conflict between Charles Lindbergh and Franklin Roosevelt at this stage centered on the United States' participation in the war in Europe. Lindbergh was vehemently opposed to it, seeing the war as a potential disaster for all the belligerents. He was also strongly anti-Communist and feared another European war would result in the spread of Soviet Communism.

President Roosevelt, on the other hand, saw the war as a way to finally overcome the horrendous economy that his policies had failed to cure and had possibly even worsened. Looking at national unemployment figures, it is hard to argue the New Deal was a success. In 1931, the year before Roosevelt was elected president, unemployment stood at 15.9 percent. The year of his election, it jumped to 23.6 percent. After seven years of New Deal policies, unemployment in 1939 was 17.2 percent. Over nine million people out of a civilian work force of 55 million remained out of work.[1]

This record looks even more dismal when we consider that the administration's much heralded make-work program, the taxpayer-funded Works Progress Administration, employed 3 million people as of March 1939. This is equivalent to 10 million Americans on the government payroll in today's labor market.[2] If these WPA employees are added back into the ranks of the unemployed, the unemployment figure is nearly 22 percent—close to what it was when Roosevelt took office.

The economy was bad even compared to Europe. "European countries, according to a League of Nations survey, averaged only about 12 percent [unemployment] in 1938," note history professor Burton Folsom Jr. and Hillsdale College's Anita Folsom. They argue, "The New Deal, by forcing taxes up and discouraging entrepreneurs from investing, probably did more harm than good."[3]

One of the architects of those failed policies, Roosevelt's treasury secretary and close friend, Henry Morgenthau, bemoaned the administration's futile attempts to fix the economy on May 9, 1939, when he offered this shockingly frank confession to a group of Democrats from the House Ways and Means Committee:

> We have tried spending money. We are spending more than we have ever spent before and it does not work. And I have just one interest, and if I am wrong...somebody else can have my job. I want to see this country prosperous. I want to see people get a job. I want to see people get enough to eat. We have never made good on our promises....I say after eight years of this Administration we have just as much unemployment as when we started....And an enormous debt to boot.[4]

Although FDR's multiplicity of stimulus programs failed to revive the economy, the president did have another option, as Amity Shlaes observes in her history of the Depression:

> A war, however, would hand to Roosevelt the thing he had always lacked—a chance, quite literally, to provide jobs to the remaining unemployed. On the junket down the Potomac, for

example, he could count 6,000 men at work at Langley Field; 12,000 men at Portsmouth Navy Yard, where there had been 7,600; and new employment in the military or the prospects of it, for Americans elsewhere. Roosevelt hadn't known what to do with the extra people in 1938, but now (1940) he did: he could make them soldiers.[5]

The month of Secretary Morgenthau's confession, Secretary of State Cordell Hull prompted New York Democrat Sol Bloom, acting chairman of the House Committee on Foreign Affairs, to introduce a resolution to revise the Neutrality Acts. In addition to imposing an embargo on the sale of weapons and other war material to nations at war, the Neutrality Acts of 1935, 1936, and 1937 had banned loans and credits to warring states. However, at Roosevelt's request, the 1937 version contained a "cash and carry" provision that allowed the sale of embargoed items to belligerents if they paid cash and could transport the items themselves. The main concern was to ensure U.S. ships would not draw attacks, as they had in World War I, by carrying weapons to warring nations.

Among Secretary Hull's proposed revisions were eliminating the embargo on war material to belligerents, and in case that was not approved, renewing the "cash and carry" provision, which was set to expire in 1939. The bill was reported to the full House, where an amendment was attached reaffirming the embargo. Defeated, Hull turned to the Senate, where the Foreign Relations Committee, under the leadership of interventionist Key Pittman of Nevada, took up his proposal.[6] Notably, throughout the debate, both sides claimed they were voting to prevent war.

The Senate committee comprised thirteen Democrats and ten Republicans, so Hull had reason to hope for a positive outcome. However, two Democrats, Guy Gillette of Iowa and Walter George of Georgia, saw the vote as an opportunity to pay back the president for opposing their reelection bids the previous year—a move Roosevelt undertook after both senators rejected his court packing scheme. The final vote was twelve against the proposed changes and eleven in favor, which effectively killed the issue for the time being.

Furious, Roosevelt ranted against Republicans in a midnight call to Treasury Secretary Morgenthau. "I will bet you an old hat, and tell your people to spread the word around, that Hitler, when he wakes up and finds out what has happened, there will be great rejoicing in the Italian and German camps. I think we ought to introduce a bill for statues of [Republican Senators] Austin, Vandenberg, Lodge, and Taft—the four of them—to be erected in Berlin and put the swastika on them."[7]

Having evidently learned a lesson about attacking powerful members of his own party, the president assiduously refrained from criticizing the two Democrats who gave the margin of victory to his opponents. But Republicans were a different story—Roosevelt was growing bolder in tying them to international fascism. "That guilt by association pattern of identifying leading isolationists with Hitler and the Nazis," writes historian Wayne S. Cole, "was to become an increasingly effective and devastating tactic used by interventionists and the Roosevelt administration to demolish their isolationist opponents."[8]

Understanding that Roosevelt's attempts to neuter the Neutrality Acts were largely a maneuver to aid England, British prime minister Chamberlain denounced the senators who defeated the president's revisions as "pig-headed and self-righteous nobodies."[9] Roosevelt refused to give up, however. A few months later, believing he could win over his opponents on the Neutrality revisions, he assured Chamberlain, "We shall repeal the arms embargo within the next month."[10]

Roosevelt's interventionism was starkly at odds with American public opinion. Surveys at the time showed Americans largely agreed with Idaho's Republican senator William E. Borah, who opposed altering the Neutrality Acts, because "our boys would follow our guns into the trenches."[11]

In September, the Elmo Roper Public Opinion Polls conducted its first wartime survey on American public opinion about the war. The results were clear: over 37 percent of respondents agreed with the statement, "Take no sides and stay out of the war entirely, but offer to sell to anyone on a cash-and-carry basis." Another 30 percent supported an even tougher stand: "Have nothing to do with any warring country—don't even trade with them on a cash-and-carry basis."[12]

Moreover, George Gallup's American Institute of Public Opinion asked voters the following: "If it appears that Germany is defeating England and France, should the United States declare war on Germany and send our army and navy to Europe to fight?" When the question was asked during the first week in September, 40 percent responded yes and 50 percent declared no. By the third week of October, an overwhelming 71 percent of voters said no to the same question, and just 29 percent said yes. Gallup said the decline in support for intervention was not due to a lack of sympathy for the Allies, whom most voters wanted to win, but instead was "another indication of the growing intense desire on the part of the public to avoid shedding American blood on the battlefields of Europe. An overwhelming majority are for staying out no matter what happens."[13]

It was no easy task to change the minds of millions of people who still recalled World War I and were dead set against getting involved in another war. But Roosevelt had a valuable ally in molding public opinion, for the British government launched a massive, secret propaganda campaign in the United States to win public support for backing England and France in the war.

Ironically, during his September 3 fireside chat, the president warned the American people to be weary of the exact kind of manipulation that the British would soon employ against them. "As I told my press conference on Friday, it is of the highest importance that the press and radio use the utmost caution to discriminate between actual verified fact on the one hand and mere rumor on the other. I can add to that by saying that I hope the people of this country will also discriminate most carefully between news and rumor. Do not believe of necessity everything you hear or read."[14]

As British historian Nicholas John Cull noted, British propaganda had been instrumental in getting the United States involved in the first war against Germany, but had left a sour taste in the mouths of millions of Americans because "Americans knew that, throughout the war, the British had shamelessly manipulated war news, had peddled pictures of bloated Prussian beasts, had invented tales of 'Hun' atrocities, and had faked the evidence to fit."[15] The man who directed these efforts out of

London, Canadian novelist Sir Gilbert Parker, had exposed the entire operation in a 1918 *Harper's* article. Parker revealed he had arranged interviews for American journalists with British political leaders, flattered Americans' "educated" opinions, and distributed propaganda to "American libraries, educational institutions and periodicals." He also "established relations with influential and eminent people of every profession in the United States" to win their support for American entry into World War I.[16]

The second British propaganda campaign to draw the United States into war was headed, at least in major part, by another Canadian, Sir William Stephenson, who was immortalized in the best-selling book, *A Man Called Intrepid*. Instead of being run out of London, this time the propaganda organization, known as British Security Co-ordination, located its headquarters on two full floors at Rockefeller Center in New York City, where one thousand people were employed.

It was from that office, and another near New York's Battery Park operating with the even less innocuous title of the British Library of Information, that British agents, according to Thomas Mahl's definitive account of the British propaganda campaign, "mounted in 1939 a massive secret political campaign in the United States (including the use of front groups, agents, collaborators, manipulation of polling data, involvement in election campaigns, etc.) to weaken the isolationists, bring the United States into the war, and influence U.S. war policy in England's favor."[17]

The British campaign had two primary goals. The first was to discredit anyone who opposed U.S. intervention in the war, including members of Congress and famous American citizens. For example, the Brits ran a six-year-long operation to defeat Congressman Hamilton Fish, a Republican non-interventionist from the president's home district in New York. Through a front organization called the Nonpartisan Committee to Defeat Hamilton Fish, British agents set up a headquarters in the district's largest city, Poughkeepsie, and spent thousands of dollars spreading rumors and lies about Fish. They even managed to get two interventionist writers, Drew Pearson and Robert S. Allen, to run columns just before Election Day suggesting that Nazis were subsidizing Fish's campaign. However, the congressman's popularity held up under the onslaught and he was reelected, though by the smallest margin he had ever received. After the election one British intelligence agent complained that the "local Democratic machine in the district was of practically no help."

Determined to unseat Fish, British agents spent the next two years spreading more false stories about him and his alleged association with Nazis. The campaign against him continued even after the attack at Pearl Harbor and American entry into the war. In the 1942 election, Fish won again, but by an even smaller margin. It was not until the 1944 election, after Fish's congressional district was separated into three pieces, that the British agents were able to drive him out of office.[18]

The second goal of the propaganda campaign was, of course, to gain the support of a majority of Americans for the position of the interventionists. Winning this support was accomplished in part by manipulating news stories coming out of Europe and feeding them to American reporters and columnists who were either naïve or pro-intervention.

Furthermore, the British agents created numerous front groups designed to do their bidding. In addition to the group dedicated to defeating Hamilton Fish, these included Friends of Democracy, the Nonsectarian Anti-Nazi League, the League for Human Rights, the Fight for Freedom Committee, the American Labor Committee to Aide British Labor, and the Committee for Inter-American Co-operation. They each gave the impression of being a homegrown organization, and each had its own set of goals. But they were all under the complete control of British secret agents determined to change public and congressional opinion and get America into the war.[19]

Perhaps the Brits' most successful endeavor was their massive effort to manipulate public opinion polls. The results of the most prestigious opinion polls would gradually change in 1940 from strong opposition to any involvement in the war, to approval of selling arms to the British and French, and then to support for most government actions just short of actually going to war. The polls were dubious, however, since British

intelligence agents had infiltrated Gallup and other polling organiza-
tions, and in some cases published their own polls.[20] Professor Tom
Mahl chides historians who unquestioningly cite the polls as proof that
Americans became increasingly enamored of joining the war:

> The first thing to know when reading the public opinion polls
> commonly cited from 1939 to 1942 is that none of them was
> produced by disinterested seekers of truth. The most promi-
> nently published polls were all under the influence of British
> intelligence, its friends, employees, and agents. At the very
> best, when questions of the war or international relations are
> considered, the major polls should be thought of as what
> modern critics call "advocacy polls." Unknown to the public,
> the polls of Gallup, Hadley Cantril, Market Analysts, Inc.,
> and Roper were all done under the influence of dedicated
> interventionists and British intelligence agents.[21]

The British manipulation of opinion polls had far-reaching effects. In
one egregious case, British agents worked to undermine the anti-inter-
ventionist leaders of the Congress of Industrial Organizations (CIO).
Led by mineworkers' leader John L. Lewis, the group of unions belong-
ing to the CIO opposed any steps that could push America into war. At
one annual CIO convention, British agents rigged a poll of delegates.
As one account related: "'Great care was taken beforehand to make
certain that the poll results would turn out as desired'.... The results
rewarded the effort: '96 percent thought defeating Hitler was more
important than keeping the U.S.A. out of the war; 95 percent said they
would advocate keeping the Japanese out of British possessions in
Asia.'" The efforts by the agents "[were] particularly appreciated by
some representatives of the Roosevelt Administration who attended the
convention as observers."[22]

Many union leaders opposed the war because they knew that it was
working-class Americans whose bodies would be strewn across European

battlefields. They must have been shocked to learn that their members were willing not only to go to war to save England from the Germans, but were also willing to fight and die to protect the British empire's possessions—which, coincidentally, was a major goal of Winston Churchill's. Many of those same members would also have been shocked to learn these were their own views.

Not to be outdone by their colleagues in the Intelligence Service, the British Foreign Office hired the services of a noted advertising company, the J. Walter Thompson Agency, to develop a plan to influence American public opinion. "This plan suggested that Britain emphasize the limited nature of the aid needed from the United States, on the theory that the Americans would be more forthcoming if they knew that their troops would not be required."[23]

In part because they claimed to use special scientific techniques to gauge the public's attitude, the polls were extremely influential. As Richard W. Steele, former historian for the Office of the Joint Chiefs of Staff, noted, "Public opinion was what the polls said it was, and as a result polls became a political weapon that could be used to inform the views of the doubtful, weaken the commitment of opponents, and strengthen the conviction of supporters."[24]

The entire covert British propaganda campaign was set in motion by then-First Lord of the Admiralty Winston Churchill before the war broke out. As previously noted, he was determined from the beginning to turn the United States into a combatant. In fact, less than two weeks after he became prime minister, he revealed to his son Randolph his key to winning the war: "I shall drag the United States in."[25]

Drag it in he did, with more than a little help from the American president. President Roosevelt paid close attention to public opinion polls, and must have been cheered as they slowly moved in his direction. Was he aware British agents were influencing them? In all probability he was, especially since he had his own mole working alongside the British inside the Gallup organization. He may even have known that Gallup had been persuaded not to publish polls that might be harmful to the British cause.[26] In fact, Roosevelt once told William Stephenson, the British agent who oversaw the campaign, "I'm your biggest undercover agent."[27] It was a stunning statement coming from a president whose administration and supporters were furiously attacking the loyalty and patriotism of his critics.

———

On October 13, 1939, Lindbergh gave his second radio address. Called "Neutrality and War," the speech discussed the proposed revisions to the Neutrality Acts and echoed the Monroe Doctrine's determination to keep European powers out of the Western hemisphere. He argued American neutrality must be built on strength, and that our armed forces "must be ready to wage war with all the resources of our nation" if any country threatened the Western hemisphere. He categorically rejected the pacifist position, insisting, "Neutrality built on pacifism alone will eventually fail."

Drawing from the American experience in World War I, Charles called the extension of cash loans and credit for $10 billion to warring European nations a step toward our involvement in that war. His theme was: first our credit, then our arms, then our young men to die once again on European battlefields. And once again, he denounced the Allies' failure to repay their debts to us after we had spilled our own soldiers' blood to help them win their war:

> After that war was over, we found ourselves in the position of having financed a large portion of the expenditures of European countries. And when the time came to pay us back, these countries simply refused to do so. They called us "Uncle Shylock." They were horror struck at the idea of turning over to us any of their islands in America to compensate for their debts, or for our help in winning their war. They seized all the German colonies and carved up Europe to suit their fancy. They took our money and they took our soldiers.[28]

Charles' invocation of World War I was powerful, for many Americans still remembered that the war had cost over 116,000 American lives and drained more than $22 billion from our treasury. In return, we received little from our victorious allies except resentment at their financial and military dependence on the United States. Taking into account the wide-spread belief among Americans that the mistreatment of the defeated Germans by France and Britain had led to this new war, it is easy to understand why a majority of Americans opposed involvement in another of "their" wars.

Some Americans even recalled with distaste the words of a young Winston Churchill in the House of Commons: "We have got all we want in territory, but our claim to be left in undisputed enjoyment of vast and splendid possessions, largely acquired by war and largely maintained by force, is one which often seems less reasonable to others than to us."[29]

In his October radio address, Lindbergh presented his own four-part program for American neutrality:

1. An embargo on offensive weapons and munitions.
2. The unrestricted sale of purely defensive armaments.
3. The prohibition of American shipping from the belligerent countries of Europe and their danger zones.
4. The refusal of credit to belligerent nations or their agents.[30]

With such arguments, Lindbergh gradually became the face of the non-interventionist movement. However, his opposition to Roosevelt's policies, especially on the revisions of the Neutrality Laws, was not total. His position on selling defensive but not offensive weapons was similar to that of former president Hoover, and meant that Britain could purchase all the anti-aircraft guns she could afford. He also supported renewal of cash-and-carry, though he opposed extending credit to countries that had not yet repaid their debts to us from the last war—and that included France and Britain.[31]

On October 26, 1939, Roosevelt gave his own radio address. Despite his May defeat, he had continued pressing for his revisions to

the Neutrality Acts, and the Senate was to vote on the matter the following day. This was a crucial vote for the president, and he had to
neutralize opponents who warned his revisions would move America
one more step toward war. Without naming anyone, the president
criticized what he called the "orators and commentators and others
beating their breast and proclaiming against sending the boys of American mothers to fight on the battlefields of Europe. The simple truth is
that no person in any responsible place in the national government in
Washington...has ever suggested...sending the boys of America's mothers to fight on the battlefields of Europe."[32]

The revisions passed the Senate by a vote of sixty-three to thirty, with
twelve Democrats voting against the president. The House passed the
measure 243 to 181, and Roosevelt signed it into law on November 4.
Cash and carry (which many non-interventionist senators had actually
supported and had tried unsuccessfully to vote on separately) resumed,
which was of help only to England and France, since Germany and Italy
did not have fleets of merchant ships that could cross the Atlantic without confronting the Royal Navy. The new law also established a maritime danger zone around Europe which U.S. ships were prohibited from
entering.

No sooner was the law signed than Roosevelt began looking for ways
to weaken the new stipulations. "He personally favored a proposal from
the U.S. Maritime Commission to reflag U.S. merchant ships as Panama-
nian without changing their ownership, which would enable them to
evade the cash-and-carry provisions." The president dropped the suggestion when several interventionist leaders, including Senator Harry Truman, objected that it was devious.[33]

Lindbergh, who had started the non-interventionist campaign virtually alone, soon found wide support for his actions. He met with both
Democratic and Republican senators in Washington who also opposed
the war, including powerful Democrats such as Harry Byrd of Virginia,
with whom Lindbergh "agreed almost a hundred percent on the necessity
of keeping the United States out of the war, and also on the best way to
handle the embargo situation."[34] Byrd introduced the colonel to other

like-minded Democratic senators, including Bailey of North Carolina, Burke of Nebraska, George of Georgia, Johnson of California, and Gerry of Rhode Island.

Perhaps most notably, Herbert Hoover asked Lindbergh to visit him at his residence in New York's Waldorf-Astoria. The former president told Lindbergh they were in agreement on the war, and he suggested that Lindbergh organize a nonpartisan, non-interventionist organization to further the cause.

———

In Europe the war continued. On November 30, the Soviet Red Army attacked Finland. The Soviets brought to bear twenty-six divisions with a total of 465,000 men, while Finland's defense relied on just nine divisions with 130,000 men. Throwing one thousand warplanes against the Finns' 150, Stalin mercilessly bombed Helsinki. Resisting tenaciously, the Finns inflicted major losses on the Soviets, which bore out Lindbergh's analysis that the Soviet war machine suffered major deficiencies. However, the hopelessly outnumbered Finns eventually capitulated, signing a treaty giving Stalin 11 percent of their territory.[35]

On the Western front, on April 9, 1940, Germany invaded Denmark and Norway. German intelligence learned from intercepted British naval transmissions that an Anglo-French force was to land at several strategic points along the Norwegian coast in an effort to deny Germany the production from Swedish iron mines that fuelled its military.[36]

With Hitler only thirty miles from the Belgian frontier, 136 German divisions, supported by paratroopers and glider troops, swept across the borders of neutral Belgium and Holland at dawn on May 10, 1940, on the way toward invading France. Later that day British prime minister Chamberlain stepped down, and Winston Churchill became both prime minister and minister of defense. Five days later Churchill sent a secret telegram to Roosevelt explaining his needs. These were, in Churchill's words:

- the loan of forty or fifty of your older destroyers;
- several hundred of the latest types of aircraft;
- anti-aircraft equipment and ammunition;
- the ability to purchase steel in the United States;
- the visit of a United States squadron to Irish ports [to fend off possible German parachute drops into that country]; and, to
- keep that Japanese dog quiet in the Pacific, using Singapore in any way convenient.[37]

The president lacked the authority to do most of what Churchill requested, except possibly to send a few Navy ships to visit an Irish port. And in truth, America was not in a strong position to dole out military equipment, because Roosevelt had largely ignored the pleas of Lindbergh and others to increase America's military preparedness. As historian Ted Morgan notes, "In the eight years since Roosevelt's election, the military had been ignored. The entire Army numbered 227,000 men, as against a German regular army of 850,000. There were only a handful of bombers and employable tanks. The P-40s and other fighters still had machine guns that were synchronized to fire through the propeller, as in 1918."[38]

In his response to Churchill, Roosevelt told him as much. Then he ordered Army chief of staff General Marshall to check all military warehouses and supply depots for unused equipment that might be of help to the British. "Scrape the bottom of the barrel," he told Marshall. The search turned up a large quantity of items left over from the last war. Mostly of British manufacture, these included 35,000 machine guns, 500,000 Enfield rifles, 500 75-millimeter artillery guns, and a supply of ammunition.[39]

On May 16, soon after the Germans' western blitz, Roosevelt addressed a joint session of Congress. Referring to the Germans' steady advances against Allied armies, he said, "These are ominous days—days whose swift and shocking developments force every neutral nation to look to its defenses in the light of new factors." He then requested nearly $1 billion for a defense fund. The money, which was in addition to all other appropriations, would be used "principally for the increase of production of airplanes, anti-aircraft guns and the training of additional personnel for these weapons." He asked Congress not to "take any action which in any way hamper or delay the delivery of American-made planes to foreign nations which have ordered them or seek to purchase more." He also said he wanted to increase the manufacture of warplanes from the current rate of 12,000 aircraft per year to 50,000.[40]

As the war spread through Europe, both non-intervention and pro-intervention groups sprang up throughout America (though some of the latter were creatures of British intelligence). As de facto leader of the non-interventionist camp, Lindbergh initially concentrated on writing articles for various publications and meeting with influential Americans both in and out of government. Like it or not, he had spoken his mind, people had listened carefully, and he had become the "nation's symbol of neutrality."[41] As such, interventionists further intensified their attacks on him.

Three days after Roosevelt's congressional speech, Charles gave his third national radio address. This one, which like the others he wrote by himself, he titled "The Air Defense of America." Without mentioning the president's speech, Lindbergh countered once again Roosevelt's impulse to build as many airplanes as possible. "The power of aviation has been greatly underrated in the past," he said. "Now we must be careful not to overrate this power in the excitement of reaction. Air strength depends more upon the establishment of intelligent and consistent policies than upon the sudden construction of huge numbers of airplanes."

He discussed the importance of new discoveries and developments in aviation and how they impact different nations. He also expressed his belief that America was fortunate, since "our people have natural ability in the design, construction and operation of aircraft. Our highly organized industry, our widely separated centers of population, our elimination of formalities in interstate travel—all contribute to the development of American aviation." He called for the nations of the Western hemisphere to work together to build a mutually advantageous defense policy against European and Asian aggressors.

Halfway through what had been a pragmatic speech, he changed the tone and spoke of America's legacy to future generations: "The greatest inheritance we can pass on to our children is a reasonable solution of the problems that confront us in our [own] time—a strong nation, a lack of debt, a solid American character free from the entanglements of the Old World."

Near the end of his fifteen-minute address, Lindbergh repeated his now standard refrain that "we need a greater air force, a greater army, and a greater navy; they have been inadequate for many years." He closed the talk by asserting, "We cannot aid others until we have first placed our own country in a position of spiritual and material leadership and strength."[42]

This speech must have struck a nerve with the president, for the next day he told Treasury Secretary Morgenthau, "I am absolutely convinced that Lindbergh is a Nazi."[43] FDR biographer Ted Morgan notes that the comment reflected Roosevelt's increasing animosity toward non-interventionists as he pushed America toward war:

> Already, [Roosevelt] was taking the attitude that those who disagreed with him were disloyal. In fact, the isolationists had a valid case, rooted in the feeling that England expected every American to do his duty. The chances of a German attack on the United States were remote, and there were sound reasons not to become involved. But to Roosevelt, the isolationists were helping Hitler, and he took extraordinary measures to combat subversion.[44]

Roosevelt had to proceed cautiously, however. Although by mid-1940 the polls, for what they were worth, showed growing public support for assisting the Allies, the public still overwhelmingly opposed direct U.S. involvement in the war. Furthermore, Lindbergh remained popular despite the vitriol hurled at him by pro-Roosevelt newspaper columnists such as Dorothy Thompson as well as Walter Winchell, a gossip maven turned foreign affairs expert. Thus, instead of attacking him directly, the White House continued to outsource the task to others.

This time it was the turn of South Carolina's James F. Byrnes, an outspoken Roosevelt supporter who was rewarded the following year with a seat on the Supreme Court. The South Carolinian's relationship with the president was so close that other Democratic senators called him the "assistant president." Byrnes, speaking over the radio on the Columbia Broadcasting System on May 22, 1940, charged that Lindbergh's call not to succumb to war hysteria was similar to "fifth column activities." He also alleged that people like Lindbergh had "lulled into a false sense of security" the governments of England and France. The truth, of course, was that Charles had urged them to avoid a war until they were prepared for one. They had not listened, however, and now German forces were sweeping across France toward Paris.

Byrnes repeatedly referred to Lindbergh as "Mr. Lindbergh" instead of Colonel Lindbergh, in an obvious attempt to downplay his Army service. He went on to claim incorrectly that Lindbergh had opposed the cash and carry provision of the Neutrality Acts. Ignoring Lindbergh's repeated calls for military preparedness, the senator blatantly misquoted Charles as advocating appeasement. Byrnes ended his attack with a vague but incendiary reference to Charles being one of "the Fifth Column's most effective fellow travelers."[45]

It would not be the last time Lindbergh heard that explosive allegation.

———

A May 20, 1940 telegram from Churchill to Roosevelt, part of their secret correspondence, outlined the English plans should there be a successful German landing in Britain: "Our intention is whatever happens to fight on to the end in this island." There would be no government in exile in Canada or Australia, or anywhere else. The prime minister, however, pointed out that while his cabinet had taken a "no surrender" position, should his ministers fall and others take their place, there would be no accounting for their actions. He emphasized that a new government might be willing to trade the British fleet for reasonable terms from Hitler.[46]

According to FDR's son Elliott, that message "helped to cinch it, so far as Father was concerned. The British must receive all possible aid short of American entry into war."[47]

General Marshall visited the offices of the British purchasing mission in Washington and handed Arthur Purvis, head of the mission, a list of the weapons that were inventoried according to the president's instructions. The British were told that the War Department could not sell them directly under the terms of even the revised Neutrality Acts, but that they could be declared surplus items not required for the defense of the United States. They would then be sold to private companies that could resell them to the British. This was a slick way around the Neutrality Acts that Congress had already revised at the president's urging.[48]

Marshall objected to including the aircraft Purvis had requested. "Our situation in bombers is very serious because we have this antiquated force in Panama [for defense of the canal] and Puerto Rico and Hawaii as well as...in the United States." He then told the secretary there was no ammunition for anti-aircraft guns "and will not be for six months." A similar situation existed for the anti-tank guns. "So if we gave them the guns they could do nothing with them."[49]

Acting as if America were already at war, Roosevelt issued instructions on May 21, 1940, for widespread wiretapping of those he called "subversives." The wiretaps, according to Ted Morgan, were "used against FDR's political enemies."[50]

Amidst Roosevelt's rush to war, some of his officials worried the poor economy was hindering his plans. At a cabinet meeting in late May, Attorney General Robert Jackson told the group they could say all they wanted about Hitler, but the truth was that the Fuhrer had provided every man a job, and so every German at least had enough to eat. Secretary Ickes interpreted Jackson's comment to mean "that we are not going to have a united country [in] back of us as long as so many of our people are in economic despair."[51]

Despite such obstacles, throughout 1940 Roosevelt worked doggedly to pull the United States, step-by-step, into the war. All the while, he denied doing so. It was also an election year, and the president was preparing to run for an unprecedented third term, something no previous president had seriously considered. He could not run on a platform of "I am going to send your sons to Europe to fight yet another war there." Despite that being his real goal, his campaign slogan was the opposite: "Your boys are not going to be sent into any foreign wars."[52]

In his autobiography, Lindbergh summarized the interventionists' disingenuous strategy for getting America into the war:

> Every poll taken showed a large majority of the American populace to be against participation in the war. Yet it was obvious that the United States was moving constantly closer to belligerency. Very cleverly, prowar organizations took advantage of the fact that Americans, although unwilling to enter an internecine war in Europe, preferred an English-French victory. A policy called "steps short of war" was therefore advocated by prowar forces—a policy that, if followed, would inevitably bring the United States into the conflict. It was a policy difficult to oppose because each step was cushioned by hypocrisy until no single one of them seemed to be of critical importance.[53]

Indeed, even as Roosevelt explicitly rejected American participation in the war, it wasn't difficult to read between the lines of his speeches to decipher his real goal. Take, for example, a fireside chat he broadcasted on the evening of May 26, 1940. Speaking from the White House, Roosevelt first made a veiled attack on opponents of his interventionist policies, referring to "the fifth column that betrays a nation unprepared for treachery. Spies, saboteurs and traitors are the actors in this new strategy. With all these, we must deal vigorously." Near the end of his talk, the president explained the goals of his internationalist policies: "We build a life for generations yet unborn. We defend and build a way of life, not for America alone, but for all mankind. Ours is a high duty, a noble task."[54]

Thus, it had suddenly become the "high duty" of the American people to defend a way of life not just for Americans, but for everyone in the world. The implication here was that Americans had a universalist mission that was much bigger than merely defending their own country.

As shown in Roosevelt's speech, the president and many of his top officials were increasingly invoking the specter of "fifth columnists," which they cited as a primary reason for the Allies' failure to defeat the Germans. This was a near total fabrication. The closest thing there was to a "fifth column" in Europe was groups of civilians who urged their country's soldiers not to confront German soldiers in their own neighborhoods. In his history of the fall of France, William Shirer cited such actions on the part of French civilians:

> Most demoralizing of all to army units still trying to fight were the efforts of civilians to prevent them from offering further resistance that might damage their homes and shops. At one village on the River Indre the local inhabitants extinguished the fuses of explosives already lit by army engineers to blow the bridge there and slow down the German advance. French troops digging in a Poiters were surprised to see the mayor driving out with a white flag to surrender the town to the Germans. He was backed by the inhabitants, who had threatened to tear down the barricades erected by the soldiers. French civilians, like so many of the troops, had no more stomach for the fighting that had started only a month before.[55]

Such actions were surely demoralizing, but it's hardly evidence of a widespread, pro-German fifth column. Undoubtedly, after the fall of France various collaborators emerged to work in the Vichy regime, but that kind of opportunism is something far different than a nation harboring an extensive, organized network of traitors working to enable a German occupation. That image was largely created by interventionists, who found it a useful concept for tarring opponents of their war plans as traitors.

Roosevelt even used the fifth column as one of the themes for his speech accepting the Democratic Party nomination for a third term. In that address, given on July 19, 1940, the president said he had sought to aid the Allies "in the face of appeaser fifth columnists who charged me with hysteria and war mongering." He did not name those "appeasers," but the majority of his listeners knew whom he meant, and Charles Lindbergh headed the list. In that same speech Roosevelt made a direct appeal to create "some form of selection by draft," claiming it was "as necessary and fair today as it was in 1917 and 1918."[56]

Meanwhile, Lindbergh continued speaking out and writing against the march to war. His position, as he said repeatedly, was that the interventionists were using the same arguments they had used when they had urged Britain and France to declare war on Germany while neither country had realistically prepared to fight a war. The British and French had "one last desperate plan remaining. They hope that they may be able to persuade us send another American Expeditionary Force to Europe, and to share with England militarily, as well as financially, the fiasco of this war."[57]

Lindbergh and other non-interventionists concerned Prime Minister Churchill, who worried over how much influence they really had. It was hard for him to tell by reading American public opinion polls, since he knew his own agents were manipulating them. Churchill, however, knew he could count on Roosevelt. In fall 1940 Churchill's primary advisor on American issues, North Whitehead, told him that "America is not in the bag. However, the President is engaged in carefully calculated steps to give us full assistance."[58]

———

Toward the end of May, the German Army pushed British and French troops in northern France into a small pocket around the English Channel port town of Dunkirk, just ten miles from the Belgian border. "On the morning of May 24 three panzer divisions and two motorized infantry divisions of General Ewald von Kleist's army group were within fifteen miles of Dunkirk. The general estimated that the city and its port could be his in less than one day."[59]

At 6:00 the previous evening, General von Rundstedt had ordered the advance to "halt tomorrow." On the 24th, Hitler visited Rundstedt's headquarters and agreed with his "halt" order. A second order, issued in

Hitler's name, commanded that all attacks on Dunkirk were to be "discontinued."[60]

Historians continue to argue over the motive behind Hitler's actions. Some believe he was still interested in coming to terms with the British as part of his design to divide the Western world between the British empire and his new German empire. Whatever the reason, it gave the English time to send virtually every craft that could float to Dunkirk and evacuate the troops cornered there. By the time the evacuation ended, nearly 340,000 troops were brought to England. This included 140,000 French and a smaller number of other Allied forces, including Czechs, Belgians, and Poles.

Even as the evacuation was in progress, British agent Arthur Purvis arrived at Secretary Morgenthau's office with a fresh list of war material the Anglo-French allies were requesting. They included advanced weapons that were then still on order for the U.S. military, including the brand new torpedo boats that Morgenthau said could never be defined as surplus equipment. The administration was sympathetic to the Allies' needs, but their problem was, as Morgenthau himself put it, "to find a way frankly to get around the law."[61]

With its army evacuated minus most of its heavy weapons and vehicles, Britain was unprepared for what it expected would be Hitler's next step, the invasion of the British Isles. French leaders urged a joint Anglo-French appeal to the United States for help, but the British war cabinet rejected the idea because it "feared such an appeal would suggest weakness, even panic, to the Americans. But it did agree to sound out the American president on an appeal." As a result, the British ambassador, Lord Lothian, met with the president. Roosevelt "did not consider such an appeal desirable. It would hinder him in getting materiel to the Allies and would slow down the crystallization of American opinion in favor of aid because it would be interpreted as an attempt by foreigners to influence the United States in the direction of war. However, Roosevelt felt that a broadcast by Churchill might be useful, with the qualification that it should be addressed to the British Empire."[62]

Churchill planned to speak to the House of Commons about Dunkirk, and arrangements were made to broadcast the address in the United

States. On June 4, Churchill gave one of his most famous speeches, dubbed the "no surrender speech." It included the now famous vow, "We shall fight on the beaches, we shall fight on the landing grounds, we shall fight in the fields and the streets, we shall fight in the hills, we shall never surrender." Overlooked by many writers is the part that was most assuredly addressed to his American audience; he said if the British Isles fell to the Germans, the British fleet and the Empire would continue to fight "until, in God's good time, the New World, with all its power and might, steps forth to the rescue and liberation of the old."[63]

Elliott Roosevelt described his father's reaction to the address. "Father scratched around for whatever was readily available for the British shopping list," he said, "and nudged Morgenthau, his liaison with the purchasing commission, into coming up with legal justification, no matter how flimsy, for what he was doing. Soon 500,000 World War I rifles were on the way for Britain's civilian Home Guard."[64]

On the same day as Churchill's speech, administration officials, including Treasury Secretary Morgenthau, Assistant Secretary of State Sumner Welles, and attorneys in the Treasury and Justice Departments, devised a plan under which the government would transfer "surplus items" to private companies that would then resell them to the British and French. While Welles agreed that "a direct sale of arms and munitions to a belligerent would violate American neutrality under international law, and would also breach the Neutrality Act," the officials seemed satisfied that their plan would not technically violate the law. Fortuitously, they also uncovered a 1919 law that would allow them to do this without the usual requirement of advertising for bidders. In actuality, the government was selling the arms to the warring nations in violation of the Neutrality Acts, but using private manufacturers as intermediaries to give the entire operation a veneer of legality.[65]

On June 7, Roosevelt made his intentions clear to former budget director Lewis Douglas. "Very many planes are actually on the way to the Allies.... We are turning in old Army and Navy material to the manufacturers who have been given orders for new and up-to-date material. I have a sneaking suspicion that the old material ... will be on its way to France in few days." He explained to Douglas that he was "not talking very much about it" because opponents would "confuse the public mind."[66]

While Roosevelt was concerned about the public becoming "confused," he had few qualms about finding ways to ignore federal laws, especially the Neutrality Acts. At a cabinet meeting on June 9, the president "became impatient" with Navy Secretary Charles Edison, who was due to leave soon for a successful run for governor of New Jersey (and would be replaced as navy secretary by a Republican interventionist, newspaper publisher Frank Knox).[67] Edison had said that the Navy's judge advocate general told him the transfer of Navy weapons to England and France that Roosevelt had ordered was "illegal." Dismissing the judge advocate general as an "old admiral" and a "sea lawyer," Roosevelt told Edison to send him on vacation and to get the attorney general to give him legal advice instead. When Secretary Edison objected, Roosevelt told him to forget what the judge advocate general had said "and do what I told you to do."[68]

———

In a speech to the graduating class at the University of Virginia at Charlottesville on June 10, the same day Italy declared war on France and Britain, Roosevelt enunciated his government's policy toward the war in Europe: "[W]e will pursue two obvious and simultaneous courses; we will extend to the opponents of force the material resources of this nation and, at the same time, we will harness and speed up the use of those resources in order that we ourselves in the Americas may have equipment and training equal to the task of any emergency and every defense."[69]

The following day, under the headline "Our Help Pledged," the *New York Times* reported the speech was "the President's only reference to plans for compulsory universal military training for which he already has expressed sympathy."[70]

The president's speech in Virginia was hailed in London. The *Times of London* saw in the speech a preparation to "revolutionize" the U.S. economy and to play a part in the war, "though not presently the same part as we." The *Telegram* interpreted the speech to mean that the United

States was "not a neutral any longer but a noncombatant associate of the Allies." The *Daily Mail* proclaimed, "America's awakening cheers and heartens the Allies." The *Daily Herald* editorialized, "To the President: We know you will not fail us."[71]

Columnist Arthur Krock noted in the *New York Times* that the Neutrality Acts were not the only legal obstacle to Roosevelt providing war supplies to the Allies. "By the terms of the Johnson Act no nation under default of its debt to this government may float private or public loans here. Two such nations are 'the opponents of force,' France and Great Britain, and money is very much a 'material resource.'"[72] Neither nation, however, would be able to purchase much on a cash and carry basis. They would both either require loans from the U.S. government or be allowed to make purchases on credit.

In March 1944, Lieutenant General Walter Bedell Smith was selected by Supreme Commander General Dwight Eisenhower to be his chief of staff. On June 11, 1940, while still a major, Smith delivered an Allied request for 500 75-mm guns and a considerable amount of ammunition for those guns to the president's military advisor and secretary, General Edwin Watson. Watson asked the major his opinion about fulfilling the request.

> I replied that if the War Department could be assured that we would not be called upon for a general mobilization within two years...the transaction was perfectly safe, but that if we were required to mobilize, after having released guns necessary for this mobilization and were found to be short in artillery material...everyone who was a party to the deal might hope to be found hanging from a lamppost. Whereupon General Watson took the paper in to the President, who ok'd the transaction.[73]

Five days later, the president requested the resignation of the most influential member of his administration who opposed the transfer of planes and weapons to the Allies, Secretary of War Harry Woodring, replacing him with outspoken interventionist Henry Stimson. A Republican,

Stimson had served as President Taft's secretary of war and President Hoover's secretary of state. Woodring probably sealed his fate when, in September 1937, he wrote a memorandum to the president observing, "It is evident that the influences which led America into the World War are again at work. The objective is the same—to commit the U.S. to the employment of armed forces to any extent necessary to support British policy in the present world situation"[74]

Stimson was a logical choice for the president. As a Republican, he would lend an air of national unity to the cabinet, and he had recently "urged in a nationally broadcast radio address that compulsory military training be made a matter of national policy and that the United States should convoy American ships carrying food and military supplies to the French and British forces."[75] Interior Secretary Ickes thought the appointment of Stimson was "excellent" because his position on the war "has been both right and courageous."

Following the announcement of Woodring's resignation, the *Topeka Kansas Capital* newspaper released a statement he had made several weeks earlier, which he had asked them not to publish before he left office. Woodring told the paper, "I am an advocate of adequate defense, but I will never stand for sending American boys into Europe's shambles. There is a comparatively small clique of international financiers who want the United States to declare war and get into the European mess with everything we have, including our man power. They don't like me because I am against stripping our own defenses."[76]

While these cabinet changes were taking place, Roosevelt was preparing to run for a third term as president. Front runners among Republicans to oppose him in the election included non-interventionist senators Robert Taft and Arthur Vandenberg. Then, to the surprise of most observers, "Wendell Willkie stole the nomination from under the noses of the party professionals. Until recently a Democrat, and having voted for FDR in 1932, Willkie had endeared himself to Republican businessmen by leading the fight against [the Tennessee Valley Authority] as president of a powerful utility."[77]

Willkie was an interventionist who publicly supported the administration's policy of aiding the British and French. His nomination by a party populated by non-interventionists left many people wondering what happened. Willkie had only switched parties in 1939, and now he was the Republicans' candidate for president. Although the president and the Republican nominee both favored the little steps that were leading the United States to war, as candidates they both publicly professed they would not engage in foreign wars. Willkie promised, "I will never send an American boy to fight in any European war," while Roosevelt pledged, "Your boys are not going to be sent into any foreign wars."

Pat Buchanan terms the 1940 presidential campaign "among the most dishonest ever held. Both FDR and Willkie were, by that time, interventionists at heart. After the election they would work together to steer America into war." The reason for their deception, he explains, was that "86 percent of Americans said they did not want to go to war against Germany and Italy."[78]

Roosevelt was swept back into the White House in the 1940 election, winning 54.7 percent of the vote. It was substantially less that the 60.8 percent he won in the 1936 election, but with his third term now secure, he could more openly pursue his war aims. As Henry Kissinger wrote, "Immediately after the election, Roosevelt moved to eliminate the requirement of the Fourth Neutrality Act—that American war materials could only be purchased for cash. In a fireside chat, borrowing a term from Wilson, he challenged the United States to become the "arsenal of democracy."[79]

The key driver behind Roosevelt's efforts was a letter Churchill wrote him on December 7, 1940. A long rambling missive, it had the backing of his war cabinet. After covering a variety of war issues, the prime minister got to the heart of the matter: "The moment approaches when we shall no longer be able to pay cash for shipping and other supplies."[80] With Britain unable to pay for her weapons, Roosevelt maneuvered to supply them on credit.

———

From June to November 1940, the Gallup polls revealed what many thought was a substantial change in American public opinion toward

the war. On June 25, over 64 percent "believed that it was more important to stay out of the war than to assist Britain." By October 20, the poll
was split 50–50, a truly radical change. On November 19, 60 percent
said it was more important to help Britain than to stay out of the war.[81]
It is impossible to decipher whether this complete reversal of public
opinion in five months was due to events in Europe or to the efforts of
British intelligence agents working inside the Gallup organization.[82]

Regardless of American public opinion, Britain continued to draw
America into its war with Germany. Several times during the year,
Churchill, who seemed to know when and how to push Roosevelt's but-
tons, requested the transfer of some U.S. Navy warships to the Royal
Navy. During a predawn meeting at the Admiralty building in London,
Churchill met with Ambassador Kennedy to ask for America's help. The
ambassador, who had been close to Chamberlain and thought the new
prime minister drank too much alcohol, wanted the United States to stay
out of the war. When Churchill asked Kennedy what the U.S. could do
to aid Britain, the ambassador explained that a great portion of the U.S.
fleet was in the Pacific, and when it came to warplanes, "We haven't
sufficient airplanes for our own use." Churchill replied that he would ask
Roosevelt directly for whatever aircraft America could spare, and "the
loan of 30 or 40 of (your) old destroyers."[83]

Later that day, Churchill sent FDR his first telegram mentioning the
request for destroyers. However, he had upped the number he wanted,
asking for "the loan of forty or fifty of your older destroyers." The
president responded that he could not take such a step without congressional approval, which he doubted he could get considering "our own
defense requirements."[84]

Churchill pressed again on June 11, the day after Roosevelt spoke at
the University of Virginia. He renewed his request for aircraft, especially
flying boats, "but even more pressing is the need for destroyers." He
closed by asserting that "nothing is so important as for us to have 30 or
40 old destroyers you already had reconditioned."[85]

The prime minister tried again on June 15. He discussed the possibility of a German invasion of England, which "will almost certainly be in
the form of dispersed landings from a large number of small craft and

the only effective counter to such a move is to maintain numerous and effective destroyer patrols. We must ask therefore as a matter of life and death to be reinforced with these destroyers."[86]

Roosevelt wanted to help, but he was concerned about what might happen if he did manage to "loan" some destroyers, old or not, to Britain. Realizing that the Atlantic Ocean was American's bulwark defense against a German assault on either North or South America, he had to maintain control of at least the Western Atlantic. "If Roosevelt lent destroyers to Churchill and then Britain lost, the United States would be still the worse off, perhaps catastrophically so. Yet, if the destroyers helped keep the British in the war, they would be of greater value than on American patrol service. That was the dilemma."[87]

Nevertheless, at some point Roosevelt clearly decided he wanted to accommodate Churchill's request for destroyers. But appearing before a congressional committee, Naval chief of staff Admiral Harold Stark complicated Roosevelt's efforts. When asked if the United States needed all the destroyers it had, his answer was an unequivocal "yes." The problem for the president was that the law only permitted the sale of "surplus equipment," and the Navy was "unwilling to consider old destroyers as surplus."[88]

At the same time, Army chief of staff General George Marshall resisted sending B-17s to Britain. The four-engine bombers known as Flying Fortresses were in short supply. Marshall was concerned that the United States would "pour our slender means into a situation...over which we have no control and reduce ourselves to the point where we can't protect our own interests....When it comes to training of pilots, we are in a difficult situation. When it comes to ammunition, we are in extremely critical ammunition times."[89]

Roosevelt was concerned that if Britain lost the war the Germans would take over the British fleet. So he tried to barter a deal with the wily Churchill, who instructed his ambassador in Washington to "discourage any complacent assumption on United States' part that they will pick up the debris of the British Empire by their present policy."[90]

Ultimately, Roosevelt offered to deliver fifty destroyers out of a total U.S. fleet of 168, as well as some torpedo boats and airplanes. In return, he wanted a two-part agreement. The first was a pledge from Churchill that should "the waters of Great Britain become untenable for British ships of war, the latter would not be turned over to the Germans or sunk but would be sent to other parts of the Empire." The second part was British authorization for the United States to establish naval and air bases on British-controlled territories along the Atlantic, from Newfoundland through Bermuda, the Bahamas, Jamaica, St Lucia, Trinidad, and British Guiana.[91]

Churchill rejected the first demand, as it would damage British public morale if word leaked out that the British government even considered the possibility that the Germans would conquer Great Britain. An agreement was reached on the second part, however, giving America 99-year leases on the base sites in exchange for the Royal Navy gaining possession of the so-called "surplus destroyers."

At a cabinet meeting, war hawks Ickes, Morgenthau, Stimson, Knox, and Wallace supported the deal. According to Conrad Black's biography of FDR, "These bases would enable the United States to maintain a very extensive patrol of the western ocean, from which Britain would clearly benefit, since Roosevelt intended, informally, to hand over to the British any information about German submarines that the U. S. Navy could provide." Naval commanders had already been instructed that anywhere within the so-called Neutrality Zone that the president pushed out from 3 to 200 miles from the coast, the movements of any submarines or other "suspicious" (i.e. German) ships should be reported not in code, but in the clear. This meant in English, which enabled any Royal Navy ships receiving the signal to know the location of the German vessel. "He planned to extend the zone toward the British Isles in large increments."[92]

The president did not seem concerned by his dubious authority for taking these steps. As Attorney General Robert H. Jackson later explained, "The President was not a legalistic minded person." He had "a tendency to think in terms of right and wrong, instead of terms of legal and illegal."[93]

Although the attorney general initially thought the deal was legally questionable, he eventually gave his approval. Edwin M. Borchard, Yale

Law School professor and specialist in international law, deemed Jackson's judgment to be "really disgraceful and [one which] abandons all vestiges of respect for law." He charged, "It would be much more honest to say that we are in a limited state of war and that under such circumstances military aid to our ally must be permitted."[94]

Diplomatic historian Frederick W. Marks III has outlined how quickly Roosevelt moved toward war at this time:

> Roosevelt found himself exempt from much of the pressure of a normal election campaign since Republicans had chosen Wendell Willkie, a candidate whose views on foreign policy coincided largely with his own. With Willkie's tacit consent, he could and did abandon all pretense to lawful neutrality. In rapid succession came Destroyers for Bases, executive endorsement of the Burke-Wadsworth selective service training bill (the first peacetime draft in American history), the secret guarantee of British possessions in the Far East, and Lend-Lease.[95]

Additionally, some 20 percent of the U.S. military's ammunition and ordinance had already been sent to the British to help replenish what they left on the beaches of Dunkirk. The American arsenal was becoming so depleted that General Marshall and Admiral Stark asked Roosevelt on June 22 to place a moratorium on future arms sales to Britain. Roosevelt flat-out refused. [96]

There were many backroom negotiations over how to tell the public, British and American, about the destroyers-for-bases deal. Roosevelt wanted to tout it as "a shrewd deal: an exchange of some overage ships that had been in mothballs, for excellent strategic bases." Churchill wanted it to appear "two friendly acts, lending destroyers and leasing bases, out of solidarity." The compromise solution was to claim the Newfoundland bases were leased "out of friendship, and the Caribbean bases leased in exchange for the loan of the destroyers."[97]

Roosevelt was concerned that he would not get the deal through Congress, even though his party controlled both houses. He told Navy

Secretary Knox, who supported the destroyer plan, "I fear Congress is in no mood at the present time to allow any form of sale."[98] He was right. On June 22, in an act designed to forestall Roosevelt from selling or otherwise transferring any naval warships, Congress "decreed that he could not transfer any warships to a belligerent until the chief of naval operations certified they were not essential to the defense of the United States."[99]

Then, in a great turn around that undoubtedly included some presidential pressure, when push came to shove, both General Marshall and Admiral Stark took "deep breaths, crossed their fingers" and certified that the destroyers FDR was going to trade the British were "obsolete" and "useless."[100] Demonstrating the farcical nature of the presidential election campaign, Roosevelt also seems to have received support for the deal from his ostensible opponent, Wendell Willkie. After the president asked newspaper editor William Allen White if he could get Willkie to support the destroyers deal, White reported, "I have talked with both of you on this subject and I know there is not two bits worth of difference between the two of you."[101]

Once he had the signatures of the Army and Navy chiefs, Roosevelt decided he could bypass Congress entirely and make the trade by executive order. After all, he had met the requirement that the naval chief approve. Roosevelt made his announcement to a group of reporters while on a tour of a war plant in Charleston, West Virginia, on September 3. He told the twenty journalists on his train about the trade, and compared its importance to the Louisiana Purchase, which was quite a stretch.

The American press leaned heavily toward supporting the trade. One conspicuous exception was a *St. Louis Post-Dispatch* editorial that called it "an act of war." The piece went on to complain that Congress had been "informed" of the arrangement rather than consulted. It also accused Roosevelt of acting like a dictator.[102]

Reactions in Congress divided largely along the lines of interventionists and non-interventionists. Some non-interventionists echoed the *Post-Dispatch* that it was an act of war and that the president acted like one of the dictators he claimed to dislike. Interventionists, meanwhile, generally overlooked the secrecy in which the agreement was made and welcomed the potential addition of more air bases for the country.[103]

On September 5, Churchill told the House of Commons, "Only ignorant persons would suggest that the transfer of American destroyers to the British flag constitutes the slightest violation of international law or affects in the smallest degree the non-belligerency of the United States."[104] But after the war, Churchill revealed his true thoughts on the deal: "The transfer to Great Britain of fifty American warships was a decidedly unneutral act by the United States. It would, according to all standards of history, have justified the German Government in declaring war upon them. The transfer of these destroyers to Britain in August 1940 was an event which brought the United States definitely nearer to us and to the war."[105]

Less than two weeks later, in mid-September, the president took the next step toward intervention in the war. He signed the Burke-Wadsworth Act, which was the first conscription for compulsory military service during peacetime in the nation's history. Roosevelt immediately asked Congress for $1.6 billion in additional funds to cover the expenses associated with housing, clothing, feeding, paying, and training the recruits.

The Selective Service Training Act, as the conscription act is better known, required all men between eighteen and thirty-five to register for service. Those men whose numbers were called in lotteries were to serve for one year, although a few months later Roosevelt asked Congress to extend the term, which it did. While many of the men were glad to have a roof over their heads and three meals a day, a great number resented having their time extended. "There were times when OHIO, chalked on latrine walls, meant 'over the hill in October,' and many of the young men cursed George Marshall, the President, [and] the Congress which (by a House vote of 203-202) extended their draft service."[106]

The approval of the draft and the supplemental funds for it finally solved Roosevelt's unemployment problem. The ranks of the unemployed were decimated as people were hired to work in manufacturing facilities to make the 3.6 million pairs of trousers, 4.8 million handkerchiefs, 1.2 million pairs of shoes the army needed, and "an equal number of field caps, raincoats, etc. [that] will be required. But the big immediate job is to build wooden barracks and other buildings for these men and to supply new camps, and additions to present posts, with water, sewerage, lights, and other essential services and equipment."[107] With the introduction of the draft, unemployment fell from 17.2 percent in 1939 to 14.6 percent in 1940. The following year, with close to one million men drafted and over $1 billion being spent, joblessness fell to 9.9 percent. In 1942, the first full year of American participation in the war, the rate fell to 4.7 percent.[108]

The draft starkly revealed how New Deal policies had failed to improve the economy: "Of the first million men selected for the draft, almost 40 percent were found unfit for general military service; one-third of the rejections were due directly or indirectly to poor nutrition." James MacGregor Burns commented, "These were evils in themselves; they also showed marked social weaknesses in a nation girding for defense."[109]

Renewing the draft, however, was another sign Roosevelt was girding for something more than defense.

———

Throughout 1940, Lindbergh's radio addresses warned against America's gradual slide toward war. In May, it was "The Air Defense of America," in June it was "Our Drift Toward War." He never attacked Roosevelt personally, only the policies he believed were wrong. Meanwhile, the president's people, both in and out of the administration, continued to assail Lindbergh as the most visible opponent of Roosevelt's war policies.

Lindbergh authored an article titled "What Substitute for War?" for *Atlantic Monthly* that was condensed and printed in the May 1940 *Reader's Digest*. He wrote, "The last war demonstrated the fallacy of sending American soldiers to European battlefields. The victory we helped win brought neither order nor justice in its wake, and these interminable wars continue unabated and with modern fury." Expressing what was, in many ways, the core of his concern, he argued America should "stand aside" to allow the Europeans to determine their own destinies, "if for no other reason than that one strong western nation may be left to preserve the flame of civilization and to lead the way from the chaos that will come to Europe if this war goes on. Somewhere among us that flame must be kept burning if this civilization, too, is not to lie with the bones of marble and of bronze that represent the greatness of Rome, Greece, and Egypt, and Babylon."[110]

On September 5, Lindbergh wrote in his diary about a meeting he had with Harry Byrd, Virginia Democratic senator. Although Byrd was distressed that Roosevelt was "headed for war if he wins the election," the senator explained he had to vote for Roosevelt because as a candidate for reelection in Virginia, he was required to pledge to vote for the party's nominee. Still, Byrd had refused to actively work for the president's reelection, and he asked Lindbergh to speak to Republican senator John Townsend of Delaware about urging Willkie to take an anti-war stand in the election.[111]

Throughout the second half of 1940, Lindbergh continued to give public speeches. On August 4, 1940, he spoke for twenty minutes at a rally sponsored by several veterans groups in Chicago. A crowd of about forty thousand people gathered under a hot sun in Soldier's Field to hear the aviator tell them, "I do not offer my opinion as an expert, but rather as a citizen alarmed at the position our country has reached in this era of experts." He talked about his time in Europe and how he had come to realize that even though a generation had passed since the Treaty of Versailles was signed, he could see that "the sons of victory and the sons of defeat were about to meet on the battlefield of their fathers."

Calling for America to develop a peace plan that "should be based upon the welfare of America," he unequivocally stated his views on defense: "I believe that we should rearm fully for the defense of America." He then made clear that he was not an "isolationist" as some called him: "While I advocate the non-interference by America in the internal affairs of Europe, I believe it is of the utmost importance for us to cooperate with Europe in our relationships with the other peoples of the earth. It is only by cooperation that we can maintain the supremacy of our Western civilization and the right of our commerce to proceed unmolested throughout the world."[112]

Interventionists responded with their typical aspersions. Calling Lindbergh "the chief of the fifth column in this country," Senator Claude Pepper, Democrat of Florida, suggested, "Maybe the Colonel would like to see American life regimented the Hitler way."[113]

Another attack on Lindbergh was leveled by the Reverend Leon M. Birkhead, a Unitarian minister who was national director of the Friends of Democracy, a front group organized by British intelligence. Birkhead announced that he had sent a telegram to the secretary of war demanding to know what the relationship was between this "apologist for Hitler," as he called Lindbergh, and the United States Army.[114] Later that year, Birkhead would become chairman of another British intelligence front group, the aforementioned Nonpartisan Committee to Defeat Hamilton Fish.[115]

Despite the predictable attacks, Lindbergh had attracted a legion of supporters. Future Secretary of State John Foster Dulles wrote him following the Soldier's Field speech saying he was "very glad you spoke out as you did." Chester Bowles, who would serve as undersecretary of state in the Kennedy administration, ambassador to India for Presidents Truman, Kennedy, and Johnson, as well as governor of Connecticut, told Lindbergh he hoped "you will keep on talking and talking in spite of all the criticism and innuendos that will undoubtedly be fired in your direction."[116] Famed architect Frank Lloyd Wright was moved to wire Lindbergh, "We knew you could fly straight, but now when everywhere is equivocation and cowardice you not only think straight but you dare speak straight."[117]

On the evening of October 14, Lindbergh gave another radio address. Recorded in the Mutual Broadcasting Company studios in Washington, it was titled "A Plea for American Independence." Referring to England, France, and Spain, Charles reminded his listeners that "during the first century and a quarter of our existence as a free and independent people we opposed, and opposed successfully, all the major powers of Europe." He then recounted the War for Independence, the creation of the Monroe Doctrine, how we had forced France to withdraw its armies from Mexico, and then drove the Spanish from the hemisphere. He asked, "Where is the blood of such leaders as Washington, Jefferson, and Lincoln; blood that stood firm on American soil against the threats, the armies and the navies of the greatest empires on earth?"

Then, in a political vein he had rarely touched on previously, he declared, "What we lack today is the type of leadership that made us a great nation; the type that turned adversity and hardship into virility and success." Praising the "fundamental courage and solidarity of Americans when our national welfare is at stake," he condemned the leaders of France and Britain who neglected their own military strength and then "told their people that security lay abroad, that the best way to defend their own countries was to fight for Poland." Now that they have failed, they want the United States to follow along behind them. Without mentioning any names, he also condemned the American leaders who neglected our defenses and ran up a huge national debt. As for the coming presidential election, he did not name any candidate when he said the future of our nation depends upon men, "regardless of their party, who will lead us to strength and peace, rather than to weakness and to war."[118]

Speaking at a campaign rally in Erie, Pennsylvania, two days later, Democratic vice presidential candidate Henry Wallace called Lindbergh "the outstanding appeaser of the nation." In Boston on the same day, Attorney General Robert Jackson claimed Lindbergh's speech was "perfectly calculated to undermine confidence in American leadership" just as the draft was about to begin.[119]

It was always the same—very little comment on the substance of Lindbergh's speech, a few responses to comments Lindbergh did not make, and always, always, the name calling. The *Christian Century*, reports Scott Berg, said the "attack launched against Lindbergh has gone far beyond the ordinary canons of debate. It has pulsed with Venom. If this man who was once the nation's shining hero had been proved another Benedict Arnold he could not have been subjected to more defamation and calumny."[120]

On the afternoon of October 30, Lindbergh drove from his home on Long Island to Yale University in New Haven, Connecticut, to speak at the invitation of a group of students who had formed the Emergency Committee to Defend America First. The group's name had since been shortened to the America First Committee. Arriving in time for dinner at the home of Professor A. Whitney Griswold, Lindbergh was greeted by one of the group's original organizers, Kingman Brewster, Jr., who would be appointed president of the university in 1963. That evening

Lindbergh gave his longest address to date, thirty minutes, to well over 3,000 packed into Woolsey Hall. He expected to be heckled by some, but the audience remained attentive to his discussion and clapped enthusiastically when he finished. He wrote in his diary that although it was not a large gathering, it was "by far the most successful and satisfying meeting of this kind in which I have taken part."[121]

Lindbergh would spend the next year traveling the country giving speeches about the need to stay out of the war and build America's defenses. He wrote all his own speeches, with input and editing from Anne, and he never received any compensation for them, even paying all his own expenses including travel and lodging. Yet he had become by far the largest draw of all the non-interventionist speakers in the nation. As Roosevelt positioned America for war, Charles continued to warn that we were courting catastrophe.[122]

Chapter Eight

❦

THE PRESIDENT
ATTACKS

anuary 1941 began a momentous year in which Roosevelt, politically secure following his third-term election, took giant steps
toward getting into the war. That month he sent his closest advisor, Harry Hopkins, to London to meet with Churchill. Ted Morgan
reports that while there, Hopkins told the prime minister, "The President
sent me here to tell you that at all costs and by all means he will carry
you through, no matter what happens to him—there is nothing he will
not do so far as he has human power."[1]

In accordance with that pledge, Roosevelt backed a proposal that
would invalidate all previous Neutrality Act legislation and place unprecedented power in the hands of the president. The policy, deceptively
named Lend-Lease, would also invalidate the Johnson Act of 1934, which
prohibited loans to nations such as Great Britain that had defaulted on
their World War I debts to the United States. Lasting through 1945, Lend-
Lease would funnel more than $50 billion (approximately $760 billion

in current dollars) worth of supplies and materials to various Allied nations, including over $31 billion to Great Britain and $11 billion to Stalin's Soviet Union.

Roosevelt had first raised the possibility of Britain exhausting its cash and credit reserves, and how the United States could finance future British purchases, at a cabinet meeting on November 8, 1940. There, the president told his top officials he believed Britain had "about $2.5 billion here in credit and property that could be liquidated. He believes," wrote Secretary Ickes, "that this money ought to be spent first, although the British do not want to liquidate their American securities. The President added, however, that the time would surely come when Great Britain would need loans or credits." The solution, Roosevelt suggested, was to lease war material, including warships, military aircraft, army vehicles, and any "property that was loanable, returnable, and insurable."

Ickes thought it was a good idea.[2] In fact, evidence suggests it was Ickes who first intimated such a program. On August 2, he wrote Roosevelt saying, "It seems to me that we Americans are like the householder who refuses to lend or sell his fire extinguishers to help put out the fire in the house that is right next door."[3]

On November 23, reporters met returning British Ambassador Lothian at New York's LaGuardia Airport. When asked how England was faring in the war, Lothian expressed confidence in final victory, but said his country "was near the end of its fiscal resources and would need financial aid in 1941." He added that England's need to purchase war supplies abroad was "becoming urgent."[4]

Lend-Lease began taking shape with a December 7 correspondence from Churchill to Roosevelt in which the prime minster reported, "The moment approaches when we shall no longer be able to pay cash for shipping and other supplies."[5] Churchill later wrote that this letter "was one of the most important I ever wrote."[6] It reached Roosevelt while he was on a post-election cruise in the Caribbean aboard the U.S. Navy heavy cruiser *Tuscaloosa*, which was touring the sites of the proposed bases for which he had traded to Britain fifty destroyers.

Roosevelt studied Churchill's letter for two days. His shipmates noted that the president "was plunged in intense thought, and brooded silently."

Then one evening as the ship sailed home, "he suddenly came out with it—the whole program. He didn't seem to have any clear idea how it could be done legally. But there wasn't a doubt in his mind that he'd find a way to do it."[7]

Back in Washington, Roosevelt met with Treasury Secretary Morgenthau on December 17 and laid out his plan for Lend-Lease: "I have been thinking very hard on this trip about what we should do for England, and it seems to me that the thing to do is to get away from the old dollar sign.... We will say to England, we will give you the guns and ships that you need, provided that when the war is over you will return to us in kind the guns and ships that we have loaned to you." Morgenthau thought it was the "best idea yet."[8]

Later that day, FDR met with the press and fed them the same line about getting away from the old dollar sign. He invoked a somewhat condescending parable so the simple people could understand his plans: "Suppose the house of the President's neighbor catches fire and he has a length of garden hose, 400 or 500 feet. He does not say his hose costs $15; pay me $15. He doesn't want $15, but his hose back when the fire is over. The neighbor gives back the hose and pays him for the use of it. If it gets smashed in the fire, the President says he was glad to lend it. The neighbor says he will replace the part destroyed."[9]

Republican senator Robert Taft offered a contrary analogy: "Lending war equipment is a good deal like lending chewing gum. You don't want it back."[10]

Discussing his Lend-Lease plans in a fireside chat on December 29, the president averred that "the Axis powers are not going to win this war." He called for labor and management at war plants to resolve any difference without either side shutting the plants down, and he once again attacked "American citizens, many of them in high places, who, unwittingly in most cases, are aiding and abetting the work" of "secret emissaries" of the Nazis.[11]

On January 10, 1941, identical Lend-Lease bills were introduced in the House and the Senate. Over the next two months, the program was passionately debated in Congress and across the country. After Secretary Morgenthau admitted that the president wanted a "blank check," General

Wood of the America First Committee charged what he really wanted was "a blank check book with the power to write away your man power, our laws and our liberties."[12] The true implications of the bill were immediately recognized by a delighted Churchill, who exclaimed to his private secretary that the legislation was "tantamount to a declaration of war by the United States."[13]

As historian Wayne S. Cole notes, at House and Senate hearings, opponents of Lend-Lease "came under increasingly damaging attacks, as their public image grew more tarnished." The denunciations became so vicious that "the fainthearted were reluctant to speak out on the non-interventionist side."[14]

Colonel Charles Lindbergh was the star witness against the bill at both the House and Senate hearings. Appearing before the House Foreign Affairs Committee on January 23, 1941, he began by reading a prepared statement urging the United States to improve its defenses and establish bases that would serve to counter any potential invader. He primarily focused on air defense, which he said "greatly strengthens our position and increases the security of this entire hemisphere from foreign attack."[15] He emphasized the difficulty a foreign power would have invading the United States, especially if we strengthened our military aviation capabilities. Committee members then quizzed Lindbergh about his suggestion that the United States should help mediate a negotiated peace in Europe. The idea was a logical outgrowth of his belief that American entry into the war "would be the greatest disaster this country has ever passed through."

Scott Berg reports, "For the pro-intervention representatives, the hearing proved to be something of a joust, in which they attempted to knock Lindbergh off his horse of staunch neutrality."[16] Still, Lindbergh managed to impress even his opponents. At the end of his four-and-a-half hours of testimony, the committee chairman, Democrat Sol Bloom, a supporter of the bill, told Lindbergh, "You have made one of the best witnesses that this committee could possibly ever hear. You answered all the questions only as a Colonel Lindbergh could answer them."[17]

The Senate hearing on February 6 was less contentious. It began with some unintended humor when Senator Claude Pepper asked the witness when he first went to Europe. Not realizing Pepper was asking about when he and his family moved to Europe, Lindbergh answered that it was in 1927—the year of his famous New York-Paris flight. The audience reacted with laughter and applause.

Addressing Lend-Lease, Lindbergh declared, "This bill is obviously the most recent step in a policy which attempts to obtain security for America by controlling internal conditions in Europe." He told the senators the policy of depleting our own military to aid England was misguided because England could not win the war without full American participation. He insisted, "Our own air forces are in deplorable condition for lack of modern equipment. The majority of the planes we now have are obsolescent on the standards of modern warfare."[18] Nevertheless, Lindbergh claimed that "the United States was the only nation in the world capable of equaling or excelling Germany in aviation."

He then argued the United States had some responsibility for the war, both through our acquiescence to the Treaty of Versailles and because our representatives in Europe had left French and British leaders with the impression that America would "ultimately participate [in another war against Germany], although he conceded that he had no proof whatever that this was the case. He based his assumption, he said, on the attitude he found among inhabitants of both countries in 1937 and 1938, when persons with whom he talked regarded war with Germany as inevitable. All these persons were counting on the armed intervention of the United States, he explained."[19]

Lindbergh's position was not difficult to defend. France and Britain had encouraged Poland to refuse Hitler's demands over Danzig, then they declared war on Germany after it invaded Poland. But the leaders of both France and England, especially the military leaders, must have been aware that Germany was more powerful than their two nations combined. It's reasonable to assume that what motivated them to declare war on a much stronger country was their assumption that the United States would eventually join the war on their side.

While Congress was dealing with Lend-Lease, Roosevelt appointed a new ambassador to Britain to replace Joseph Kennedy. John G. Winant was a Progressive Republican who had served two non-consecutive terms as governor of New Hampshire.

True to his nature of "not letting the left hand know what the right hand is doing," the president then found a way to bypass the ambassador and the State Department in his dealings with Churchill. He appointed 49-year-old businessman and banker Averell Harriman as a "defense expeditor" and sent him to England. When reporters asked what Harriman's relationship would be to the U.S. Embassy in London, Roosevelt responded with an expletive, "I don't know, and I don't give a—you know!"[20] In his memoirs, Harriman reports that his instructions from Roosevelt were: "I want you to go over to London and recommend everything that we can do, short of war, to keep the British Isles afloat."[21]

Both Winant and Harriman traveled with Churchill to visit various cities the Germans had bombed. The three became very close, especially after the prime minister discovered that Harriman could play his favorite card game, bezique. At one point Churchill, speaking of Winant and Harriman, told his war cabinet, "These two gentlemen were apparently longing for Germany to commit some overt act that would relieve the President of his election and pre-election declaration regarding keeping out of the war." He added that Harriman "had said that the United States might be prepared to escort their own ships outside the prohibited area. He was working out a scheme whereby United States ships would take over the long hauls, leaving us with the short hauls. They were also planning a very big merchant ship-building program, which would mature in 1942."[22]

Thus, eleven months before the Japanese attack on Pearl Harbor brought the United States into the war, the Roosevelt administration was looking to provoke the Germans into causing an incident in the Atlantic comparable to their 1915 torpedo attack on the *Lusitania*—a British ship carrying American passengers and, covertly, war materials for Britain, whose sinking was a major cause of America's entry into World War I.

To Roosevelt's frustration, however, Hitler refused to take the bait. Having a healthy respect for America's military potential, the Fuhrer was keen at this point to keep the United States out of the war. He repeatedly told German businessman and confidant Ernst Hanfstaengl, "The only thing that brought our defeat in 1918 was that America entered the war."[23]

Hitler's caginess presented a real problem for Roosevelt, who needed a drastic event like war to shore up the economy. As FDR began his third term, the U.S. economy continued to limp along. Unemployment at the end of 1940 stood at nearly 15 percent, with more than 8 million out of work despite massive government programs that employed millions. On the day of Roosevelt's inaugural, January 20, 1941, the liberal daily newspaper *PM,* published by leftist journalist Ralph Ingersoll in New York City, carried a front-page photograph of "row upon row of men on the benches of a Bowery mission. They sat, their heads lowered, not in prayer, but on the hard narrow top of the bench ahead, their coats pulled up over their heads, babbling, coughing, snoring, scratching."

These were some of the 7,000 men in the city who were both unemployed and homeless. At night, many of them found refuge in the missions or flophouses of the Bowery area, but during the day, they wandered the streets in search of a handout or some free food to fill their empty stomachs. The article was, according to FDR biographer James MacGregor Burns, "a cruel comment on the end of two terms of 'Relief, Recovery, and Reform' under Roosevelt. But it was not unfair."[24]

The *PM* story was an accurate description of a nation suffering after eight years of a failed presidency. Perhaps if Roosevelt had faced an opponent who exposed and rejected his war plans, his path to a third term would not have been a cakewalk. But with Willkie towing the interventionist line, Americans were deprived of a meaningful choice. Thus, Roosevelt could celebrate his successful re-election campaign, but he faced a serious problem as he began his third term. Seeing a wartime economy as the only hope for economic improvement, but with Hitler refusing to enable his war plans, the president scrambled to find a pretext to get America into the war.

———

While the press generally supported Roosevelt's interventionism, the president's efforts encountered resistance from a surprising source: Kansas newspaper editor William Allen White, a stalwart interventionist and Roosevelt supporter. During the congressional battles over the Neutrality

Act revisions, "Roosevelt asked the esteemed Kansas editor and [Progressive] Republican William Allen White to organize a Non-Partisan Committee for Peace through Revision of the Neutrality Act," also known as the White Committee. White went on to help organize and served as chair of the Committee to Defend America by Aiding the Allies.[25]

White shocked his fellow interventionists when he wrote Scripps-Howard Newspapers president Roy Howard a letter that Howard published in the form of an interview. In the letter, White wrote, "The only reason in God's world I am in this organization is to keep this country out of war." Denying that he and his organization favored U.S. ships participating in British convoys, he wrote, "The Johnson Act should not be repealed and we are not for it. It is not true even remotely that we favor repealing (the Neutrality Law) to carry contraband of war into the war zone. That would be leading us to war and our organization and I personally are deeply opposed to it." He added that a good motto for the committee would be "The Yanks Are Not Coming."[26]

One of the first public responses to White's declaration came from Charles Lindbergh. In a statement first published in the *New York World Telegram* and picked up by other papers, Lindbergh said that White's remarks had "given us new hope for a united America at a time in our history when unity is essential."[27]

Roosevelt's supporters immediately swung into action against White. Among the first to attack was New York City mayor Fiorello La Guardia, a Progressive Republican and New Deal supporter who would soon be appointed director of Roosevelt's new Office of Civilian Defense. In a letter addressed to White that La Guardia released to the press, the mayor accused him of "doing a typical Laval"—a reference to Pierre Laval, a French collaborator in the Vichy government who would be executed for high treason in 1945.[28] La Guardia added that White should head up a group called the Committee to Defend America by Aiding the Allies with Words, "while the rest of us would join a 'Committee to Defend America by Aiding the Allies with Deeds.'"

White was soon forced to resign from the organization he had created on the president's behalf, while Roosevelt remained silent on the fall of his old friend. As Eleanor Roosevelt once noted about her husband, "The

President uses those who suit his purposes. He makes up his own mind and discards people when they no longer serve a purpose of his."[29]

Meanwhile, despite the warnings of Lend-Lease opponents that the policy would hand dictatorial powers to Roosevelt, the bill, which the administration had misleadingly named "An Act Further to Promote the Defense of the United States," was approved by Congress and signed into law by the president on March 11, 1941. Although the bill easily passed the Senate by a vote of 60 to 31, it sparked heated opposition from senators who understood that Lend-Lease, despite Roosevelt's entreaties to the contrary, was a huge step toward American participation in the war. Henrik Shipstead, a Farmer-Labor Party member from Minnesota, passionately warned his fellow senators, "We will pay the bill with our money, our resources and the precious blood of American boys." The Progressive Republican from California Hiram Johnson, a former Roosevelt supporter, wrote his son after the vote, "We assassinated liberty under the pretext of aiding a belligerent in the war."[30]

As World War II historian Ian Kershaw writes, the reaction in London to the passing of Lend-Lease was quite different:

> For Churchill, it was "a wonderful decision," bringing new hope and conviction through the knowledge that "the United States are very closely bound up with us now." He spoke of it as a "climacteric"—an "intense turning-point"—in Britain's war effort. It meant an "irrevocable commitment" to the alliance of the United States with Great Britain, a "point of no return" in American policy against Nazi Germany, "a major step towards war." The Wehrmacht leadership interpreted it as "a declaration of war." . . . Hitler immediately decided to extend the combat zone in the North Atlantic as far west as the territorial waters of Greenland.[31]

The law gave the president incredible—many argued unconstitutional—authority, including the power "not withstanding the provisions of any other law" to "sell, transfer title to, exchange, lease, lend, or otherwise dispose of" any "defense article" to "the government of any country whose defense the President deems vital to the defense of the United States." The first appropriation bill for Lend-Lease, for $7 billion, passed thirteen days later.[32]

Within three months, the Lend-Lease powers would place the president in a quandary. Following the German invasion of the Soviet Union on June 22, 1941, Joseph Stalin, the brutal Soviet dictator, suddenly became a potential recipient of American aid. Just two days after the invasion, some Democratic senators voiced their opposition to aiding the Soviets. Senator Bennet Clark of Missouri remarked, "It's a case of dog eat dog. Stalin is as bloody-handed as Hitler. I don't think we should help either one." Senator William Bulow of South Dakota declared, "I would not be in favor of helping Russia at all. Hitler will soon have so much territory he will have plenty of trouble handling it."

Senator Robert La Follette, Progressive of Wisconsin, predicted that the interventionists would begin "the greatest whitewash act in history" in order to aid Stalin. "The American people," he proclaimed, "will be told to forget the purges in Russia by the OGPU, the confiscation of property, the persecution of religion, the invasion of Finland, and the vulture role Stalin played in seizing half of prostrate Poland, all of Latvia, Estonia, and Lithuania. These will be made to seem the acts of a 'democracy' preparing to fight Nazism."[33]

La Follette's predictions were largely on target; the Soviet Union would be the recipient of $11 billion worth of Lend-Lease aid and would use the war against Germany to expand its own oppressive empire across all of Eastern Europe.

———

In April, Lindbergh joined the America First Committee, instantly becoming their most popular leader. Over the next few months, he would be the featured speaker at thirteen AFC rallies around the country. The first was scheduled for April 17, at the Chicago Arena.

Lindbergh came under renewed attack even before he gave his AFC address. Throughout the previous year, to counter Lindbergh, the administration had orchestrated a series of speeches by pro-intervention Democratic senators. Assistant Secretary of State Adolf A. Berle was instrumental in writing those speeches, including ones given by Senators Byrnes of South Carolina (May 1940), Pittman of Nevada (June 1940), and Lucas of Illinois (August 1940). Berle also "helped former Assistant Secretary of War Louis A. Johnson write the speech that he broadcast in response to Lindbergh's address of October 14, 1940."[34]

Recent Gallup polls revealed that 80 percent of Americans were "against going to war against Hitler." Considering what we know about the infiltration of U.S. polling companies by British intelligence, it is startling that the polls continued to report such a huge majority of Americans were against getting involved in the war. However, the Brits' priority at the time was maintaining the supply of U.S. war material, and the polls dutifully showed more than 70 percent of Americans favored the U.S. government taking action to protect the supplies shipped to England from U-boat attacks.[35]

The subject of British intelligence activities in the Unites States was addressed at a cabinet meeting the same week that Lindbergh gave his first AFC address. An entry in Secretary of State Harold Ickes' diary reveals the attitude of most members of the cabinet: "[Attorney General] Bob Jackson objected to the British establishing an intelligence service here. Morgenthau said that the information they send in from time to time is of great help to the Treasury. No one seems to be very excited about it except Jackson." The attorney general held the view—apparently unique in Roosevelt's cabinet—that "it is improper for a foreign government to operate an intelligence service in the United States."[36]

There is no indication if anyone asked Secretary Morgenthau whether he considered the "information" those British agents provided the Treasury Department to be truthful or propaganda—and propaganda, after all, is what those agents were assigned to produce.

Although the administration could tolerate British intelligence operations on American soil, it had less patience with Lindbergh and America First. On April 13, four days before Lindbergh's inaugural America First speech, the president's most forceful mouthpiece, Interior Secretary Ickes, kicked off the new campaign against Lindbergh by labeling him the "No.1 Nazi fellow traveler" in America. According to the *New York*

Times, Ickes also "depicted General Robert E. Wood, national chairman of the America First Committee, as 'apparently a fellow-traveler.' He declared that the America First Committee should be renamed the America 'Next' Committee, adding that it attracts 'antidemocrats, appeasers, labor baiters, and anti-Semites.'"[37]

Attacking Lindbergh as a Nazi sympathizer was standard rhetoric for Roosevelt's men, but the assault on General Wood marked a new low in the campaign against non-interventionists. A West Point graduate, Wood had served in the Philippines during the insurrection and the Panama Canal Zone during the construction. He retired from the Army in 1915, returning two years later as America headed toward entry into World War I. In Europe, he served as a lieutenant colonel in the 42nd (Rainbow) Division. By war's end, he had been promoted to brigadier general and was made acting quartermaster general of the Army. Wood received the Distinguished Service Medal; the French made him a Knight of the Legion of Honor; and the British awarded him the Companion Order of St. Michael and St. George.

General Wood pulled no punches in his reply to Ickes: "It is an old trick for a war party to claim a monopoly of patriotism, but the people are wise to it. Secretary Ickes speaks for the swivel chair patriots. America First speaks for the boys who will have to fight and die if Secretary Ickes and others involve this country in the war."[38]

On the evening of April 17, General Wood introduced Colonel Lindbergh to an enthusiastic crowd of around 10,000 people inside the Chicago Arena. With the venue packed to capacity, another 4,000 people listened from the streets outside. In his twenty-five minute address, the colonel explained that America First was formed to give voice to the many people who oppose sending American soldiers to fight another war in Europe. He expressed his belief, based on his personal observations of Europe's military forces, that "this war was lost by England and France even before it was declared." Only American participation can win the war for them, he asserted, adding that it would be "a tragedy to the world, even to Germany, if the British Empire collapses" as a result of the war.

He then attacked "the people who, under the guise of 'steps short of war,' have led us to the verge of war itself. They now demand that we convoy ships to England with the American Navy. If we do this, it is inevitable that we will have American battleships sunk and American sailors killed. Under no guise of imagination can this be called a step 'short of war.'"[39] "Steps short of war" had become a favorite term of administration officials and other war supporters to describe what was in truth steps *toward* war, such as urging that U.S. warships convoy merchant vessels to England through the Atlantic war zone.

History has proven that Lindbergh was essentially correct in his assessment that Britain and France had lost the war before it even began. Neither country, nor the combination of both, was equipped to beat the German juggernaut that swept the Allied armies before it right up to the French coast. France fell within weeks and surrendered its capital to the Germans. The RAF eventually fended off the Luftwaffe in the Battle of Britain, but the English were incapable of confronting and defeating the German army on the continent, as demonstrated by their retreat from Dunkirk. It was only the intervention of outside forces, namely the Soviet Union and the United States, that enabled France and Britain to prevail over Germany.

On one important point Lindbergh was wrong, however: in his fear that someone would draw America into war, he underestimated Hitler's reluctance to do so. Not only were U.S. warships tracking German U-boats and reporting their locations to British warships, but U.S. ships actually fired on U-boats in several incidents. One such event took place on April 11, 1941, when the U.S. Destroyer *Niblack* dropped three depth chargers on what it suspected was a nearby submarine. Despite strong objections from German naval commander Admiral Erich Raeder, Hitler refused to permit attacks on U.S. ships. To make himself clear, he issued an order specifying that "in the extended zone of operations U.S. merchant ships, whether single or sailing in English or American convoys and if recognized as such before resort to arms, are not to be attacked."[40]

Looking back on this time, Hanson W. Baldwin, former military editor of the *New York Times*, wrote, "In retrospect, it is easy to see that the so-called short-of-war measures taken by Washington in rapid succession in 1940-41 might ultimately have involved the United States in all-out war against Germany and Italy whether or not there had ever been a Pearl Harbor."[41]

The interventionists' campaign against Lindbergh continued after his Chicago speech. The Committee to Defend America by Aiding the Allies accused him of being ignorant of history and having a "blind spot which prevents him from seeing the value of moral imponderables."[42] In one startling attack, a federal judge officiating at the swearing-in ceremonies of 268 newly naturalized American citizens in Cleveland told the new citizens that Lindbergh "was one of those who seek to undermine all that we hold dear." Judge Robert N. Wilkin then labeled Lindbergh "a defeatist, a pacifist and isolationist."[43]

But Charles was unbowed. His next address, billed as an anti-convoy rally, was on April 23 at New York's Manhattan Center. The building was once again jammed with supporters, and the police reported another 15,000 to 20,000 on 34th Street outside. This time Lindbergh shared the platform with the famous novelist Kathleen Norris. Along with supporters, there were pickets from the British front group Friends of Democracy, whose members called the rally "the largest gathering of pro-Nazi and pro-Fascists" since the German American Bund rallies years earlier. Another British concoction, the Non-Sectarian Anti-Nazi League, distributed handbills bearing the heading, "What One Hitler Medal Can Do"—a reference to Lindbergh's medal from Goring. The left-wing newspaper *PM* reported that the crowd contained "a liberal sprinkling of Nazis, Fascists, anti-Semites, [and] crackpots." Gossip columnist Walter Winchell said that "every hate spreader they could find showed up for that meeting."[44]

The day following the New York rally, Eleanor Roosevelt told reporters that Lindbergh gave the American people "very little credit for much ability, much courage, or much common sense." She added that he "seems to have a strange lack of confidence in his own people."[45]

Some public figures, discomfited by the vituperation heaped on Lindbergh, spoke out in his defense. At a forum at Washington's Wardman Park Hotel titled "How Can We Make Democracy More Vital for Youth?" one speaker was Dr. Oscar F. Blackwelder, president of the Washington Federation of Churches. Praising Lindbergh as a fine illustration of courage, Dr. Blackwelder asked the two hundred civic leaders and educators present, "Why can't he speak without being pilloried by his elders?"[46]

In New York City, Mayor La Guardia told a group of reporters that he thought Lindbergh lacked a proper understanding of European history. But he also said he believed Lindbergh was a good American and not a Hitler supporter.[47] It was a note of civility entirely uncharacteristic of the interventionists' campaign against Lindbergh—a campaign whose central argument was that one of America's chief cultural icons was a despicable traitor.

——

At this time, President Roosevelt was preparing for his first public attack on Lindbergh. Roosevelt biographer Frank Freidel explains that Lindbergh's speeches theretofore were "relatively mild" and he was "careful in what he said, not even mentioning Roosevelt by name." However, "because of his potential following, he most aroused the president's animus."[48]

An astute politician, Roosevelt set a trap for his politically naïve opponent.[49] A few weeks earlier, he had asked John F. Carter, a secret White House operative, to do research on the Copperheads—northerners who criticized Lincoln's policies during the Civil War and were sympathetic to the South. On April 22, Carter gave the president a fifty-five page report including details about Clement L. Vallandigham, a former Democratic congressman, newspaper editor, and leading Copperhead who was imprisoned by federal authorities and later expelled to Confederate territory.[50]

At Roosevelt's next press conference, on April 25, a reporter conveniently asked the president why Lindbergh, who was a colonel in the Army Air Corps reserve, had not been called to active duty. In response, the president launched into a "folksy history lesson" about Vallandigham and the Copperheads, and their attempts to get Union soldiers to quit fighting. After a brief tangent discussing "appeasers at Valley Forge trying to persuade George Washington to quit and arguing that the British could not be defeated," Roosevelt returned to the Civil War, arguing that many "liberty-loving people" had fought on both sides of the conflict, while certain people were not called to serve. The implication was that traitors were not called to the colors. When a reporter asked if he was still talking about Lindbergh, the president responded with a simple "yes."[51]

Roosevelt's attack prompted newspaper headlines around the country proclaiming that the president had called Lindbergh a Copperhead and had implied that Charles was a traitor whose commission would be ignored in wartime.

Lindbergh was shocked when friends informed him of the president's charges. They were so personal, and most upsetting to Charles, they touched on his honor as an Army officer. "If it had been only a political attack, without any connection to my commission, I would pay little attention to it," he wrote in his diary that day. But since it was "a point of honor," he thought he might have to resign his commission. This was something he did not want to do, since "my commission in the Air Corps has always meant a great deal to me, and I would prefer to hold it."

The attack provoked some deep introspection from Lindbergh, who saw a bitter irony in his position. "What luck," he wrote in his diary, "it is to find myself opposing my country's entrance into a war I *don't* believe in, when I would much rather be fighting for my country in a war I *do* believe in. Here I am stumping the country with pacifists and considering resigning as a colonel in the Army Air Corps, when there is no philosophy I disagree with more than that of the pacifist, and nothing I would rather be doing than flying in the Air Corps."

Anger soon crept into Lindbergh's writing: "Sometimes I feel like saying, 'Well, let's get into the war if you are so anxious to. Then the responsibility will be yours.' In comparison to the work I am now doing the fighting would be fun." But he became more measured as he looked at the bigger picture: "My mind tells me we better face our problems and let Europe face hers without getting messed up in this war. I have an interest in Western civilization, and I have an interest in my race, or culture, or whatever you want to call it, and I have an interest in the type of world my children are going to live in." England and France, he still believed, had even more responsibility for the war than Germany, because, "They declared war without consulting us."[52]

Charles talked the situation over with Anne. Opposed to his resigning his commission, she wrote, "I feel rather sick about it." Charles told her that the reason he had not been called to duty may be that the Army did not want officers who thought the war could not be won. She had trouble sleeping, caused by, she writes, "a kind of dumb misery over C. giving up his commission. The army meant so much to him. It was the open world, his first chance; he blossomed there. How he worked, what it meant to him, he has told me."[53]

Seeking to discuss the situation with some Army friends, Charles drove into Manhattan that night and took a late train to Washington. The following morning, April 26, he had breakfast with Truman Smith, his old friend who had recruited him in Europe to report on the Luftwaffe's development. Although Smith agreed it was a point of honor, he opposed Lindbergh resigning his commission. Charles recorded that he also met with Senator Bennett Clark, Democrat from Missouri, but we do not know if they discussed the resignation.

He took a 6:00 p.m. train back to New York. He had made up his mind by then to resign. This was obviously a difficult decision, but he felt it was the only "honorable course" open to him. "If I do not tender my resignation, I would lose something in my own character that means more to me than my commission in the Air Corps. No one else might know it, but I would. And if I take this insult from Roosevelt, more, and worse, will probably be forthcoming."[54]

Returning home, he informed Anne of his decision, ignoring her warnings that the move could hurt him politically. Lindbergh spent most of Sunday working on his letters, one to the president and the other to Secretary of War Stimson. When he finished writing the letter to Roosevelt, he gave it to Anne to read. She suggested a final sentence, which he added, and their secretary, Christine Gawne, typed it for him. Both letters were mailed on Monday morning, and that afternoon copies were released to the press. The letter to Roosevelt read:

> My Dear Mr. President:
> Your remarks at the White House press conference on April 25 involving my reserve commission in the United States

Army Air Corps have of course disturbed me greatly. I had hoped that I might exercise my right as an American citizen, to place my viewpoint before the people of my country in time of peace without giving up the privilege of serving my country as an Air Corps officer in the event of war.

But since you in your capacity as President of the United States and Commander in Chief of the Army, have clearly implied that I am no longer of use to this country as a reserve officer, and in view of other implications that you, my President and my superior officer, have made concerning my loyalty to my country, my character, and my motives, I can see no honorable alternative to tendering my resignation as colonel in the United States Army Air Corps Reserve. I am therefore forwarding my resignation to the Secretary of War.

I take this action with the utmost regret, for my relationship with the Air Corps is one of the things that has meant most to me in life. I place it second only to my right as a citizen to speak freely to my fellow countrymen, and to discuss with them the issues of war and peace, which confront our Nation in this crisis.

I will continue to serve my country to the best of my ability as a private citizen.

Respectfully,

Charles A. Lindbergh

Making light of the situation with the headline "Lone Eagle's Feathers Ruffled," the *Washington Post* noted, "Army officials, however, did say that it was the War Department's general policy not to accept resignations from reserve officers during the emergency period." The article explained that since there was no regulation covering the issue, acceptance was entirely up to the Secretary of War.[55] And indeed, the War Department released a statement reporting that Secretary Stimson had accepted Lindbergh's resignation.

The White House had a little more to say. After conferring with the president in FDR's bedroom, Press Secretary Early attended the regular daily press briefing. He told the assembled reporters that he understood Lindbergh "is returning his commission," and wondered if he was also "returning his decoration to Mr. Hitler." Then, to demonstrate the White House had not forgotten or forgiven Lindbergh's opposition to the air-mail contract cancellations seven years earlier, Early complained that Lindbergh, by releasing his letter to the press, showed the same discourtesy he had shown in 1934. He ended his comments with the snide remark, "Now there is a commission that someone else can hold."[56]

In an editorial titled "An Unhappy Incident," the *New York Times* took both Lindbergh and Roosevelt to task. It said the president "spoke impetuously last Friday when he went back three-quarters of a century into the bitterness of a Civil War to find a disparaging epithet for Charles A. Lindbergh." It then called Lindbergh's resignation "a petulant action in relinquishing his commission." Returning to Roosevelt, the editorial claimed, "No evidence justified the President's comparison of Mr. Lindbergh with Clement Vallandigham." As for Lindbergh, it said no member of the military is "big enough to take the position that he will not serve his country because he has been, as he believes, unjustly reprimanded by his Commander-in-Chief or any other superior."[57]

Predictably, interventionists hailed Lindbergh's resignation as a great victory, while non-interventionists decried that the colonel was forced to take such a drastic step. Among the latter was North Dakota Republican senator Gerald P. Nye, who issued a statement saying, "None undertake to answer the arguments of Col. Lindbergh, but columnists and the President proceed with an effort to tear him limb from limb as a rank 'Copperhead' for his brilliant exercise of his right as an American to freedom of speech and expression."[58]

———

Somewhat lost in all the reporting over Charles' resignation was a comment made by the president in the same press conference in which he denounced Lindbergh. Roosevelt announced that the Navy's so-called "neutrality patrols" were to be extended "as far as the oceans of the world as necessary for hemisphere safety." He claimed that Navy warships would not be undertaking convoy duty, but instead would "engage in reconnaissance of certain areas to find out if there is any aggressive ship in that area or anywhere that might be coming toward the Western Hemisphere." He refused to answer a question about what one of these patrol vessels would do if they came on a German craft firing on a British convoy. However, he did say that patrol vessels have instructions to report back to him anything they see at sea. According to the *Washington Post*, "The White House has already disclosed that these reports are radioed back to shore in plain English, making it simple for British war vessels in the vicinity to tune in."

The *Post* said that reporters were "left with the impression that the neutrality patrol ships will act as scouts for the British convoys, the advance eyes and ears of the British Navy."

The U.S. Navy, an armed service of a nation that was supposed to be neutral in the war, had warships patrolling vast sections of the Atlantic Ocean. These warships were reporting the locations of any German or Italian warships or submarines they sighted. These reports were made in such a manner that British warships could pick up the transmissions and possibly speed to the locations to attack the sighted vessel. Although Hitler continued to ignore these provocations, non-interventionists in Congress constantly complained that this was clearly an act of war.

At the same press conference, the president indicated he was considering taking some kind of action over Greenland, which the United States had taken temporarily under its protection. He alluded to secret reports about German bombers flying over the giant Arctic island, but did not specify what he was going to do about it.[59]

As the president continued his machinations, Charles returned to the public circuit. On May 3, he spoke to 15,000 cheering supporters in St. Louis; the following week it was 10,000 in Minneapolis. His speeches now carried a different tone. Previously, he had patiently laid out the historical, moral, and political case against intervention, without ever mentioning Roosevelt's name. But the president's attack changed all that.

On May 23, Charles spoke to 25,000 people at Madison Square Garden, with a similar-sized crowd in the surrounding streets listening through loudspeakers. In his most strident speech to date, he attacked the administration's intolerance of dissent. "We have been shouting against intolerance in Europe, but it has been rising in America. We deplore the fact that the German people cannot vote on the policies of their government—that Hitler led his nation into war without asking their consent." Then, in a slap at Roosevelt as well as Willkie, who became an even more fervent interventionist after he lost the election, Lindbergh declared, "We in America were given just about as much chance to express our beliefs at the election last Fall as the Germans would have been given if Hitler had run against Goring."

Interrupted numerous times by the cheering crowd, Lindbergh explained what made America unique. Aside from the fact that we were a democracy that eschewed British and French-style empires, he argued,

> The United States is a nation of mixed races, religions and beliefs. We came from every part of Europe and from every portion of the earth. Here, in this country, we have learned to live peacefully together. Here we have developed a racial tolerance such as the world has never known before. Here we have developed a civilization in many ways never previously approached. Why must all this be jeopardized by injecting the wars and the hatreds of Europe into our midst?

Lindbergh closed with several appeals to his listeners, who were asked to join their local America First Committee; to demand that elected officials keep their promises; and to organize in their communities and attend rallies such as this one. "Our American ideals," he told them, "our independence, our freedom, our right to vote on important issues, all depend on the sacrifice we are willing to make and the action we take at this time."[60]

On May 29, Lindbergh addressed the Philadelphia Arena, which was packed to capacity with about 9,000 people, as another 6,000 gathered outside. Here he mocked the interventionists who ignored him when he was "advocating a stronger air force for America and England. In those days there was still time to have prevented this war, the people who shout so loudly now were hard to find." He decried the fact that he "could find very few people interested in military aviation when the German air force was being built." Lindbergh drew a roar of cheers and laughter from the crowd when he wondered how it was that "now there are thousands of experts on transatlantic bombing."

Then, focusing on the Allies, especially the British, he declared, "Always they demand more assistance from America. First they said, 'Sell us the arms and we will win.' Then it was, 'Lend us the arms and we will win.' Now it is, 'Bring us the arms and we will win.' Tomorrow it will be, 'Fight our war for us and we will win.'" He demanded that the government be accountable to the people and stop treating them like children. "We demand the truth from our leaders. We demand that they tell us where they are leading us."[61] Lindbergh's speeches continued in this vein right up until the attack on Pearl Harbor.

Roosevelt continued to try to push Germany into some overt act of war, but Hitler refused all provocations. On April 18 FDR moved the so-called "neutrality zone" so far east that it encompassed Greenland. Soon thereafter American forces took up residence there. On July 7, a brigade of four thousand U.S. Marines was shipped to occupation duty in Iceland. When he sent orders to the commander of the Atlantic Fleet, Admiral Ernest King, to transport the Marines to Iceland, Admiral Stark, who was by far one of the most ardent interventionists in the administration, told King, "I realize that this is practically an act of war."[62]

Returning home from a summit with Roosevelt in Newfoundland, Churchill told his war cabinet that Roosevelt had assured him "that he would wage war, but not declare it, and that he would become more and more provocative." As far as the Germans were concerned, if they "did not like it they could attack American forces." Churchill also explained that Roosevelt told him he had ordered the Navy warships on escort duty "to attack any U-boat which showed itself, even if they were 200 to 300 miles from the convoy."[63]

An ironic aspect of the Lindbergh–Roosevelt conflict, and the larger dispute between interventionists and non-interventionists, is that both sides were focused on Germany. In the meantime, Roosevelt finally got the incident he had hoped Hitler would orchestrate to bring America into the conflict—but it came at the hands of the Japanese, not the Germans. However, because Roosevelt had promised Churchill that whatever happened, war against Hitler would come first, the Pacific theater was ignored for several months as American troops, including many conscripted through Roosevelt's draft, prepared to fight and die now that the president had secured his long-sought-after war.

Chapter Nine

❦

"LINDBERGH IS A NAZI"

Of all the aspersions that Roosevelt's supporters hurled against Charles Lindbergh, the one that most damaged his reputation—an allegation that endures even today—was that Lindbergh was a Nazi sympathizer, and perhaps even an outright Nazi.

In addition to the insinuations of disloyalty conveyed in his "Copperhead" remarks, President Roosevelt himself privately declared he was "convinced" Charles was a Nazi, as previously described. The day after he made the allegation, the president wrote to Henry Stimson that he was concerned about "fifth column" activities in the country. "When I read Lindbergh's speech I felt that it could not have been better put if it had been written by [Nazi propaganda minister Joseph] Goebbels himself. What a pity that this youngster has completely abandoned his belief in our form of government and has accepted Nazi methods because apparently they are efficient."[1]

That same day, Roosevelt instructed Attorney General Robert H. Jackson to use the FBI to obtain information through "listening devices" about people "suspected of subversive activities against the government of the United States, including suspected spies." Jackson objected that this would involve wiretapping, which was outlawed by the Federal Communications Commission Act of 1934—legislation that was upheld twice by the Supreme Court in the face of appeals from FBI director J. Edgar Hoover that it be overturned. The president cavalierly told Jackson, a future Supreme Court justice himself, that he was sure the court did not intend its rulings to apply to "grave matters involving the defense of the nation."[2]

Jackson was disgusted that Roosevelt ordered him to ignore a Supreme Court ruling. He told Hoover he "did not want to authorize specific wiretaps and did not want to know who was being tapped."[3]

Wiretaps were nothing new to Roosevelt. In 1973, when President Nixon was being attacked for secretly taping Oval Office conversations, Roosevelt's son John commented, "I can't understand all the commotion in this case. Hell, my father just about invented bugging. He had them spread all over, and thought nothing of it."[4]

The creation of a secret White House "intelligence unit" to monitor the president's political rivals was another common thread in those two administrations; Nixon's so-called Plumbers, it turns out, had a precedent in the Roosevelt administration. Soon after the 1940 election, Roosevelt created the first of these units, headed by Secretary Ickes. Professor Richard W. Steele, former National Archives archivist and historian for the Joint Chiefs of Staff, describes Ickes as "a civil libertarian of sorts." But as far as Ickes was concerned, civil liberties extended to those with whom he agreed, such as "dissidents on the left, persecuted minorities, labor organizers, and the like. His contempt for isolationist dissenters left him unmoved by any claim to free expression they might have."[5]

Perhaps it was this view of civil liberties that endeared Ickes to the president. In his sympathetic biography of Roosevelt, James MacGregor Burns was forced to admit that the "wartime White House was not dependably a source of strong and sustained support for civil liberties in specific situations."[6]

When the Ickes group did not work out, according to Steele, Roosevelt was left "without an effective way of exposing the roots of isolationism. British Intelligence, which included among its varied activities in the United States manipulating public opinion and discrediting opponents of intervention, was a continuous source of inspiration and help."[7]

In February 1941, Roosevelt created a new, secret spy unit that reported directly to him. The head spook was John Franklin Carter, who worked for Roosevelt in this capacity right up until the president's death in 1945. A former mystery novelist and newspaper columnist, Carter's first assignment was to find some dirt on Senator Burton Wheeler, a Montana Democrat and prominent non-interventionist. When that effort proved unsuccessful, Roosevelt sent Carter after the leaders of the recently formed America First Committee. Unfortunately for Roosevelt, not only did Carter fail to find any Nazi connections or influence in the organization, but he reported that the committee's first national chairman, General Robert Wood, "had no use for Nazis or their doctrines, and would not tolerate any dealings with them if he knew of such dealings."[8]

Within months Carter had a staff of eleven people, all paid with State Department funds. His services were called upon again in 1943, after Roosevelt learned of the massacre of over 10,000 Polish Army officers in the Katyn Forest by Soviet secret police agents. The Poles were shot in the back of their heads and thrown into large mass graves, where Soviet agents pummeled survivors with their rifle butts. When the Germans uncovered the graves, Stalin, who had personally ordered the operation, claimed the Nazis had perpetrated the killings. Few believed him, since the Poles were prisoners of the Soviets when they were murdered.

FDR ordered Carter to look into the massacre. In a report submitted for the president's eyes only, Carter found the Soviets guilty—the same conclusion reached by a British investigation as well as an inquiry by the U.S. naval attaché in Istanbul, Lieutenant Commander George H. Earle. But Roosevelt was not interested in discovering anything that would impugn the reputation of his future wartime ally. As historian Thomas Fleming notes, "FDR told Carter before he began this task that he thought the Russians were probably guilty, but he 'didn't want to believe it.' If he eventually did believe the Russians had killed the Poles, he would 'pretend not to' believe it."[9]

While Roosevelt's "see no evil" approach to Stalin was appalling, his operations against his American political opponents were equally objectionable. The White House routinely forwarded to the FBI telegrams and letters it received criticizing the president's foreign policy. Later, when a controversy arose over the use of U.S. Navy ships to escort Allied convoys, letters supporting Lindbergh's opposition to the convoy duty were sent from the White House to the Secret Service.[10]

According to historian Athan G. Theoharis, the president's press secretary, Stephen Early, told J. Edgar Hoover, "It was the President's idea" that the FBI "might" record the names and addresses of those writing letters and telegrams opposing Roosevelt's position on intervention in the war. What exactly Roosevelt wanted to do with these ostensible subversives is not entirely clear. As Theoharis notes, in response to FDR's request, Hoover

> forwarded to the White House reports detailing whatever derogatory information the FBI had already collected on the identified critics. When the FBI had no preexisting file, a special inquiry was initiated with the results also sent to the White House. Hoover's reports provoked no protest from the White House, even though they confirmed that the FBI was monitoring political activities that did not violate federal statutes. The Roosevelt White House, instead, expressed appreciation and invited further submissions of information. There ensued a continuing flurry of FBI reports.[11]

Unsurprisingly, the FBI compiled a detailed file on Lindbergh running 1,368 pages long. Other than some angry, baseless charges by his opponents, there was not one shred of evidence that he in any way supported Nazi Germany. Roosevelt biographer Conrad Black observes, "The public battle between Roosevelt and Lindbergh would continue for another two years, but it was already an unequal contest. Roosevelt routinely referred to Lindbergh in private as a Nazi. Roosevelt subjected him to wiretaps, seeking evidence of Nazi connections, but no direct links came to light."[12]

And Lindbergh was far from the only target of Roosevelt's operation. As Theoharis notes, "Insofar as many of the adherents of the anti-Roosevelt America First Committee were prominent American civic and political leaders, including Charles Lindbergh and U.S. senators Burton Wheeler (D. MT) and Gerald Nye (R. ND), FBI intelligence reports on their speeches and strategies furthered the president's political interests—providing information about planned lobbying and congressional initiatives."[13]

Even the British intelligence agents working in the United States got into the act. In one rigged poll of members of the Congress of Industrial Organizations convention, the survey claimed that convention delegates had voted Lindbergh "U. S. Fascist Number One and Senator Wheeler U. S. Fascist Number Two."[14]

Richard W. Steele notes that FDR's domestic spying efforts were part of a larger campaign to smear his opponents: "FDR led an education campaign that portrayed his domestic critics as part of the Nazi conspiracy. His efforts gained credibility from the fifth column myth that, due in part to the propaganda efforts of the administration and its interventionist supporters, had established a firm grip on the American imagination."

Steele pinpoints a series of articles co-written by William J. Donovan as the most influential of the administration's efforts to portray Roosevelt's opponents as Nazis. The four-part series appeared in almost every major American newspaper in August 1940, and "purportedly derived from Donovan's observations on a trip through Europe. In fact, it was based on material supplied by British Intelligence. The story authoritatively informed the American people that Hitler's success could be explained by the democracies' susceptibility to internal subversion."[15]

"Wild Bill" Donavan was the founder of the CIA's World War II precursor, the O.S.S. (which was created at the suggestion of British intelligence chief William Stephenson). Harboring a near-paranoid fear of domestic Nazi sympathizers, Donovan went so far as to claim that "in the United States an organization of Nazis is being trained in arms.

As matters now stand, it is conceivable that the United States possesses the finest Nazi-schooled fifth column in the world."[16]

The entire concept was a figment of the imaginations of British intelligence, yet many Americans swallowed the myth of a pro-Nazi fifth column hook, line, and sinker. Meanwhile, the man who probably knew the most about the topic, FBI director J. Edgar Hoover, "privately minimized the alleged fifth column."[17]

As a result of these kinds of baseless allegations, however, Lindbergh and the entire non-interventionist movement became widely perceived as Nazi sympathizers. In her book *Why America Fights*, Susan A. Brewer describes the true beliefs of non-interventionists. The movement "included conservatives, liberals, socialists, communists, and pacifists." In other words, it was a cross-section of the American public. As for their motivation, she writes, "They viewed the American entry into World War I as a mistake not to be repeated. Some feared it would mean bigger government or the dismantling of the New Deal reforms or another crackdown on civil liberties" as Americans had experienced under the Wilson administration during the Great War.[18]

As Steele notes, FDR viewed non-interventionist sentiment through the lens of his own political fortunes: "Isolationism confronted the President with serious problems of public leadership, but his responses in many instances bore no close relationship to the 'threat.' FDR's enemies did not constitute a fifth column—a conclusion verified by the FBI, the Justice Department, and even his own personal investigator. FDR's decision to disregard this information and to act instead on the necessarily suspect suggestions of British intelligence suggests that his judgment was strongly conditioned by the hopes of using the loyalty issue to smear his critics."[19]

Professor Justus D. Doenecke, a renowned authority on the period, writes that the world inhabited by those opposed to intervention "differed markedly from that of the Roosevelt administration. Aside from blaming Nazism first on Versailles, then on allied appeasement, the isolationists held no brief for Germany. 'No one,' said Senator Hiram Johnson [a progressive California Republican and former FDR supporter who broke with the president over the war] could wish more ardently than I do for the defeat of Hitler.'"[20]

Anne Lindbergh colorfully described the anti-interventionists as "not smart, not rich, not intellectual, dowdy, hard-working good people, housewives, shopkeepers, etc." She depicted the interventionists rather sarcastically as "the East, the secure, the rich, the sensitive, the academic, the good."[21]

The playwright Robert Sherwood, who was a speechwriter for President Roosevelt and originator of the term "arsenal of democracy," was an outspoken interventionist and supporter of British intelligence front groups operating inside the United States. In his history of FDR and Harry Hopkins, Sherwood attempted to clarify who were the "isolationists": "Actually, in the first year or more of war, the ranks of the isolationists included the overwhelming majority of the American people who would have been glad to see the European war end on almost any inconclusive terms merely as a guarantee that the United States would not be drawn into it." Following a discussion of the differences between the anti-war motivations in 1914–17 and in 1939–41, he wrote, "Americans in 1939 were fortified with the experience that the previous generation had conspicuously lacked, the experience of involvement in European war, and they wanted no more of it."[22]

Here Sherwood touched upon the heart of the matter. There was a great deal of animosity among the American population over World War I. People felt we had saved England and France from German domination and were resented for it in both countries. They did not want to see a new generation of young Americans sent to fight and die in Europe. This was confirmed by Sir Robert Bruce Lockhart, the famous British spy and director of propaganda during the war, who visited the United States on a speaking tour in 1939. He said Americans told him, "We Americans went into the last war to save democracy. We pulled you out of a hole and we received very grudging thanks. At Versailles and after Versailles you trampled on democratic ideals. Now, largely through your own fault, you are in trouble again and you want our help. Well, we've learnt our lesson."[23]

For the most part, the president remained publicly silent on non-interventionists. He let his officials and supporters counter them on his behalf, which allowed him to appear above the fray. One such official was Robert Sherwood himself. In a radio address on August 26, 1940, carried in both the United States and Canada, and later rebroadcast over the BBC, Sherwood attacked Lindbergh and Henry Ford for having what he called "a traitorous point of view." He assured his British listeners that the voice "of our country is not expressed by Lindbergh, or the other bootlickers of Hitler." Lindbergh and Ford, he said, were "machine worshipers" who admired the regimentation of German industries and "wish we could have the same system over here."[24]

By the time he published his book on Hopkins and Roosevelt in 1948, Sherwood seemed somewhat more understanding of Lindbergh, although he still considered him a "forcible and persuasive although unwitting purveyor of Nazi propaganda." Following that gratuitous introduction, Sherwood described what it was that prompted Lindbergh to become "undoubtedly Roosevelt's most formidable competitor on the radio":

> Largely because of personal tragedy, and the refusal of the more sensational press to allow him and his family to lead anything resembling a normal life, Lindbergh had lived for several years in Europe before the war. He had seen the flabby weakness of the England of Stanley Baldwin and Neville Chamberlain, and the chaotic disunity of France, and the apparent deficiency of Russian industry, as contrasted with... Germany, which presented a model of efficiency to his technological mind. A retiring and taciturn man by nature as well as by force of cruel circumstances, Lindbergh became a violent and extremely eloquent crusader for the cause of isolationism.[25]

Despite the unwarranted description of the mild mannered Lindbergh as "violent," Sherwood seems to have concluded that Lindbergh was not a Nazi lackey after all.[26]

Among those who passionately opposed intervention was a small group of students at Yale University Law School who formed what became known as the America First Committee. The founding members of the group's executive committee, all of whom opened themselves up to the typical charges of disloyalty made against non-interventionists, comprised an unlikely group of alleged Nazi sympathizers. They were Robert D. Stuart Jr., an army reserve lieutenant who would become president of the Quaker Oats Company and U.S. ambassador to Norway; future member of Congress and president of the United States Gerald Ford; future Associate Justice of the U.S. Supreme Court Potter Stewart; and future U.S. ambassador to Pakistan Eugene Locke.[27]

More than 800,000 Americans eventually joined the America First Committee's 500 local chapters across the country. Membership was "open to all patriotic American citizens," while "Fascists, Nazis, Communists, and members of the Bund" were explicitly banned.[28] Among the group's members was former President Herbert Hoover, whom *Life* magazine called "the nation's most effective isolationist."[29] Other well-known adherents included President Theodore Roosevelt's daughter Alice Roosevelt Longworth; future undersecretary of state and ambassador to India Chester Bowles; future president of Yale, Kingman Brewster; the actress Lillian Gish; and best-selling novelist Kathleen Norris.[30]

Liberal economist John T. Flynn, who was chair of the New York City AFC chapter, described the price many of these people paid for their stand against another European war: "No one will [ever] know what...odium has been heaped upon honorable men and women because they dared to lift their voices for peace and for our country."[31]

Lindbergh himself became so politically toxic that people who merely associated with him often found themselves subject to furious attacks. One was Truman Smith, the former U.S. military attaché in Berlin and Lindbergh's old friend from his tours of the Luftwaffe. Promoted to lieutenant colonel and retired from the Army because of diabetes, in mid-1940 Smith was working as an analyst and advisor on German military matters to Army chief of staff General George C. Marshall. The chief of staff had personally arranged for Smith's new role because, as

General Albert C. Wedemeyer wrote, General Marshall "personally admired Truman Smith and highly respected his professional abilities, particularly his judgments concerning military affairs in Europe. He considered Smith's retirement a serious loss to the Intelligence Division of the General Staff and arranged for him to participate in intelligence evaluations on a schedule that would not further endanger his health."[32]

Smith's value to the Army did not forestall presidential press secretary Stephen Early from condemning him to Army officials as a "friend of Lindbergh." Early wrote to Roosevelt's military secretary and close friend General Edwin Watson on May 27, 1940, claiming that Dwight Davis, secretary of war under President Coolidge, said that Smith was the inspiration behind Lindbergh's radio addresses. He then mentioned that Lindbergh had been a guest in Smith's home in Berlin, which was no secret, and best of all, "he was known to be pro-Nazi."[33]

Typical of an official in an administration that carelessly threw around incendiary charges against opponents, Early offered no evidence for the validity of Davis' statement.

There, the great bugaboo accusation often silenced anyone even suspected of opposing the president's foreign policies. In this case it did not work. Even after Treasury Secretary and ardent interventionist Morgenthau suggested to General Marshall that Smith be fired, Marshall resisted, considering Smith too valuable to him and the Intelligence Division. Instead, Smith went to Fort Benning Georgia for a few weeks until matters cooled down. When Lindbergh continued his speeches while Smith was away, Marshall considered the matter closed and brought him back.

Then the attacks on Smith were taken up by Roosevelt's supporters in the press. In a campaign believed to have been instigated by Secretary Ickes and Roosevelt advisor Felix Frankfurter, Smith was denounced in columns by interventionists Drew Pearson, Dorothy Thompson, and Walter Winchell for allegedly showing pro-German bias in the reports to Washington he and Lindbergh had sent from Berlin. Echoing accusations that were hurled at Lindbergh, they charged Smith had exaggerated the strength of the Luftwaffe in order to frighten the Americans, French, and

British out of resisting Hitler. In fact, the reports had been accurate, and when combined with information from other sources, they were used to develop U.S. military policy toward Germany. The campaign against Smith finally ended when presidential advisor Bernard Baruch spoke to Roosevelt about the situation, reportedly telling the president that the attacks on Smith could harm relations between the administration and the Army.[34]

In September 1941, a medical retirement board at Walter Reed Hospital overruled Marshall and ordered Smith retired for health reasons effective January 31, 1942, allowing him to utilize his remaining leave time. A few days after the attack on Pearl Harbor, General Marshall called Smith and asked him to return to the Intelligence Division if he felt up to the task. Smith returned to duty on February 1 with the rank of full colonel. On January 19, 1945, Colonel Truman Smith was awarded the Distinguished Service Medal by Secretary of War Stimson. The citation accompanying the medal outlines his service and asserts, "His contribution to the war effort of the nation has been of major significance." Smith retired permanently from the Army in June 1946, after thirty years of honorable service to his country, despite the best efforts of Roosevelt's men.[35]

In writing about this officer whose greatest offense was being a friend of Lindbergh, General Wedemeyer said, "The attempt to disparage Truman Smith has long seemed to me a grave injustice."[36]

The entire campaign to paint Lindbergh as a Nazi sympathizer was made through innuendo, mistruths, and guilt-by-association, since he never expressed any pro-Nazi sentiments in his numerous articles and speeches. The only evidence his critics could cite was the instance of Charles receiving a medal from Goring. Although the real circumstances of that event were known publicly, Lindbergh's detractors were not interested in those details, nor were they impressed by his service as a quasi-spy against the very regime they accused him of supporting.

In his definitive biography of Lindbergh, Scott Berg came to the following conclusion about the aviator's loyalties: "In truth, Charles Lindbergh was never associated with any pro-Nazi or anti-Semitic organization; he never attended any Bund meetings; and since more than

four months before the outbreak of war in Europe, he had neither con-
sorted nor consulted with anyone known to have any connections with
the Third Reich."[37]

The late Professor Wayne S. Cole, one of the leading authorities on
the foreign policy debates of the prewar period, concurred. "Lindbergh
did not like Hitler or Nazism," he wrote. "He did not favor a Nazi dic-
tatorship either for Germany or for the United States. He did not want
Nazi Germany to triumph in Britain or in the United States. Whatever
one may think of his views, Lindbergh formulated them in terms of his
own judgment of what was best for the United States and for Western
Civilization. He thought the United States should not be guided in its
conduct of foreign affairs by the wishes of any foreign government (German, British, or Russian) but, rather, by what Americans thought best
for the United States."[38]

Professor Robert Smith Thompson addresses the issue forthrightly in
his history of the interlude between the world wars: "Lindbergh may have
been foolish and Lindbergh may have been wrong. But no one in 1940,
and for that matter no one in the half century since, has proven Lindbergh
to be a Nazi."[39]

———

In addition to allegations of Nazi sympathies, Charles Lindbergh was
widely accused of being an anti-Semite—another charge that is commonly
believed today, although a few historians have begun questioning the
conventional wisdom.

The accusation stems from Lindbergh's speech at an America First
Committee rally at the Coliseum in Des Moines, Iowa, on September 11,
1941. In earlier speeches, such as his May 23 address in New York, he
attacked government leaders, claiming that the country lacked "only a
leadership that places America first—a leadership that tells what it means
and what it says. Give us that and we will be the most powerful country
in the world. Give us that and we will be so united that no one will dare
to attack us." In that speech he also insisted Americans must "demand

an accounting from a government that has led us into war while promising peace."[40]

He stepped up his rhetoric six days later in Philadelphia. After Roosevelt gave a pro-war radio address in which he proclaimed that "an unlimited national emergency exists" and declared that the Cape Verde Islands off the west African coast were vital to America's security, Lindbergh charged that the president had gone beyond "even Hitler" in his actions.[41]

The Des Moines speech was different in that Lindbergh identified the larger groups he believed were pushing America into the war. He titled this address, "Who Are the War Agitators?" In a strange twist, the president gave another radio address just before Charles' speech was scheduled to begin. The rally organizers decided to broadcast Roosevelt's talk over the public address system in the Coliseum. In that address, Roosevelt discussed a confrontation that had taken place in the North Atlantic on September 4. Here is how he described the incident:

> The United States destroyer *Greer*, proceeding in full daylight toward Iceland, had reached a point southeast of Greenland. She was carrying American mail to Iceland. She was flying the American flag. Her identity as an American ship was unmistakable. She was then and there attacked by a submarine. Germany admits that it was a German submarine. The submarine deliberately fired a torpedo at the *Greer*, followed by another torpedo attack.... The German submarine fired first upon this American destroyer without warning and with deliberate design to sink her."

Because of this and other incidents, Roosevelt explained, he had ordered the Navy to attack any German or Italian "vessels of war" that "enter the waters the protection of which is necessary for American defense."[42]

This has been known ever since as Roosevelt's "shoot-on-sight" speech. Of course, by that time the area deemed vital to the protection of the United States constituted well over half the Atlantic Ocean, almost to the European coast. The attack on the *Greer* nearly gave the president the incident he was looking for to push a war declaration through Congress. But Roosevelt did not pursue it—he needed a better provocation, since he had blatantly misconstrued this one.

The truth, as later revealed by the ship's deck log, was that the destroyer, which was transporting military supplies along with mail to U.S. forces stationed on Iceland, had been tracking the German submarine U-562 and reporting its position to nearby Lockheed Hudson patrol bombers of the British Coastal Command, stationed at Iceland. The U-boat, commanded by Lieutenant George-Werner Fraatz, quickly dived after it was spotted on the surface by a British bomber. The aircraft, which was specifically designed and used for anti-submarine warfare, dropped several depth charges on the sub, to no effect.

At about that time, the *Greer* arrived on the scene and began sweeping the area with radar while the bomber returned to its base to refuel and restock its depth charges. For the next three hours, the destroyer's radar remained locked on the submarine, awaiting the arrival of a second British bomber, which also dropped a series of depth charges, all missing their target. At some point, Fraatz must have raised his submarine to periscope level to see who was tracking him and dropping depth charges on his boat, and he saw the destroyer. Whether he realized it was a U.S. ship—which he was prohibited from attacking—is not clear. In retaliation for the depth charges, he fired two torpedoes at the *Greer*, both of which passed under her hull. The destroyer responded by launching nineteen depth charges, but all missed the target, and the U-boat sped away from the ship's radar. The destroyer's commander later "drew angry comments from Atlantic Fleet commander Ernest King" for not being more aggressive or calling in other forces to help sink the submarine.[43]

According to historian Robert Dallek, the Navy reported to Roosevelt on September 9 that there was "no positive evidence" that the sub knew the ship was American. Obfuscating the truth of what had happened, the president called the encounter an act of "piracy—piracy legally and morally."[44]

Following Roosevelt's broadcast, Lindbergh gave his twenty-five minute address to 7,500 people at the Des Moines Coliseum—an audience that he later learned included some opposition-paid hecklers.[45] In his speech, Charles broached a sensitive topic, declaring, "National polls showed that when England and France declared war on Germany, in 1939, less than 10 percent of our population favored a similar course for America. But there are various groups of people, here and abroad, whose interests and beliefs necessitated the involvement of the United States in the war. The three most important groups who have been pressing this country toward war are the British, the Jewish and the Roosevelt administration." He added that lesser pro-war groups included capitalists, Anglophiles, and Communists, the latter having been "opposed to intervention until a few weeks ago," when Germany invaded the Soviet Union.[46]

Scott Berg wrote of the speech, "Lindbergh had reduced his comments about the Jews to three paragraphs. They were the only public comments he ever made during the Great Debate in which he mentioned them. Although he felt he was showing his sympathy for a long-persecuted tribe, each additional sentence would be used to burn the brand of anti-Semite deeper into his public persona."[47]

Here are Lindbergh's exact remarks that caused so much furor:

> It is not difficult to understand why Jewish people desire the overthrow of Nazi Germany. The persecution they suffered in Germany would be sufficient to make bitter enemies of any race. No person with a sense of the dignity of mankind can condone the persecution of the Jewish race in Germany. But no person of honesty and vision can look on their pro-war policy here today without seeing the dangers involved in such a policy both for us and for them. Instead of agitating for war, the Jewish groups in this country should be opposing it in every possible way for they will be among the first to feel its consequences.
>
> Tolerance is a virtue that depends upon peace and strength. History shows that it cannot survive war and devastations.

A few far-sighted Jewish people realize this and stand opposed to intervention. But the majority still do not. Their greatest danger to this country lies in their large ownership and influences in our motion pictures, our press, our radio and our government. I am not attacking either the Jewish or the British people. Both races I admire. But I am saying that the leaders of both the British and Jewish races, for reasons which are as understandable from their viewpoint as they are inadvisable from ours, for reasons which are not American, wish to involve us in the war.

We cannot blame them for looking out for what they believe to be their own interests, but we also must look out for ours. We cannot allow the natural passions and prejudices of other people to lead our country to destruction.[48]

Lindbergh never blamed American Jews for their attitude toward the war. To the contrary, even as he criticized Jewish support for war, he expressed sympathy and understanding for the Jewish position. Nevertheless, Lindbergh's enemies ignored the substance of his Des Moines speech and vilified Charles as an anti-Semite. It was a devastating charge that was easy for many Americans to believe, since his critics had already planted the idea that he was a German sympathizer, a fifth columnist, and even an outright Nazi.

When Anne read the Des Moines speech in advance, it threw her into a "black gloom." Although she thought her husband was expressing himself "truthfully, moderately, and with no bitterness and rancor," she tried to remove the Jewish references, correctly foreseeing that they would be portrayed as an attack on Jews and that Charles would suffer for it. Charles responded that the point was not the effect his words had on him, but whether he spoke the truth and if his statements would help keep us out of the war. He clearly did not anticipate that the charge would be repeated thousands of times over the years until millions came to believe it.[49]

One of the first to strike at Lindbergh was White House press secretary Stephen Early, who used the opportunity to once again tie Charles to the Nazis: "You have seen the outpourings of Berlin in the last few days. You saw Lindbergh's statement last night. I think there is a striking similarity between the two."[50] That was just the beginning of the invective, which included outright attacks on Lindbergh's character and patriotism, as well as some smaller slights. The latter included the city of Charlotte, North Carolina, changing the street name of "Lindbergh Drive," and Little Falls, Minnesota, painting over the announcement on a water tower proclaiming it as the birthplace of Charles Lindbergh.[51]

Lindbergh's enemies rejoiced, while many of his friends distanced themselves from him for fear of being tarred with the anti-Semitic brush. He remained as chief speaker for the America First Committee, but the Des Moines speech had harmed his reputation and that of the AFC so badly that it ceased to serve as an effective counter-balance to the administration's pro-war efforts. Lindbergh still drew huge crowds after the speech, and he never again mentioned the Jews, but the damage was done.

Thus, we see that Lindbergh's famed anti-Semitism came down to a single claim he made—that Jews were among the influential groups that shaped America's war policies. This was enough for history to forever record Lindbergh as a strident Jew-hater.

It is notable that hardly anyone remembers Roosevelt or his cabinet members this way. One might consider the case of Robert H. Jackson, who had been Roosevelt's attorney general, and later an associate justice of the U.S. Supreme Court. Writing in the early 1950s about Roosevelt's decision to insist on an unconditional surrender from Germany, Jackson, who also served as the U.S. chief prosecutor at the Nuremberg trials, recalled, "Then too there was a very large Jewish influence in public sentiment. That favored a very strong or severe peace, to which unconditional surrender was preliminary."[52] Apparently, citing strong Jewish influence is unremarkable coming from a Roosevelt man, but unforgiveable coming from Lindbergh.

Socialist leader Norman Thomas, although embarrassed by Lindbergh's comment about the Jews, claimed that Lindbergh was "not as anti-Semitic as some who seize the opportunity to criticize him."[53] Perhaps Thomas had Roosevelt himself in mind when he made that charge, since the president apparently agreed with Lindbergh's sentiments on Jewish influence. In a diary entry for early July 1939, Secretary Ickes reports that he once gave the president a copy of a London newssheet with an article attacking Ambassador Kennedy. The piece charged that Kennedy "goes so far as to insinuate that the democratic policy of the United States is a Jewish production." Ickes relates, "The President read this and said to me: 'It is true.'"[54]

Roosevelt indeed was not particularly fond of the Jewish people. British historian Paul Johnson, in his *A History of the Jews*, observes that FDR was "anti-Semitic, in a mild way, and ill informed. When the topic came up at the Casablanca Conference, he spoke of 'the understandable complaints which Germans bore towards the Jews in Germany, namely that while they represented a small part of the population, over 50 percent of the lawyers, doctors, schoolteachers, college professors in Germany were Jews.'" Johnson points out that FDR had grossly exaggerated the figures—the actual numbers were 16.3, 10.2, 2.6, and 0.5 percent, respectively.[55]

This was no isolated incident; throughout his life, Roosevelt frequently made disparaging remarks about Jews. In 1937, when the owner of the *New York Times* died, leaving his family with a potential inheritance tax bill in the millions of dollars. Roosevelt, who was sometimes upset by the newspaper's reporting, expected that the Sulzbergers would have to sell a large block of their stock in the *Times* to pay the tax. Instead, Arthur Sulzberger "found a legal way to use the corporation's money to pay the family's tax bill. And not a single share of voting stock was lost." In response to the maneuver Roosevelt thundered, "It's a dirty Jewish trick."[56]

In November 1941, Roosevelt complained during a cabinet meeting that there were too many Jews among federal employees in Oregon. Evidently, some Oregon Democrats had complained about this, so he was limiting the appointments of Jews there. When Secretary Morgenthau asked about this two weeks later, Roosevelt tried to explain how to handle the problem of having too many Jews. "Let me give you an example," he told Morgenthau. "Some years ago a third of the entering class at Harvard were Jews and the question came up as to how it should be handled. It was decided that over a period of years, the number of Jews should be reduced one or two per cent a year until it was down to 15%."[57] Evidently, 15 percent was an acceptable number of Jews. Ted Morgan notes that Roosevelt knew this story because he personally was "a member of the board of overseers" who "helped to formulate" the decision to cut Jewish attendance at Harvard.[58]

In January 1942, Roosevelt let loose another slur against both Jews and Catholics. The president told Leo T. Crowley, a Catholic economist, that the United States was "a Protestant country and the Catholics and Jews are here on sufferance. It is up to both of you [Crowley and Morgenthau] to go along with anything that I want at this time." After Crowley told Morgenthau about the comment, Morgenthau, who was Jewish, asked him, "What am I killing myself for at this desk if we are just here by sufferance?"[59]

The following year Secretary Morgenthau and his Treasury Department became involved in efforts to save some 70,000 Jews in Rumania from Nazi extermination. Frustrated by stalling tactics from the State Department and a maddening silence from the president on the subject, Treasury official Randolph Paul "prepared a memorandum summarizing the saga of delay and obfuscation. It had an explosive title 'Report to the Secretary on the Acquiescence of this Government in the Murder of the Jews.'"[60]

When it came to efforts to save the Jews of Europe, Roosevelt's record was hardly inspiring. In May 1939, the *St. Louis* sailed from Hamburg to Cuba carrying 936 passengers, all but six of them Jewish refugees from Nazi Germany. The ship was turned away from Havana harbor and sailed up the Florida coast, where the captain sought permission to land. Seven hundred and thirty-four passengers were already on the quota lists for entry visas to the United States. Despite numerous petitions and even entreaties from Secretary Morgenthau, Roosevelt refused to allow the ship to dock in the United States. It eventually returned to Europe and was permitted to land its passengers in Belgium. A year later that country was overrun by German troops followed by Gestapo agents, and most of the former passengers of the *St. Louis* were shipped off to extermination camps.[61]

Morgenthau, who appears to be the only cabinet member concerned about the fate of Europe's Jews, spoke to the president often about what could be done to save them. At one point Roosevelt told him to "give me a list of the thousand richest Jews in the United States" so he could pressure them to contribute to some effort to relocate Jews. "FDR was willing," writes Ted Morgan, to "'spread the Jews thin all over the world,' as he put it, but he did not want them entering the United States in large numbers."[62]

In his history of the Holocaust, David S. Wyman, founder and chairman of the Wyman Institute for Holocaust Studies, explains the politics behind Roosevelt's policy on European Jewry: "It appears that Roosevelt's overall response to the Holocaust was deeply affected by political expediency. Most Jews supported him unwaveringly, so an active rescue policy offered little political advantage."[63]

Roosevelt's hostility toward Jews was a long-standing family trait. Discussing the history of anti-Semitism in the Roosevelt family, Morgan wrote this about FDR's mother, Sara Delano Roosevelt:

> Jews were "horrid"—anti-Semitism was a Delano trait.... When she first met the Henry Morgenthaus in July 1918, she wrote: "The wife is very Jewish but appeared very well." (i.e., in spite of being Jewish). Once Franklin was married, one of Eleanor's mother-in-law problems was how to deal with Sara's offensive anti-Semitic remarks at the luncheon table. She would remind Sara that one of her ancestors was Jewish. Sara indignantly responded: "Eleanor, how can you say such a thing?" and Eleanor would reply, "But mother, he was."[64]

FDR's half-brother Rosy held high the family banner of anti-Semitism throughout his life. He delighted in openly expressing his contempt for Jews, commenting, to take just two examples, that the village of Lake Placid, New York, "reeks of Jews," and that Bermuda was crowded with "mostly an awful class of Jews, most objectionable when sober, and worse when drunk."[65]

One might ask, if Roosevelt was an anti-Semite, as it certainly appears, why did he have so many Jewish advisers? U.S. Court of Appeals judge Jerome Frank, a close associate of Roosevelt, answered the question: since Jews were not viewed as viable presidential candidates, Roosevelt believed they "would not become political threats."[66]

In light of what we now know about the casual anti-Semitism of FDR and his family, consider a comment made by Anne Lindbergh about Charles to journalist Herbert Mitgang in 1980: "He was accused of being anti-Semitic, but in the 45 years I lived with him I never heard him make a remark against Jews, not a crack or a joke, neither did any of my children."[67]

One close friend, who knew Lindbergh better than perhaps any other, was Harry Guggenheim, the Jewish financier, philanthropist, and one-time owner and publisher of *Newsday*. When asked about Lindbergh, Harry insisted Charles "has never had the slightest anti-Semitic feeling."[68]

We may wonder why Lindbergh never fought back against the charge of anti-Semitism. *New Yorker* writer Brendan Gill offered some insight on this question in writing about Charles' refusal, despite Anne's objections, to remove his remarks on Jews from his Des Moines speech: "Lindbergh was so confident of his being known to be a man of virtue and therefore incapable of embracing anti-Semitism that he refused to do so."[69]

The campaign against Lindbergh was so intense that, despite the profound unfairness of the allegation of anti-Semitism, it is debatable whether he could have salvaged his reputation even if he had actively refuted the charge. Regardless, the colonel thought that a dignified silence was the best response to such a scurrilous accusation. As it turned out, however, silence was not enough to counter the Roosevelt smear campaign, which destroyed Lindbergh's reputation as an American patriot and even as a decent human being. Today, when we speak of the politics of personal destruction, we should consider the interventionists' attacks on Charles Lindbergh as Exhibit A.

Chapter Ten

❧

THE SMEAR
CONTINUES

On Sunday morning, December 7, 1941, over 350 aircraft from six Japanese carriers swept down on the Pearl Harbor naval base in Hawaii. The planes came in two waves and included dive-bombers, torpedo planes, fighters, and bombers. Caught unprepared, the U.S. Navy suffered four battleships sunk and four others damaged. In addition, the attackers sank or damaged three cruisers, three destroyers, one mine-laying ship, and an anti-aircraft training ship. The Japanese also struck Army airfields, where 188 aircraft were destroyed, many on the ground. The attack resulted in the deaths of 2,402 military personnel, and another 1,282 wounded.

After listening to radio reports of the attack, Lindbergh asked a question many Americans were asking: "How did the Japs get close enough [to attack America], and where is our Navy?" He then reasoned, "The Japanese can, of course, raid the Hawaiian Islands, or even the West Coast, with aircraft carriers. But the cost in carriers and planes lost is going to be awfully high unless our Navy is asleep—or in the Atlantic. The question in my mind is how much of it has been sent to the Atlantic to aid Britain."[1]

Early on Monday, December 8, 1941, Lindbergh called Robert Stuart of the America First Committee to suggest that the rally planned for December 12 in Boston be cancelled. Stuart agreed. The speech Lindbergh was writing for that rally only exists in draft form. In many ways, it may have been his most powerful speech for the AFC. Tentatively titled "What Do We Mean by Democracy and Freedom?" it would have been his most direct attack yet against Roosevelt. In this undelivered speech Charles declared, "I believe in freedom and I believe in democracy, but I do not believe in the form of freedom and democracy toward which our President is leading us today. I say that democracy is gone from a nation when its people are no longer informed of the fundamental policies and intentions of its government. I say freedom is a travesty among men who have been forced into war by a President they elected because he promised peace."

Later in the address he asked, "Have you ever stopped to think how ridiculous it is that this democratic nation has twice, within a generation, been carried to war by Presidents who were elected because they promised peace?"

Lindbergh also denounced Roosevelt for sending Marines to Iceland, which he described as "a European island"—a part of the world that Roosevelt himself had "recognized as a war zone by banning it to American shipping." Addressing the president, he assailed Roosevelt for making the decision to send these forces on "your own initiative, as a dictator would have made it, without any warning to our people, and without laying the matter before our Congress. Is this your standard of integrity, after promising us again, and again, that our boys would not be sent to fight in foreign wars?"

"The record of the Roosevelt Administration," he continued, "has been a record of subterfuge masquerading as a crusade for freedom. 'Cash and Carry,' 'Steps Short of War,' 'Aid to the Democracies,' 'Neutrality Patrols,' 'Lease and Lend'; every one of these slogans was used to deceive the American people."

Lindbergh then challenged the president, "Before we crusade for freedom and democracy abroad, let us decide how these terms are to be applied to the Negro problem in our own southern states." The "Negro problem" to which Lindbergh referred was the inequality, segregation, and deprivation of voting rights suffered by African-Americans in the former Confederate states, all tightly controlled by Roosevelt's Democratic Party.

On the issue of who our allies would be in the coming war, Lindbergh revealed his strong anti-Communist streak with the statement, "One year Russia is a totalitarian monster, and the next year she is a democratic friend."

As the speech concluded, Lindbergh challenged the president by demanding, "Before we send our youth to die defending the freedom and democracy of the British Empire, let us decide how freedom and democracy are to be applied to British Imperialism in India. Before we send American soldiers to fight for Soviet Russia, let us inquire why a nation as brave and as respected as Finland, a nation that has fought for freedom and democracy with the utmost courage, let us inquire why such a nation has been fighting on the other side."[2]

After speaking with Stuart, Lindbergh called General Wood, who said of the president, "Well, he got us in [the war] through the back door."[3] Following these conversations, Lindbergh sat down and wrote out a statement that the AFC could release to the press the following day. In Lindbergh's declaration, released by the AFC headquarters in Chicago, he expressed what quickly became the primary view of AFC members: in light of the Japanese attack, Americans should rally to their country's defense, regardless of the administration's past mistakes. Charles also took one last subtle but unmistakable jab at Roosevelt:

> We have been stepping closer to war for many months. Now it has come and we must meet it as united Americans regardless of our attitude in the past toward the policy our government has followed. Whether or not that policy has been wise, our country has been attacked by force of arms and by force of arms, we must retaliate. Our own defenses and our own

military position have already been neglected too long. We must now turn every effort to building the greatest Army, Navy and Air Force in the world. When American soldiers go to war it must be with the best equipment that modern skill can design and that modern industry can build.[4]

Lindbergh listened to the president's now famous war address to Congress, broadcast around the world by commercial radio on Monday afternoon, December 8. It began with the words, "Yesterday, December 7, 1941—a date which will live in infamy—the United States of America was suddenly and deliberately attacked by the naval and air forces of the Empire of Japan." He asked Congress for a declaration of war against Japan, and the Senate responded with an 82 to 0 vote in favor. In the House, the vote was 388 to 1, with the lone dissenter being Republican congressman Jeanette Rankin of Montana, who had also voted against war in 1917.

What the world did not know at the time was that Secretary of War Stimson had urged Roosevelt to ask Congress to include both Germany and Italy in the declaration of war. The president refused because, as he told British ambassador Lord Halifax, "I seem to be conscious of a still lingering distinction in some quarters of the public between war with Japan and war with Germany."[5]

Perhaps Roosevelt feared that a war declaration including the two European fascist states—neither of which, after all, had attacked America—would yield only narrow approval in Congress. Even worse, it might delay a final war vote until the issue was resolved in meetings. In a few days, however, Hitler and Mussolini would solve this dilemma for the president.

Furthermore, FDR's critics had accused him for two years of covertly seeking war against Germany. Therefore, asking for war against Germany absent a German attack might seem to vindicate the opposition. As historians Thomas Bailey and Paul Ryan point out, "[Roosevelt] was already deeply involved in an undeclared shooting war with Hitler that had featured pitched battles between four U.S. Navy vessels, on the one hand, and at least four different U-boats, on the other. He was willing to let the informal fighting in the North Atlantic drag out indefinitely in this informal fashion without a formal declaration of war on either side."[6]

Following the president's broadcast, Lindbergh jotted down in his diary,

> We have been asking for war for months. If the President had asked for a declaration of war before, I think Congress would have turned him down with a big majority. But now we have been attacked, and attacked in home waters. We have brought it on our own shoulders; but I can see nothing to do under these circumstances except to fight. If I had been in Congress, I certainly would have voted for a declaration of war.[7]

In a fireside chat on the evening of Tuesday, December 9, Roosevelt tried hard to link Germany and Hitler to the attack on Pearl Harbor. After denouncing the "criminal" Japanese attacks against Hawaii, the Philippines, Guam, Wake, and Midway, he declared, "Powerful and resourceful gangsters have banded together to make war upon the whole human race. The course that Japan has followed for the past ten years in Asia has paralleled the course of Hitler and Mussolini in Europe and in Africa. Today, it has become far more than a parallel. It is collaboration, actual collaboration." Ignoring the fact that it was the Japanese, not the Nazis, who had attacked America, the president claimed the attack was "a thoroughly dishonorable deed, but we must face the fact that modern warfare as conducted in the Nazi manner is a dirty business."

Further implicating Germany in the attack, Roosevelt stated, "Your government knows that for weeks Germany has been telling Japan that if Japan did not attack the United States, Japan would not share in dividing the spoils with Germany when peace comes." This statement was either a deliberate lie with no substantiating evidence, or a demonstration of Roosevelt's complete lack of understanding of Germany's alliance with Japan. The truth was that Hitler did not want Japan to attack the United States, and was surprised when it did. He wanted Japanese forces to attack the Soviet Union through Siberia and force Stalin into fighting a two-front war.

Approaching the end of his talk, Roosevelt made as close to a decla-ration of war against Germany and Italy as he could when he charged that "Germany and Italy, regardless of any formal declaration of war, consider themselves at war with the United States at this moment just as much as they consider themselves at war with Britain or Russia."[8]

If there was any truth to this last statement, it was largely because U.S. Navy warships were either firing on Axis ships and submarines throughout the North Atlantic, or signaling their position to nearby Brit-ish warships, as the president had ordered.

On December 11, Adolf Hitler made the major strategic blunder of declaring war on the United States. After months of turning the other cheek to U.S. provocations, he based his move on the hope that his Japanese allies would respond in kind by declaring war against the Soviet Union. It did not happen. The result was that Hitler, along with Mus-solini who trailed behind him, had effectively brought into the war the one power that could defeat him on the western front. Congress quickly obliged the fascist dictators by declaring war on Germany and Italy.

———

The following day Lindbergh was expressing doubts in his diary over his hasty resignation from the Army Air Corps Reserve, although he tried to keep a stiff upper lip by telling himself he had "no honorable alterna-tive." With the United States facing a two-front war, the aviator won-dered how he could contribute best to "my country's war effort." His first thought was to write directly to the president, explaining that despite his past opposition, he was now prepared to do whatever he could to help. He decided against this because he understood that even among his friends, Roosevelt was considered "a vindictive man." Lindbergh sus-pected the president would use his letter for some political purpose while assigning him "to some position where I would be completely ineffective and out of the way."[9]

All around him, other prominent AFC members were joining the war effort. The tone was set by former president Herbert Hoover, the first prominent non-interventionist to react publicly to the Japanese attack.

Hoover told the press, "American soil has been treacherously attacked by Japan. Our decision is clear. It is forced upon us. We must fight with everything we have."

Brigadier General Wood, a well-known AFC member, volunteered his services to General Marshall, who immediately accepted and assigned him to the staff of the Army Ordinance Chicago District as a full-time advisor. But when Wood, who was sixty-two years old and in excellent health, sought a return to active Army status in a combat role, the president stopped him. Demonstrating a lingering resentment of his former opponents, Roosevelt wrote a confidential memo to Army chief Marshall in which he claimed, "I do not think that General R. E. Wood should be put into uniform. He is too old and has, in the past, shown far too great approval of Nazi methods. If General Arnold wishes to use him in a civilian capacity in the supply situation, I have no serious objection."[10]

General Arnold accepted Wood's offer to work for him because "our supply depots were not organized for maximum efficiency or economy," and he needed expert advice to deal with the situation. In his autobiography, Arnold wrote of Wood's valuable contribution to the war effort: "For the next three years he spent his time going around from one depot to another, from one supply center to another, with a view to simplifying our methods of operation, of cutting down overhead, of eliminating unnecessary items. By June of 1942, as a result of his efforts, we had cancelled contracts for 355 million dollars' worth of unnecessary supplies!" Arnold tried to get Wood a commission but was always halted by Roosevelt's "hostility."[11]

Other AFC members managed to escape Roosevelt's wrath and serve the military with distinction. Robert Stuart, one of the AFC's founders and its permanent secretary, had retained his first lieutenant's commission in the Army field artillery reserve. Volunteering for active duty, he was accepted, eventually promoted to major, and served on Eisenhower's staff. He entered combat after landing in Europe shortly after D-Day.

Another AFC member, Major General Thomas S. Hammond, commanded the Army Ordinance District in Chicago throughout the war. AFC national vice chairman Hanford MacNider, one of the nation's most decorated soldiers of World War I, volunteered for the army and served as a combat officer in the South Pacific, eventually rising to brigadier general. Philip F. La Follette, a former Wisconsin governor, advisor to the AFC, and outspoken critic of Roosevelt's foreign policy, was forty-four years old, married, and the father of three when he volunteered for service. He served on Douglas MacArthur's staff in the Southwest Pacific from October 1942 until June 1945, rising to the rank of colonel.[12]

Although he was a leading authority on aviation as America entered a war that would rely on air power, Lindbergh was not welcomed back into the fold. After all, he had been the face of the opposition, in both the airmail contract cancellations and the non-interventionist movement. Roosevelt and his officials were determined to keep him out of the war.

On December 20, Lindbergh wrote to General Arnold offering his services to the Air Corps. "I wrote it in such a way that he could take action or not, as he felt most advisable," Charles later recalled.[13] He did not hear back from Arnold, but heard it announced on the radio, and read in the *New York Times* of December 31, that the general had said his offer to serve "indicates a definite change from his isolationist stand and expresses his deep desire to help the country along the lines in which he trained himself for many years." When reporters asked Roosevelt at a press conference the same day if the Army would accept Lindbergh's offer, he told reporters he knew nothing about it.[14]

In true Roosevelt fashion, this response was disingenuous. Only the previous day, the vindictive Interior Secretary Harold Ickes had written a secret memo to Roosevelt about Lindbergh's offer. The complete memo reads as follows:

> I notice that Lindbergh has just offered his services to the Army Air Corps. I believe that, taking the long view, it is of the utmost importance that his offer should not be accepted.
>
> An analysis of Lindbergh's speeches and articles—and I have a complete, indexed collection of them—has convinced me that he is a ruthless and conscious fascist, motivated by a hatred for you personally and a contempt for democracy in general. His speeches show an astonishing identity with those

of Berlin, and the similarity is not accidental. His actions have been coldly calculated with a view to attaining ultimate power for himself—what he calls "new leadership." Hence it is important for him to have a military service record.

It is a striking historic fact that every single dictator and half-dictator of post-war Europe had a military service record. Mussolini was a war veteran, [Turkey's] Mustapha Kemal Pasha was a war veteran, [Poland's] Pilsudski was a war veteran, [Hungary's] Horthy was a war veteran, Hitler was a war veteran. The same is true of fascist leaders who never achieved power, but came close to doing so: Colonel de la Rocque in France and Starhemberg in Austria, for example.

To accept Lindbergh's offer would be to grant this loyal friend of Hitler's a precious opportunity on a golden platter. It would be, in my opinion, a tragic disservice to American democracy to give one of its bitterest and most ruthless enemies a chance to gain a military record. I ardently hope that this convinced fascist will not be given the opportunity to wear the uniform of the United States. He should be buried in merciful oblivion.[15]

Ickes seemed to completely disregard the fact that the men he named all came to their positions as a result of World War I. The war was fought across the maps of their countries, and few men of their age did not participate as members of their respective countries' armed forces. Millions of others also had a military service record, but very few seized political power. He wove a thin thread in attempting to link military service with dictatorial aspirations. Years later, journalist R. Cort Kirkwood wrote that Ickes' memo was "as notable for its stratospheric hyperbole as for its contemptible lies."[16] Despite his claim of ignorance, Roosevelt had responded to Ickes that same day, telling him, "What you say about Lindbergh and the potential danger of the man, I agree with wholeheartedly."[17]

The president forwarded Ickes' memo to other cabinet members without revealing the name of the author. Deceptively, Roosevelt had his press secretary, Stephen Early, write Secretaries Knox and Stimson identical "confidential" memos in which he claimed Ickes' memo attacking Lindbergh was written by "one of the President's friends."[18] Neither Early nor Roosevelt ever explained why they kept secret from these two cabinet members the fact that Ickes had written the memo.

All the war hawks lined up against Lindbergh. Navy Secretary Knox wrote Roosevelt that if it were a Navy matter, he would allow Lindbergh to enlist as an air cadet—an entry-level trainee position meant to belittle Charles. Secretary of War Stimson told FDR he agreed wholeheartedly with the president's instructions to him that Lindbergh's request be placed in limbo, without a firm reply. If asked by reporters, their response would be that Lindbergh's request was "under consideration." The memo that gave these instructions ends with a request that it be returned to FDR "for my files."[19] Perhaps he did not want evidence lying around that Lindbergh was being kept out of the war due to political and personal prejudice. When Lindbergh's name came up a short time later in a meeting with several senators, Roosevelt sneered, "I'll clip that young man's wings."[20]

The *New York Times* felt much differently about Lindbergh's offer to serve than did Roosevelt and his circle. In an editorial titled "Mr. Lindbergh Volunteers," the editors wrote hopefully,

> The first Japanese bomb that fell at Pearl Harbor made this a united nation. From that moment forward there were no "isolationists," no "interventionists." There were only Americans rallying to the defense of their country in an hour of great need. Mr. Lindbergh's action in volunteering his services to the Army Air Corps, a step announced yesterday by the War Department, follows as a logical consequence of the position he took then and, indeed, of the position in which every good American found himself.
>
> There cannot be the slightest doubt that Mr. Lindbergh's offer should be and will be accepted. It will be accepted not only as a symbol of our newfound unity and an effective means of burying the dead past; it will be accepted also

because Mr. Lindbergh can be useful to his country. He is a superb air man, and this is primarily and essentially an air war. Whether he has passed the age when he can be used for active service in the field is a matter for competent authorities to decide. But there can be no question of his great knowledge of aircraft and his immense experience as a flier. Nor have we any doubt that he will serve in the line of duty with credit to himself and to his country.[21]

The *Times* editors either did not understand their president's unforgiving nature, or they were attempting in vain to encourage him to overcome it and focus on what was best for the country.

Lindbergh spent the first few weeks of January 1942 searching for a way to contribute to the war effort, but with little result. On January 8, he met with Colonel "Wild Bill" Donovan, who was building a new organization that would become the OSS, the predecessor of the CIA. Donovan told Lindbergh he would be glad to have him, if Roosevelt approved, but thought he could better serve the country working with the Air Corps.

Even as Lindbergh sought a way to join the war, the British intelligence front groups continued their campaign to discredit him. The Non-Sectarian Anti-Nazi League demanded he return any medals he had received as a result of his 1927 flight from nations that were now part of the Axis "as evidence of the sincerity of your change of feeling."[22]

The Friends of Democracy circulated to the press a report on an alleged meeting Lindbergh had attended on December 16 in New York City at which he supposedly spoke for an hour attacking "the British and the fools in Washington." Some papers ran with the story without checking its veracity. The *New York Times* had a reporter interview the man who hosted the gathering at his home. It turned out to be an engagement party at which Lindbergh spoke for less than ten minutes and urged those present, who were mostly former AFC members, to get behind the war effort. The *Times* decided not to run the story.[23]

After several attempts, Lindbergh finally met with Secretary of War Stimson, along with the Assistant Secretary of War Robert A. Lovett and

General Arnold. Charles was not aware that Roosevelt had already ordered his request indefinitely placed "under consideration." Stimson told Lindbergh, as he confirmed in a follow-up memo to the president, that he thought Charles had a different view of America's friends and enemies than the government. He also said he was unwilling to place Lindbergh in command of troops because he thought he lacked "faith in our cause."[24]

During a second discussion, with Lovett and Arnold, Lindbergh realized that the only way he was going to get any post, either civilian or military, from the administration was to issue a statement retracting all his previous statements against intervention. They also seemed concerned about his personal feelings toward Roosevelt and whether he could respect FDR as his commander in chief. Lindbergh told them he was withdrawing his offer and perhaps they could revisit again in the future. Taken by surprise, Lovett and Arnold at first hesitated but then agreed withdrawal was the best course of action. When Lindbergh asked if there would be any objection to him joining a commercial company, both men said the War Department would have no problem with that.[25]

Of course, Lindbergh's problem was not so much with the War Department as with the White House. Several airlines and aircraft manufacturers wanted to hire him, but pressure from the White House stopped them all. Pan American's Juan Tripp told Lindbergh the White House had gotten angry with him when he brought up the possibility of Lindbergh re-joining the company. Roosevelt's vindictiveness closed doors to one of the nation's leading authorities on aviation simply out of a desire for personal revenge, whatever the cost to the country.[26]

Lindbergh finally caught a break on March 21, 1941, in the form of a phone call from Detroit. The caller was Harry Bennett, Henry Ford's director of personnel, labor relations, and plant security. Ford wanted Charles' help to set up a new factory for manufacturing B-24 Liberator bombers, a large four-engine workhorse aircraft. Ford had promised the government he would be able to build one bomber per hour of plant operation time, and he needed Lindbergh's expertise.

Lindbergh jumped at the opportunity and traveled to Detroit to meet Ford and some of his executives. Ford was a rare boss who did not have to worry about Roosevelt's reaction to his hiring of Lindbergh, since the Ford company's production was vital to the war effort. As Wayne Cole relates, Ford "was no more impressed or awed by Roosevelt than was Lindbergh."[27] Predictably, Lindbergh's critics cited his decision to work for Ford as further proof of his anti-Semitism, since Ford himself had repeatedly disparaged the Jews. What was typically omitted from this guilt-by-association argument was that Lindbergh only took the job after finding he had been blacklisted in both the military and the private sector due to White House pressure.

Lindbergh had finally found employment, far more important work than even he thought it would be. The entire family soon moved to the Detroit suburb of Bloomington Hills, and Charles immersed himself in the design, production, and test flights of aircraft pouring out of Ford's plants. He even volunteered to be a human guinea pig for the Mayo Clinic's Aeronautical Unit for Research in Aviation Medicine. For ten days, he was subjected to a grueling series of experiments designed to determine how pilots could survive in the new, high-altitude airplanes.

Charles also flew bombers and innovative bomber escort fighters like the Air Force's P-47 Thunderbolts to test their vulnerability to altitude, speed, and maneuverability. He eventually worked with United Aircraft, a company that had previously been intimidated by the White House from hiring him. At United, he helped develop the Corsair F-4U for the Marines.

Lindbergh's accomplishments at Ford and United over the next few years—deeds that were vital for the war effort—could fill its own volume. For example, United needed an investigator to visit the Pacific theater to look into conflicting reports concerning both single engine and twin-engine aircraft. Lindbergh met with Marine Brigadier General Louis E. Wood on January 5, 1944, and explained why he was the right man to study the performance of the Corps' warplanes in combat conditions. The next day he was given permission to go to the war zone as a "technician" wearing a Navy officer's uniform sans rank and insignia. If the Japanese captured him, he was on his own.

Eventually Lindbergh began flying combat missions. After flying more than a dozen such missions with the Marines in New Ireland and

New Britain off the coast of New Guinea, he moved on to the Army Air Corps units on Hollandia to gain experience with the twin-engine P-38 Lightning fighter aircraft. He flew twenty-five more missions, even engaging in his first dogfight and shooting down a Japanese fighter. Colonel Charles MacDonald, commander of the "Satin's Angels" squadron, reported that Lindbergh "flew more missions than was expected of a regular combat pilot. He dive-bombed enemy positions, sank barges and patrolled our landing forces."

When news reached General Douglas MacArthur, Theater Commander, that Lindbergh was showing army pilots how to increase the range of the planes by adjusting their fuel consumption, he sent for him. Lindbergh explained how the P-38 could easily reach a range of 700 miles with plenty of fuel for a safe landing and without major or costly modifications. MacArthur told him if he could teach his pilots this technique he could "have any plane and do any kind of flying he wanted to." As a result of Lindbergh's training, the pilots learned to stretch their missions from 6–8 hours to a full 10 hours, allowing them to go deeper into Japanese territory.[28]

After the war, President Eisenhower restored Lindbergh's commission and promoted him to brigadier general in the Air Force. Roosevelt had died in 1945 and his clique of supporters no longer commanded power. Having been awarded the Congressional Medal of Honor and the first Distinguished Flying Cross for his flight in 1927, Lindbergh received numerous additional awards after the war, including a Pulitzer Prize for his autobiography. In later life, his interests turned toward wilderness preservation and in typical Lindbergh fashion, he threw himself wholeheartedly into conservation activities.

———

Despite the sincerity and patriotism of Lindbergh's campaign against intervention, many continue to label him a Nazi or an anti-Semite. Both charges, like the accusation of racism often used today, put the accused in an impossible position; if he ignores the allegations, as Lindbergh did, they stand unrefuted and gain credibility. But if he constantly denies them, his protestations seem defensive, as if to confirm the charges.

Writers today still hurl the same old accusations at Lindbergh, though they offer scant evidence of their validity. One example is Charles Higham, whose book *American Swastika* (Doubleday, 1985) reads like a piece of 1930s yellow journalism. The chapter dealing with America First begins by mischaracterizing the engagement party Lindbergh attended on December 17, 1941, as an AFC meeting, and then lifts quotes originating with false newspaper reports about the party—reports that the *New York Times* investigated and dismissed. Charges are flung without footnotes or sources to explain where they originated.

Another is Max Wallace's *The American Axis* (St. Martin's Press, 2003). This book purports to prove that Lindbergh and Henry Ford were tools of the Nazis and Lindbergh was destined to be the leading Nazi in America. *Publishers Weekly* called it "a highly speculative rehash of material handled much better in A. Scott Berg's *Lindbergh* and Robert Lacey's *Ford: The Man and the Machine*." The review chides Wallace for seeing "a conspiracy in what he presents as Ford's pro-Nazi partnership with Lindbergh: a dark and powerful alliance designed to hinder the Allies at every turn. Once war was declared, both Lindbergh and Ford helped the Allied effort. Were they Nazi agents either before or after the start of hostilities? Wallace fails to make the case."

In his book *In Crises: Lindbergh, Roosevelt, Churchill, Truman, and Big City Bosses* (CreateSpace, 2008), Roy Hensen claims, "Charles was friendly with the Nazi party and accepted a medal from Hermann Goering." He offers no proof whatsoever of the first part of that charge, and does not explain that the medal took Charles completely by surprise, or that the U.S. ambassador to Germany later praised him for not causing an international incident by rejecting the overture.

Perhaps the worst offender of all does not even purport to be true. Philip Roth, the author of *Portnoy's Complaint*, turned his pen to more political issues with his novel *The Plot Against America* (Houghton Mifflin, 2004), in which Charles Lindbergh is elected president, beating FDR in 1940. Our anti-hero then immediately begins making deals with Nazi

Germany and Imperial Japan. In Lindbergh's America, Jews are forced to assimilate by a new federal agency, the Office of American Absorption.

Unsurprisingly, the literary establishment loved the book since it maligned someone they obviously disdain, and did so unrestrained by any obligation to historical accuracy. One of the book's attributes that endeared it to the reviewers, as identified in a friendly review by *Washington Post* writer Jonathan Yardley, was a possible subtext giving "every appearance of being an attack on George W. Bush and his administration."

Still, a few critics noted the story's inherent absurdity. Even Yardley had to admit that Roth's treatment of Lindbergh "is an imaginative leap I find hard to believe."[29] This sentiment was echoed by historian Thomas Fleming, who asked in the *Wall Street Journal*, "What does all this add up to? Less than one would have hoped for. The ultimate explanation for Lindbergh's pro-German behavior, a secret we learn at the end, strains credulity beyond the breaking point."[30] Likewise, Ross Douthat, writing in *Policy Review*, said the power of some of the novel's "passages is undone, again and again, by the creaking gears of the political 'plot,' which is never convincing, never plausible, and which constantly undermines the drama of persecution unfolding in the streets."[31]

Finally, Bill Kaufman writing in the *American Conservative*, claims "Roth writes in sodden clichés: for instance, FDR 'inspired millions of ordinary families like ours to remain hopeful in the midst of hardship.' This is Time-Life prose. There is not a felicitous sentence in this book; nor is there a spark of wit or a single subversive thought. The literary critics of the Department of Homeland Security will pronounce it fit for best-sellerdom."[32]

In the end, the question we must ask is this: Why Lindbergh? Why does the liberal-left in this country continue relentlessly attacking him long after his death in 1974? The clear answer is that he is condemned because he dared to speak out, not once, but twice, against a liberal icon, Franklin D. Roosevelt. The same Roosevelt who used military tribunals to prosecute and execute German saboteurs who landed on our beaches. The same Roosevelt who imprisoned thousands of people because they or their parents came here from Japan, Italy, or Germany. The same Roosevelt whose anti-Semitism was manifested not only in his numerous anti-Jewish slurs, but in his callous indifference to the fate of European Jewry under the Nazi regime.

The kinds of vituperative personal attacks used against Lindbergh—accusations of anti-Semitism, racism, and Nazism—are still employed today, and often have a similarly devastating effect on their subjects. As was the case with Lindbergh, the truth of the accusations is largely irrelevant; if they are repeated enough times, especially in the mainstream press, they simply become conventional wisdom.

Tea party protestors—average Americans speaking out against what they regard as irresponsible government spending—are a primary example. In March 2010, a group of black congressional representatives claimed tea party protestors had yelled the "N" word at them up to fifteen times during a protest at the Capitol building in Washington, D.C. The allegation was widely reported as fact, playing into a wider campaign portraying tea partiers as inveterate racists. Eventually, some commentators began noting that none of the abundant footage of the incident actually recorded anyone yelling any racial epithets. Even after a website offered a $100,000 reward for such footage, none surfaced—even though at least one of the alleged victims himself had filmed the incident. Although the *New York Times* later published a short retraction of the report, by then the fictitious abuse had been reported far and wide in newspapers, talk shows, and other venues. "Racist tea partiers" have now become a prominent meme throughout the media.

Like Lindbergh, the tea partiers make an argument that deserves to be discussed on its own merits. But it is difficult for them to make their case when they constantly have to defend themselves from spurious allegations of racism. Those who are orchestrating this campaign know very well that an easy way to kill a message is to ignore it and discredit the messenger. After all, it worked against Charles Lindbergh.

ACKNOWLEDGMENTS

There are many people for me to thank who contributed in various ways to the writing of this book. Foremost among them is my wife, Kathleen, who over the years of our marriage never let me lose sight of the "important" book I wanted to write. Her encouragement knew no bounds. Others include my daughters—Alexandra for her research assistance, and Olivia for her support; my sister Patricia; and several friends, especially Michele Del Monte, Joanne Luna, and Angelo Catania, each of whom read portions of the manuscript and offered sound advice. A special thank you goes to author Thomas Fleming for his encouragement.

I owe a debt of gratitude to the staffs of several libraries for their help, including the research assistants at the Franklin D. Roosevelt Presidential Library and Museum, especially Matt Hanson whose knowledge and willingness to help was outstanding, and Bob Clark, supervisory archivist, for his guidance. Also helpful in finding sometimes hard to locate books were the staffs associated with the Somerset County (NJ) Library System, especially the Bound Brook Free Library, and the Raritan Valley Community College Library. Thanks also to the staffs of the Rutgers University Library and the Syracuse University Library.

At Regnery Publishing, I want to thank Executive Editor Harry Crocker for making a home for this book. I will be forever grateful to my editor, Jack Langer, whose talent and hard work, as well as his understanding of what happened to Lindbergh, have made this a much better book in many ways.

James P. Duffy

BIBLIOGRAPHY

Arnold, H. H. *Global Mission*. New York: Harper & Brothers, Publishers, 1949.

Bailey, Thomas A., and Paul B. Ryan. *Hitler vs. Roosevelt: The Undeclared Naval War*. New York: The Free Press, 1979.

Baldwin, Hanson W. *The Crucial Years 1939-1941: The World at War*. New York: Harper & Row, Publishers, 1976.

Beard, Charles A. *American Foreign Policy In The Making, 1932-1940*. New Haven, CT: Yale University Press, 1946.

Berg, A. Scott. *Lindbergh*. New York: G. P. Putnam's Sons, 1998.

Black, Conrad. *Franklin Delano Roosevelt: Champion of Freedom*. New York: PublicAffairs, 2003.

Blum, John Morton. *Roosevelt and Morgenthau: From the Morgenthau Diaries*. Boston: Houghton Mifflin Company, 1970

Borden Jr., Norman E. *Air Mail Emergency: 1934*. Freeport: The Bond Wheelwright Company, 1968.

Bradford, Sarah. *The Reluctant King: The Life & Reign of George VI 1895-1952*. New York: St. Martin's Press, 1989.

Breitman, Richard, et al., eds. *Advocate for the Doomed: The Diaries and Papers of James G. McDonald 1932-1935*. Bloomington: Indiana University Press, 2007.

———. *Refugees and Rescue: The Diaries and Papers of James G. McDonald 1935-1945*. Bloomington: Indiana University Press, 2009.

Brewer, Susan A. *Why America Fights: Patriotism and War Propaganda from the Philippines to Iraq*. New York: Oxford University Press, 2009.

Browder, Robert Paul and Thomas G. Smith. *Independent: A Biography of Lewis W. Douglas*. New York: Alfred A. Knopf, 1986.

Brown, Anthony Cave. *Wild Bill Donovan: The Last Hero*. New York: Times Books, 1982.

Buchanan, Patrick J. *A Republic, Not an Empire: Reclaiming America's Destiny*. Washington: Regnery Publishing, 1999.

———. *Churchill, Hitler, and the Unnecessary War*. New York: Crown Publishers, 2008.

Bullitt, Orville H., ed. *For the President, Personal & Secret*. Boston: Houghton Mifflin Company, 1972.

Burns, James MacGregor. *Roosevelt: The Soldier of Freedom 1940-1945*. New York: Harcourt Brace Jovanovich, Inc. 1970.

Christy, Joe et. al. *American Aviation: An Illustrated History.* Blue Ridge Summit: TAB Books, 1987.

Churchill, Winston S. *The Second World War, Volume 2: Their Finest Hour.* New York: Houghton Mifflin Company, 1949.

Coit, Margaret L. *Mr. Baruch.* Boston: Houghton Mifflin, 1957.

Cole, Wayne S. *Senator Gerald P. Nye and American Foreign Relations.* Minneapolis: The University of Minnesota Press, 1962.

————. *Charles A. Lindbergh and the Battle Against American Intervention in World War II.* New York: Harcourt Brace Jovanovich, 1974.

————. *Roosevelt & the Isolationists, 1932-45.* Lincoln: University of Nebraska Press, 1983.

Copp, DeWitt S. *A Few Great Captains: The Men and Events That Shaped the Development of U. S. Air Power.* McLean: EPM Publications, 1980.

Cull, Nicholas John. *Selling War: The British Propaganda Campaign Against American "Neutrality" in World War II.* New York: Oxford University Press, 1995.

Dallek, Robert. *Franklin D. Roosevelt and American Foreign Policy, 1932-1945.* New York: Oxford University Press, 1979.

Davis, Kenneth S. *FDR: The New Deal Years 1933-1937: A History.* New York: Random House, 1983.

Dodd, William E., Jr., & Martha Dodd, eds. *Ambassador Dodd's Diary 1933-1938.* New York: Harcourt, Brace and Company, 1941.

Doenecke, Justus D. "American Isolationism, 1939-1941." *The Journal of Libertarian Studies* Vol. VI, Nos. 3–4 (Summer/Fall 1982): 201–16.

———. "Edwin M. Borchard, John Bassett Moore, and Opposition to American Intervention in World War II." *The Journal of Libertarian Studies* Vol. VI, No. 1 (Winter 1982): 1–34.

———. "Explaining the Antiwar Movement, 1939-1941: The Next Assignment." *The Journal of Libertarian Studies* Vol. VIII, No. 1 (Winter 1986): 139–62.

———. "The Anti-Interventionism of Herbert Hoover." *The Journal of Libertarian Studies* Vol. VIII, No. 2 (Summer 1987): 311–40.

———. *In Danger Undaunted*. Stanford: Hoover Institution Press, 1990.

Duffy, James P. *Hitler Slept Late and Other Blunders That Cost Him the War*. New York: Praeger Publishers, 1991.

Farley, James A. *Jim Farley's Story: The Roosevelt Years*. New York: McGraw-Hill Book Company, 1948.

———. *Behind The Ballots: The Personal History of a Politician*. Westport: Greenwood Press, 1972.

Fish, Hamilton. *FDR: The Other Side of the Coin*. New York: Vantage Press, 1976.

Fleming, Thomas. *The New Dealer's War: F.D.R. and the War Within World War II*. New York: Basic Books, 2001.

———. *The Illusion of Victory: America in World War I*. New York: Basic Books, 2003.

Folsom Jr., Burton W. *New Deal or Raw Deal?: How FDR's Economic Legacy Has Damaged America*. New York: Simon & Schuster, 2008.

Foulois, Major General Benjamin. *From The Wright Brothers to the Astronauts.* New York: McGraw-Hill Book Company, 1968.

Freedman, Max. *Roosevelt and Frankfurter: Their Correspondence 1928-1945.* Boston: Little, Brown and Company, 1967.

Freidel, Frank. *Franklin D. Roosevelt.* Boston: Little, Brown and Company, 1990.

Fried, Albert. *FDR and His Enemies.* New York: St. Martin's Press, 1999.

Gilbert, Martin. *The Second World War: A Complete History.* New York: Henry Holt and Company, 1989.

———. *Churchill and America.* New York: Free Press, 2005.

Gill, Brendan. *Many Masks: A Life of Frank Lloyd Wright.* New York: Da Capo Press, 1998.

Goodwin, Doris Kearns. *No Ordinary Time: Franklin and Eleanor Roosevelt: The Home Front in World War II.* New York: Simon and Schuster, 1995.

Henderson, Sir Neville. *Failure of a Mission.* New York: G. P. Putnam's Sons, 1940.

Herndon, Booton. *Praised and Damned: The Story of Fulton Lewis, Jr.* New York: Little, Brown and Company, 1954.

Hertog, Susan. *Anne Morrow Lindbergh: Her Life.* New York: Doubleday, 1999.

Hixson, Walter L. *Charles A. Lindbergh, Lone Eagle.* New York: Pearson Longman, 2007.

Hunt, Frazier. *The Untold Story of Douglas MacArthur*. New York: The Devin-Adair Company, 1954.

Jackson, Robert H. *That Man: An Insider's Portrait of Franklin D. Roosevelt*. New York: Oxford University Press, 2003.

James, D. Clayton. *The Years of MacArthur, Volume I 1880-1941*. Boston: Houghton Mifflin Company, 1970.

Janeway, Eliot. *The Struggle for Survival: A Chronicle of Economic Mobilization in World War II*. New Haven: Yale University Press, 1951.

Johnson, Paul. *A History of the Jews*. New York: Harper & Row, 1987.

Jonas, Manfred. *Isolationism in America 1935-1941*. Ithaca: Cornell University Press, 1966.

Kessler, Ronald. *The Bureau: The Secret History of the FBI*. New York: St. Martin's Paperbacks, 2003.

Kurth, Peter. *American Cassandra: The Life of Dorothy Thompson*. Boston: Little, Brown and Company, 1990.

Lash, Joseph P. *Roosevelt and Churchill, 1939-1941*. New York: W. W. Norton & Company, 1976.

Lasky, Victor. *It Didn't Start With Watergate*. New York: The Dial Press, 1977.

Lawrence, Harry. *Aviation and the Role of Government*. Dubuque: Kendall/Hunt Publishing, 2004.

Levin, Linda Lotridge. *The Making of FDR: The Story of Stephen T. Early, America's First Modern Press Secretary*. Amherst: Prometheus Books, 2008.

Lewis, W. David, ed. *Airline Executives and Federal Regulation.* Columbus: Ohio State University Press, 2000.

———. *Eddie Rickenbacker: An American Hero in the Twentieth Century.* Baltimore: The Johns Hopkins University Press, 2005.

Liddell Hart, B. H. *History of the Second World War.* New York: G. P. Putnam's Sons, 1970.

Lindbergh, Anne Morrow. *North to the Orient.* New York: Harcourt, Brace and Company, 1935.

———. *The Flower and the Nettle: Diaries and Letters, 1936-1939.* New York: Harcourt Brace Jovanovich, 1976.

———. *Hour of Gold, Hour of Lead: Diaries and Letters, 1929-1932.* New York: Harcourt Brace Jovanovich, 1973.

———. *Listen! The Wind.* New York: Harcourt, Brace and Company, 1938.

———. *Locked Rooms and Open Doors: Diaries and Letters 1933-1935.* New York: Harcourt Brace Jovanovich, 1974.

———. *War Within and Without: Diaries and Letters, 1939-1944.* New York: Harcourt Brace Jovanovich, 1980.

Lindbergh, Charles A. *The Wartime Journals of Charles A. Lindbergh.* New York: Harcourt Brace Jovanovich, 1970.

———. *Autobiography of Values.* New York: Harcourt Brace Jovanovich, 1977.

Lindbergh, Charles A, Sr. *Your Country At War and What Happens to You After a War.* Philadelphia: Dorrance & Company, 1934.

Lipsner, Capt. Benjamin B. *The Airmail: Jennies to Jets.* Chicago: Wilcox & Follett, 1951.

Loewenheim, Francis L. et. al., eds. *Roosevelt and Churchill: Their Secret Wartime Correspondence.* New York: E. P. Dutton, 1975.

Luckett, Perry D. *Charles A. Lindbergh: A Bio-Bibliography.* Westport: Greenwood Press, 1986.

MacCracken, William P., et al. *Extracts from the Congressional Record.* Washington: GPO, 1934 & 35.

MacMillan, Margaret. *Paris 1919: Six Months That Changed the World.* New York: Random House, 2001.

Mahl, Thomas E. *Desperate Deception: British Covert Operations in the United States, 1939-1944.* Washington: Brassey's, 1998.

Manchester, William. *The Glory and the Dream: A Narrative History of America, 1932- 1972.* New York: Bantam Books, 1975.

Marks III, Frederick W. *Wind Over Sand: The Diplomacy of Franklin Roosevelt.* Athens: The University of Georgia Press, 1988.

Mosley, Leonard. *Lindbergh: A Biography.* Garden City: Doubleday & Company, 1976.

Newman, Roger K. *Hugo Black: A Biography.* New York: Pantheon Books, 1994.

Newquist, Gloria Winden. *James A. Farley and the Politics of Victory: 1928-1936.* Volumes I and II. USC Ph.D. Dissertation. Ann Arbor: University Microfilms, Inc. 1966.

Nicolson, Nigel, ed. *Harold Nicolson: Diaries and Letters 1930-1939*. New York: Athenaeum, 1966.

Osborn, Michael and Joseph Riggs. *"Mr. Mac": William P. MacCraken on Aviation, Law, Optometry*. Memphis: Southern College of Optometry, 1970.

Parrish, Thomas. *To Keep the British Isles Afloat: FDR's Men in Churchill's London, 1941*. New York: HarperCollins Publishers, 2009.

Porter, David L. *The Seventy-sixth Congress and World War II, 1939-1940*. Columbia: University of Missouri Press, 1979.

Powell, Jim. *FDR's Folly: How Roosevelt and His New Deal Prolonged the Great Depression*. New York: Crown Forum, 2003.

———. *Wilson's War: How Woodrow Wilson's Great Blunder Led to Hitler, Lenin, Stalin, and World War II*. New York: Crown Forum, 2005.

Riley, Sam. *Biographical Dictionary of American Newspaper Columnists*. Westport: Greenwood Press, 1995.

Roosevelt, Elliott, and James Brough. *A Rendezvous With Destiny: The Roosevelts of the White House*. New York: G. P. Putman's Sons, 1975.

Rose, Norman. *Churchill: The Unruly Giant*. New York: The Free Press, 1994.

Rosenbaum, Herbert D. and Elizabeth Bartelme, eds. *Franklin D. Roosevelt: The Man, the Myth, the Ear, 1882-1945*. Westport: Greenwood Press, 1987.

Rosenberg, Barry and Catherine Macaulay. *Mavericks of the Sky: The First Daring Pilots of the U.S. Air Mail*. New York: William Morrow, 2006.

Ross, Walter S. *The Last Hero: Charles A. Lindbergh*. New York: Harper & Row, 1964.

Sarles, Ruth. *A Story of America First: The Men and Women Who Opposed U.S. Intervention in World War II*. Westport: Praeger Publishers, 2003.

Schachtman, Tom. *The Phony War 1939-1940*. New York: Harper & Row, 1982.

Schlesinger, Arthur M. *The Age of Roosevelt, II: The Coming of The New Deal*. Cambridge: The Riverside Press, 1958.

Sherwood, Robert E. *Roosevelt and Hopkins: An Intimate History*. New York: Harper & Brothers, 1948.

Shirer, William L. *The Rise and Fall of the Third Reich*. New York: Simon and Schuster, 1960.

Shlaes, Amity. *The Forgotten Man: A New History of the Great Depression*. New York: HarperCollins, 2007.

Smith, Geoffrey S. *To Save a Nation: American Countersubversives, the New Deal, and the Coming of World War II*. New York: Basic Books, Inc., 1973.

Smith, Henry Ladd. *Airways: The History of Commercial Aviation in the United States*. New York: Alfred A. Knopf, 1942.

Smith, Jean Edward. *FDR*. New York: Random House, 2007.

Solomon, Burt. *FDR v. Constitution: The Court-Packing Fight and the Triumph of Democracy*. New York: Walker & Company, 2009.

Steele, Richard W. "The Pulse of the People. Franklin D. Roosevelt and the Gauging of American Public Opinion." *Journal of Contemporary History* Vol. 9 no. 4 (October 1974).

———. "Franklin D. Roosevelt and His Foreign Policy Critics." *Political Science Quarterly* Vol. 94, No. 1 (Spring 1979).

Stenehjem, Michele Flynn. *An American First: John T. Flynn and the America First Committee*. New Rochelle: Arlington House, 1976.

Stevenson, William. *A Man Called Intrepid: The Secret War*. New York: Harcourt Brace Jovanovich, 1976.

Sykes, Christopher. *Nancy: The Life of Lady Astor*. New York: Harper & Row, 1972.

Tate, Dr. James P. *The Army and Its Air Corp: Army Policy Toward Aviation, 1919-1941*. Maxwell AFB: Air University Press, 1998.

Theoharis, Athan G., ed. *The FBI: A Comprehensive Reference Guide,* Phoenix: The Oryx Press. 1999.

Thompson, Robert Smith. *A Time for War*. New York: Prentice Hall Press, 1991.

Tifft, Susan E. and Alex S. Jones. *The Trust: The Private and Powerful Family behind The New York Times*. Boston: Little, Brown, 1999.

Van der Linden, F. Robert. *Airlines and Air Mail: The Post Office and the Birth of the Commercial Aviation Industry*. Lexington: The University Press of Kentucky, 2002.

Waite, Robert G. L. *The Psychopathic God: Adolf Hitler.* New York: Da Capo Press, 1993.

Wallace, Max. *The American Axis: Henry Ford, Charles Lindbergh, and the Rise of the Third Reich.* New York: St. Martin's Press, 2003.

Weiner, Ed. *Let's Go to Press: A Biography of Walter Winchell.* New York: G. P. Putnam's Sons, 1955.

Werner, Morris R. *Privileged Characters.* New York: Arno Press, 1974.

Whalen, Richard J. *The Founding Father: The Story of Joseph P. Kennedy.* New York: The New American Library, 1964.

Wheeler-Bennett, John W. *King George VI: His Life and Reign.* New York: St. Martin's Press, 1958.

Wright, Gordon. "Ambassador Bullitt and the Fall of France." *World Politics* Vol. 10, No. 1 (October 1957): 63–90.

Zelizer, Julian E. *Arsenal of Democracy: The Politics of National Security—From World War II to the War on Terrorism.* New York: Basic Books, 2010.

NOTES

Preface

1.   Among these authors are Jim Powell, *FDR's Folly: How Roosevelt and His New Deal Prolonged the Great Depression* (New York: Crown Forum, 2003); see also, Amity Shlaes, *The Forgotten Man: A New History of The Great Depression* (New York: HarperCollins Publishers, 2007), and Burton W. Folsom Jr., *New Deal or Raw Deal? How FDR's Economic Legacy has Damaged America* (New York: Simon & Schuster, 2008).

Introduction

1.   A. Scott Berg, *Lindbergh* (New York: G. P. Putnam's Sons, 1998) 152.
2.   Ibid., 164.
3.   Ibid., 237–75.
4.   Ibid., 27.
5.   Ibid., 35.
6.   Ibid., 42.
7.   Charles A. Lindbergh Sr., *Your Country At War* (Philadelphia: Dorrance & Company, 1934), 7.
8.   Ibid., 18.

Chapter 1

1.   *Newsweek*, March 17, 1934

2.   Ibid.

3.   Calculation generated by: data.bls.gov/cgi-bin/cpicalc.pl [accessed August 9, 2010].

4.   W. David Lewis, *Eddie Rickenbacker* (Baltimore: Johns Hopkins University Press, 2005), 312.

5.   Captain Benjamin B. Lipsner, *The Airmail: Jennies to Jets* (Chicago: Wilcox & Follett Company, 1951), 12–25; see also, F. Robert van der Linden, *Airlines and Air Mail: The Post Office and the Birth of the Commercial Aviation Industry* (Lexington: University Press of Kentucky), 1–2.

6.   William E. Leuchtenburg, *Herbert Hoover* (New York: Times Books, 2009), 53.

7.   Joe Christy, *American Aviation* (Blue Ridge Summit, PA: Tab Books, 1987), 83.

8.   A. Scott Berg, *Lindbergh*, 84.

9.   David Burner, *Herbert Hoover: A Public Life* (New York: Knopf, 1979), 164.

10. Roger K. Newman, *Hugo Black: A Biography* (New York: Fordham University Press, 1997), 94, 98.

11. Ibid., 140.

12. Booton Herndon, *Praised and Damned: The Story of Fulton Lewis Jr.* (New York: Duell, Sloan and Pearce, 1954), 26–31.

13. Gerald T. Dunne, *Hugo Black and the Judicial Revolution* (New York: Simon and Schuster, 1977), 152.

14. Van der Linden, *Airlines and Air Mail: The Post Office and the Birth of the Commercial Aviation Industry*, 262–63.

15. James A. Farley, *Jim Farley's Story: The Roosevelt Years* (New York: McGraw-Hill Book Co., 1948), 272.

16. Van der Linden, *Airlines and Air Mail*, 261.

17. Dewitt S. Copp, *A Few Great Captains: The Men and Events That Shaped the Development of U.S. Air Power* (McLean, VA: EPM Publications, 1989), 157.

18. William E. Berchtold, "The Air Mail Affair," *The North American Review*, Vol. 237, No. 5 (May 1934), pp. 438–47; available at: http://www.jstor.org/stable/25114446 [accessed August 9, 2010]; Van der Linden, *Airlines and Air Mail*, 208, 265, 271; A. Lee Fritschler, et al, *Study on Universal Postal Service and The Postal Monopoly*, George Mason University School of Public Policy, November 2008; James A. Farley, *Behind the Ballots: The*

Personal History of a Politician (Westport, CT: Greenwood Press, 1972), 83; James A. Farley, *Behind the Ballots* (New York: Harcourt, Brace, and Company, 1938), 270; and "Fort Worth Aviation History," B-36 Peacemaker Museum, Inc.; available at: http://www.b-36peacemakermuseum. org/History/history.htm [accessed August 9, 2010].

19. Meier Schlesinger, *The Coming of the New Deal* (Mariner Books, 1988), 451.
20. Kenneth S. Davis, *FDR: The New Deal Years 1933–1937* (New York: Random House, 1986), 358.
21. Major General Benjamin D. Foulois, *From the Wright Brothers to the Astronauts* (New York: McGraw-Hill, 1968), 236–37.
22. *New York Times*, February 10, 1934, 1.
23. Dr. James P. Tate, *The Army and Its Air Corps, Army Policy toward Aviation, 1919-1941* (Maxwell AFB, Alabama: Air University Press, 1998), 132.
24. *Newsweek*, March 3, 1934, 9.
25. *New York Times*, February 11, 1934, 1.
26. Ibid.
27. Norman E. Borden Jr., *Air Mail Emergency: 1934* (Freeport, ME: The Bond Wheelwright Company, 1968), 28–29.
28. Meier Schlesinger, *The Coming of the New Deal*, 452.
29. *New York Times*, January 12, 1934, 3.
30. Leonard Mosley, *Lindbergh: A Biography* (Garden City: Doubleday & Company, 1976), 179.
31. Max Freedman, *Roosevelt and Frankfurter: Their Correspondence, 1928–1945* (Boston: Little, Brown and Company, 1967), 196–97.
32. Robert Paul Browder and Thomas G. Smith, *Independent: A Biography of Lewis W. Douglas* (New York: Alfred A. Knopf, 1986), 110.
33. Ibid., 111.
34. *New York Times*, February 12, 1934, 1.
35. Max Freedman, *Roosevelt and Frankfurter*, 196–97.
36. Ibid.
37. Meier Schlesinger, *The Coming of the New Deal*, 452.
38. *New York Times*, February 14, 1934, 15.
39. *New York Times*, February 15, 1934, 11.
40. *New York Times*, February 19, 1934, 1.
41. W. David Lewis, *Eddie Rickenbacker: An American Hero in the Twentieth Century*, 312.
42. *New York Times*, February 11, 1934, 38.

43. *New York Times*, February 13, 1934, 16.

44. *Business Week*, February 17, 1934, 7.

45. Letter to Early, February 15, 1934, FDR Library Air Mail Folder #19.

46. Linda Lotridge Levin, *The Making of FDR: The Story of Stephen T. Early, America's First Modern Press Secretary* (Amherst, NY: Prometheus Books, 2008), 120.

47. *New York Times*, February 14, 1934, 21.

48. *New York Times*, February 12, 1934, 217.

49. *Time*, March 5, 1934

50. *New York Times*, February 15, 1934, 21.

51. *New York Times*, February 18, 1934, 10.

52. Norman E. Borden, *Air Mail Emergency: 1934* (The Bond Wheelwright Company, 1968), 52–56.

53. Edward V. Rickenbacker, *Rickenbacker* (Englewood Cliffs, N.J.: Prentice-Hall, 1967), 184.

54. Ibid., 186–88.

55. H. H. Arnold, *Global Mission* (New York: Harper & Brothers, 1949), 143.

56. Benjamin B. Lipsner, *The Airmail: Jennies to Jets*, 250.

57. *Newsweek*, February 24, 1934, 8.

58. Farley, *Jim Farley's Story: The Roosevelt Years*, 46–47.

59. Ibid., 47.

60. *The New Republic*, February 21, 1934, 29–30.

61. *The New Republic*, March 7, 1934, 85.

62. *The New Republic*, March 21, 1934, 141–42.

63. *The Nation*, February 21, 1934, 203–4.

64. Ibid.

65. *New York Times*, February 15, 1934, 11.

66. Nick A. Komons, *Bonfires to Beacons: Federal Civil Aviation Policy Under the Air Commerce Act, 1926–1938* (Washington, D.C.: Government Printing Office, 1978), 71; see also, Van der Linden, *Airlines and Air Mail*, 13.

67. *Newsweek*, March 24, 1934, 10.

68. Leonard Mosley, *Lindbergh*, 181–82.

69. *New York Herald Tribune*, March 20, 1934 as quoted in Berg, *Lindbergh*, 295.

70. Benjamin D. Foulois and C. V. Glines, *From the Wright Brothers to the Astronauts*, 254–55.

Chapter 2

1. Arthur M. Schlesinger, *The Coming of the New Deal*, 452.

2. *Time Magazine*, March 5, 1934.

3. Virginia Van Der Veer Hamilton, "Barnstorming the U. S. Mail," *American Heritage Magazine*, August 1974, 32.

4. Max Freedman, *Roosevelt and Frankfurter: Their Correspondence, 1928–1935*, 193.

5. Ibid., 195.

6. Major General Benjamin D. Foulois, *From the Wright Brothers to the Astronauts*, 257–59.

7. Ted Morgan, *FDR: A Biography* (New York: Simon and Schuster, 1985), 408.

8. Dewitt S. Copp, *A Few Great Captains: The Men and Events That Shaped the Development of U.S. Air Power*, 215; and, Frazier Hunt, *The Untold Story of Douglas MacArthur* (New York: Devin-Adair, 1956), 158–60.

9. Ibid.

10. D. Clayton James, *The Years of MacArthur, Volume 1: 1880-1941* (Boston: Houghton Mifflin Company, 1970), 438–39.

11. Norman E. Borden, *Air Mail Emergency: 1934*, 114.

12. *New York Herald Tribune*, March 13, 1934.

13. Dr. James P. Tate, *The Army and Its Air Corps: Army Policy Toward Aviation, 1919-1941*, 144.

14. *New York Times*, March 16, 1934, 1.

15. *New York Times*, March 17, 1934, 1.

16. Ibid.

17. *New York Times*, March 18, 1934, 24.

18. A. Scott Berg, *Lindbergh*, 294–95.

19. Karl A. Crowley to Cornelius V. Mitchell, May 17, 1934, Entry 42, Kohler Aviation Corp., Folder 96221, Box 34, Record Group 28, NARA; Van der Linden, *Airlines and Air Mail*, 285.

20. *Time*, April 9, 1934.

21. *Time*, September 15, 1958.

22. *New York Times*, February 16, 1934, 18.

23. *Time*, April 30, 1934.

24. Information available at: http://www.historylink.org/ [accessed February20, 2010].

25. A. Scott Berg, *Lindbergh*, 295–96.

26. *The Nation*, March 21, 1934, 330.

27. Norman E. Borden, *Air Mail Emergency: 1934*, 134.

28. S.3012, *A Bill To Revise the Air Mail Laws*, 73rd Cong., 2nd Sess. March 12 to March 20, 1934, Wording of the Bill, 73.

29. *New York Times*, February 5, 1935, 16.

30. David D. Lee, "Senator Black's Investigation Of The Airmail, 1933-1934," *Historian*, Vol. 53 (Spring 1991), 423–42.

31. Harry W. Lawrence, *Aviation and the Role of Government* (Kendall Hunt Publishing, 2008), 106.

32. *Time Magazine*, July 28, 1941.

33. *New York Times*, October 4, 1928, 3.

34. *New York Times*, October 5, 1928, 27.

35. Arthur M. Schlesinger, *The Coming of the New Deal*, 455.

36. William E. Berchtold, "The Air Mail Affair," *The North American Review*, Vol. 237, No. 5 (May, 1934), pp. 438–47; available at: http://www.jstor.org/stable/25114446 [accessed August 9, 2010].

37. Walter S. Ross, *The Last Hero: Charles A. Lindbergh* (New York: Harper & Row, 1968), 260.

38. *New York Times*, February 24, 1934, E1.

39. Leonard Mosley, *Lindbergh*, 182.

40. Kenneth S. Davis, *FDR: The New Deal Years 1933–1937*, 361.

41. Ibid., 360.

42. Conrad Black, *Franklin Delano Roosevelt: Champion of Freedom* (New York: PublicAffairs, 2003), 322.

43. *Business Week*, February 17, 1934, 7.

44. Albert Fried, *FDR and His Enemies* (New York: St. Martin's Press, 1999), 93.

Chapter 3

1. Arthur M. Schlesinger, *The Coming of the New Deal*, 455.

2. Benjamin D. Foulois and C. V. Glines, *From the Wright Brothers to the Astronauts*, 263.

3. Dewitt S. Copp, *A Few Great Captains: The Men and Events That Shaped the Development of U.S. Air Power*, 223.

4. *New York Times*, August 31, 1934, 6.

5. *Washington Post*, September 1, 1934.

6. Benjamin D. Foulois and C. V. Glines, *From the Wright Brothers to the Astronauts*, 258.

7. Ibid., 272.

8. Ted Morgan, *FDR*, 409–10.

9. Harold L. Ickes, *The Secret Diary of Harold L. Hickes* (Da Capo, 1974), 173.

10. *Time Magazine*, June 19, 1939.

11. A. Scott Berg, *Lindbergh*, 273.
12. Charles A. Lindbergh, *Autobiography of Values* (New York: Harcourt Brace Jovanovich, 1978), 143–44.
13. A. Scott Berg, *Lindbergh*, 308.
14. Charles A. Lindbergh, *Autobiography of Values*, 144.
15. Anne Morrow Lindbergh, *Locked Rooms and Open Doors* (New York: Harcourt Brace Jovanovich, 1974), 332.
16. *New York Times*, December 24, 1935, 2,14
17. *Time*, "The Press: Hero & Herod," January 6, 1936.
18. *New York Times*, December 26, 1935, 3.
19. *New York Journal American*, August 24, 1941.
20. Lawrence O. Christensen, *Dictionary of Missouri Biography* (Columbia MO: University of Missouri Press, 1999), 536–37; and, *Time*, January 6, 1936.
21. "Kelly-Nash Machine," Encyclopedia of Chicago; available at: www.encyclopedia.chicagohistory.org/pages/686.html [accessed August 10, 2010].
22. *New York Times,* December 25, 1935, 2.
23. Nigel Nicolson, ed., *Harold Nicolson: Diaries and Letters 1930–1939* (New York: Atheneum, 1966), 131–2.
24. Anne Morrow Lindbergh, *The Flower and the Nettle* (New York: Harcourt Brace Jovanovich, 1976), 27–35.
25. Nigel Nicolson, ed., *Harold Nicolson*, 247.
26. Albert Speer, *Inside The Third Reich,* trans. Richard Winston and Clara Winston (New York: Mamillan, 1970), 85.
27. Anne Morrow Lindbergh, *The Flower and the Nettle*, 31–32; Susan Hertog, *Anne Morrow Lindbergh* (New York: Doubleday, 1999), 287–88.
28. Frederick W. Marks III, *Wind Over Sand: The Diplomacy of Franklin Roosevelt* (Athens, GA: The University of Georgia Press, 1988), 134.
29. Ted Morgan, *FDR*, 438.
30. A. Scott Berg, *Lindbergh*, 353–54.
31. Ibid., 354.
32. Walter S. Ross, *The Last Hero: Charles A. Lindbergh*, 261.

Chapter 4

1. Robert Hessen, ed., *Berlin Alert: The Memoirs and Reports of Truman Smith* (Stanford, CA: Hoover Institution Press, 1984), vii.
2. Ibid., 60.
3. Henry Harold Arnold, *Global Mission*, 146–8.

4. Walter S. Ross, *The Last Hero: Charles A. Lindbergh*, 259.

5. Robert Hessen, *Berlin Alert*, 89.

6. Ibid., 87–93.

7. Anne Morrow Lindbergh: *The Flower and the Nettle*, 80–81.

8. Ibid., 85–87.

9. Ibid., 87.

10. A. Scott Berg, *Lindbergh*, 357.

11. Charles A. Lindbergh, *Autobiography of Values*, 146.

12. Ibid., 146.

13. Anne Morrow Lindbergh, *The Flower and the Nettle*, 101.

14. Charles A. Lindbergh, *Autobiography of Values*, 147.

15. Harold Nicolson, *The Harold Nicolson Diaries: 1907–1963* (Phoenix, 2005), 272.

16. Wayne S. Cole, *Charles A. Lindbergh and the Battle Against American Intervention in World War II* (New York: Harcourt Brace Jovanovich, 1994), 34.

17. Richard Breitman, et al (eds.), *Advocate for the Doomed: The Diaries and Papers of James G. McDonald* (Bloomington, IN: Indiana University Press, 207), 48.

18. Freedman, *Roosevelt & Frankfurter: Their Correspondence, 1928–1945*, 173–74.

19. William E. Dodd, Jr. Martha Dodd, eds., *Ambassador Dodd's Diary, 1933–1938* (New York: Harcourt, Brace and Company, 1941), 5.

20. Robert Hessen, *Berlin Alert*, 104.

21. Ibid., 105.

22. Ibid.

23. Walter S. Ross, *The Last Hero: Charles A. Lindbergh*, 269.

24. Robert Hessen, *Berlin Alert*, 98.

25. Kenneth S. Davis, *FDR: The New Deal Years 1933–1937*, 632.

26. Thomas Fleming, *The New Dealers' War: F.D.R. and the War Within World War II* (New York: Basic Books, 2001), 59.

27. Ted Morgan, *FDR: A Biography* (New York: Simon and Schuster, 1985), 471.

28. Thomas Fleming, *The New Dealers' War*, 60.

29. Ibid., 475.

30. Ibid., 478.

31. Frank Freidel, *Franklin D. Roosevelt: A Rendezvous with Destiny* (Boston: Little, Brown and Company, 1990), 239.

32. Walter Trohan, *Political Animals* (Garden City NY: Doubleday & Co., 1975), 99.

33. Thomas Fleming, *The New Dealers' War*, 62.

34. Ted Morgan, *FDR: A Biography*, 495–96.

35. *New York Times*, October, 19, 1937, pp. 37, 40.

36. Ted Morgan, *FDR: A Biography*, 482.

37. Thomas Fleming, *The New Dealers' War*, 101.

38. Ibid., 63.

39. Harold Nicolson, *The Harold Nicolson Diaries: 1930-1939*, 283.

40. Charles A. Lindbergh, *Autobiography of Values*, 147–48.

41. Ibid., 148–51.

42. Robert Hessen, *Berlin Alert*, 112; "Fieseler Fi 156 Storch ('Stork')," Warbird Alley; available at: www.warbirdalley.com/storch.htm [accessed August 10, 2010].

43. Ibid., 113.

44. *New York Times*, October 25, 1944, p. 13.

45. Robert Hessen, *Berlin Alert*, 120–21.

46. Charles A. Lindbergh, *Autobiography of Values*, 167.

47. Ibid., 164.

48. Ibid., 166–67.

49. Orville H. Bullitt, ed., *For the President, Personal and Secret: Correspondence Between Franklin D. Roosevelt and William C. Bullitt* (Boston: Houghton Mifflin Company, 1972), 106–7.

50. Ibid., 200.

51. Robert Hessen, *Berlin Alert*, 154–57.

52. Eliot Janeway, *Struggle for Survival: A Chronicle of Economic Mobilization in World War II* (New Haven: Yale University Press, 1951), 24–25.

53. Margaret L Coit, *Mr. Baruch* (Boston: Houghton Mifflin Company, 1957), 466–68.

54. Robert Hessen, *Berlin Alert*, 127.

55. Ibid., 128.

56. Ibid., 132–33.; Charles A. Lindbergh, *Autobiography of Values*, 180–81; Wayne S. Cole, *Charles A. Lindbergh and the Battle Against American Intervention in World War II* (Houghton Mifflin Harcourt, 1974), 41–42; Charles A. Lindbergh, *The Wartime Journals* (New York: Harcourt Brace Jovanovich, 1970), 102–3.

57. Robert Hessen, *Berlin Alert*, 133.

58. Ibid., 134.

59. *New York Times*, October 20, 1938, p. 1.

60. A. Scott Berg, *Lindbergh*, 379.

61. *New York Times*, December 19, 1938, p. 5.

62. Harold L. Ickes, *The Secret Diaries of Harold L. Ickes: The Inside Struggle: 1936-1939*, (New York: Simon and Schuster, 1954), 553.

63. Robert Hessen, *Berlin Alert*, 136.

64. Anne Morrow Lindbergh, *The Flower and the Nettle*, xxiv.

65. Charles A. Lindbergh, *The Wartime Journals*, 115.

66. Anne Morrow Lindbergh, *The Flower and the Nettle*, xxv.

67. Henry Harold Arnold, *Global Mission*, 188.

68. Truman Smith Papers, Hoover Institute, "Scope & Content Note," 1.

69. A. Scott Berg, *Lindbergh*, 379–80.

70. William L. Shirer, *The Rise and Fall of the Third Reich* (New York: Simon and Schuster, 1960), 440–52.

71. Anne Morrow Lindbergh, *The Flower and the Nettle*, 554.

72. Charles A. Lindbergh, *The Wartime Journals*, 174–75.

Chapter 5

1. A. Scott Berg, *Lindbergh*, 384.

2. Henry Harold Arnold, *Global Mission*, 169.

3. *New York Times*, January 31, 1939, p. 16.

4. Charles A. Lindbergh, *The Wartime Journals*, 182–83.

5. Henry Harold Arnold, *Global Mission*, 188–89.

6. Charles A. Lindbergh, *The Wartime Journals*, 186–87.

7. Frank Freidel, *Franklin D. Roosevelt: A Rendezvous with Destiny*, 308.

8. Ted Morgan, *FDR: A Biography*, 507.

9. Walter L. Hixson. *Charles A. Lindbergh: Lone Eagle*. (New York: Pearson Longman, 2007), 109.

10. Frank Freidel, *Franklin D. Roosevelt: A Rendezvous with Destiny*, 309.

11. Charles A. Lindbergh, *The Wartime Journals*, 197.

12. Henry Harold Arnold, *Global Mission*, 179.

13. Telegram to Halifax from Lindsay, September 20, 1938, quoted in Lash P. Joseph, *Roosevelt and Churchill* (W. W. Norton and Company, 1980), 23.

14. Frank Freidel, *Franklin D. Roosevelt: A Rendezvous with Destiny*, 309, 311.

15. Ted Morgan, *FDR: A Biography*, 302–3; and Henry Harold Arnold, *Global Mission*, 185–86.

16. Ted Morgan, *FDR: A Biography*, 503.
17. Frank Freidel, *Franklin D. Roosevelt: A Rendezvous with Destiny*, 311.

Chapter 6

1. *New York Times*, May 18, 1939, p. 5.
2. *New York Times*, May 20, 1939, p. 2.
3. *Daily Express*, November 17, 1936.
4. Martin Gilbert, *The Second World War: A Complete History* (New York: Henry Holt and Company, 1989), 199.
5. A. Scott Berg, *Lindbergh*, 282.
6. Charles A. Lindbergh, *Autobiography of Values*, 186.
7. David McCullough, *Truman* (New York: Simon & Schuster, 1992), 262.
8. Ibid., 262–63.
9. Mark S. Watson, *The War Department: Chief of Staff; Prewar Plans and Preparations*, vol. 1 (Washington: G. P. O., 1950), 300.
10. Bullitt, *For the President*, 11.
11. Gordon Wright, "Ambassador Bullitt and the Fall of France," *World Politics*, Vol. 10, No. 1 (October, 1957), 70.
12. Margaret MacMillan, *Paris 1919: Six Months That Changed the World* (New York: Random House, 2001), 219.
13. Patrick J. Buchanan, *Churchill, Hitler, and The Unnecessary War: How Britain Lost Its Empire and the West Lost the World* (New York: Crown Publishers, 2008), 97.
14. Sir Neville Henderson, *Failure of a Mission* (New York: G. P. Putnam's Sons, 1940), 225.
15. "Statement by Prime Minister in House of Commons on March 31, 1939," The British War Blue Book, archived by the Avalon Project, Yale Law School; available at: http://avalon.law.yale.edu/wwii/blbk17.asp [accessed August 12, 2010].
16. B. H. Liddell Hart, *History of the Second World War* (Da Capo Press, 1999), 11.
17. Sir Neville Henderson, *Failure of a Mission*, 227.
18. Charles A. Lindbergh, *The Wartime Journals*, 171–72.
19. William L. Shirer, *The Rise and Fall of the Third Reich*, 635.
20. Charles A. Lindbergh, *The Wartime Journals*, 249.
21. *New York Times*, September 4, 1939, p. 6.
22. Charles A. Lindbergh, *The Wartime Journals*, 251.

23. Joseph P. Lash, *Roosevelt and Churchill, 1939–1941* (New York: W. W. Norton & Company, 1976), 23.

24. Norman Rose, *Churchill: The Unruly Giant* (New York: The Free Press, 1995) 356.

25. Orville H. Bullitt, ed., *For the President, Personal and Secret: Correspondence Between Franklin D. Roosevelt and William C. Bullitt*, 304.

26. *New York Times*, April 12, 1939, p. 1.

27. *New York Times*, April 14, 1939, p. 22.

28. John W. Wheeler-Bennett, *King George VI: His Life and Reign* (New York: St Martin's Press, 1958), 390–91; and, Sarah Bradford, *The Reluctant King: The Life & Reign of George VI 1895–1952* (New York: St. Martin's Press, 1989), 297.

29. Charles A. Lindbergh, *The Wartime Journals*, 252.

30. Ibid., 254–5.

31. Harold L. Ickes, *The Secret Diary of Harold L. Ickes: The Lowering Clouds: 1939–1941*, 11.

32. *Washington Post*, September 23, 1939, p. 2.

33. Jean Edward Smith, *FDR* (New York: Random House, 2007), 578–80.

34. Frank Freidel, *Franklin D. Roosevelt: A Rendezvous with Destiny*, 323; and, Charles A. Lindbergh, *The Wartime Journals*, 257.

35. Charles A. Lindbergh, *The Wartime Journals*, 258.

36. Frank Freidel, *Franklin D. Roosevelt: A Rendezvous with Destiny*, 323.

37. Conrad Black, *Franklin Delano Roosevelt: Champion of Freedom*, 533.

38. Ibid., 534.

39. *Washington Post*, September 16, 1939, p. 7; and, *New York Times*, September 16, 1939, p. 9.

40. *Washington Post*, May 15, 1940, p. 15.

41. *Washington Post*, September 20, 1939, p. 11.

42. Peter Kurth, *American Cassandra: The Life of Dorothy Thompson* (Boston: Little, Brown and Company, 1990), 312.

43. Harold L. Ickes, *The Secret Diaries of Harold L. Ickes, The Inside Struggle: 1936-1939*, 20.

44. Peter Kurth, *American Cassandra: The Life of Dorothy Thompson*, 515 n91.

45. Sam Riley, *Biographical Dictionary of American Newspaper Columnists* (Westport: Greenwood Press, 1995), 184.

46. *Washington Post*, September 22, 1939, p. 13.

47. *Washington Post*, September 23, 1939, p. 2.

48. Anne Morrow Lindbergh, *War Within and Without: Diaries and Letters 1939–1944* (New York: Harcourt Brace Jovanovich, 1980), xxiv.
49. Ibid., xxiii.
50. Charles A. Lindbergh, *Autobiography of Values*, 193.
51. *New York Times*, October 4, 1941, p. 1.
52. Leonard Mosley, *Lindbergh: A Biography*, 261.

Chapter 7

1. U. S. Bureau of Labor Statistics
2. Richard Vedder, "Explaining the Great Depression," *Claremont Review of Books*, Spring 2010, 48.
3. Burton Folsom Jr. and Anita Folsom, "Did FDR End the Depression?" *The Wall Street Journal* (April 12, 2010).
4. Burton W. Folsom Jr., *New Deal or Raw Deal? How FDR's Economic Legacy Has Damaged America* (New York: Simon & Schuster, 2008), 2. Quoted from the Morgenthau Diary, May 9, 1939, Franklin D. Roosevelt Presidential Library.
5. Amity Shlaes, *The Forgotten Man: A New History of the Great Depression*, 381.
6. Charles A. Beard, *American Foreign Policy in the Making, 1932-1940* (New Haven: Yale University Press, 1946), 226.
7. Tom Shachtman, *The Phony War 1939-1940* (New York: Harper & Row, 1982), 5–6; Freidel, *Roosevelt*, 315.
8. Cole, *Roosevelt and the Isolationists*, 315.
9. Thomas E. Mahl, *Desperate Deception: British Covert Operations in the United States, 1939-1944* (Dulles, VA: Brassey's, 1998), 5.
10. Black, *Roosevelt*, 532.
11. Freidel, *Roosevelt*, 323.
12. Sherwood, *Roosevelt and Hopkins*, 127–28.
13. *The New York Times*, October 20, 1939, 7.
14. *The New York Times*, September 4, 1939, 6.
15. Nicholas John Cull, *Selling War: The British Propaganda Campaign against American "Neutrality" in World War II* (New York: Oxford University Press, 1995), 9.
16. Walter Millis, *Road to War* (Boston: Houghton Mifflin Company, 1935) 66–72 as quoted in Cull, *Selling War*, 9.
17. Mahl, *Desperate Deception*, vii.
18. Ibid., 107–35.

19. Ibid., 23–45.
20. Ibid., 8.
21. Ibid., 69–70.
22. Cull, *Selling War,* 167–68; William Stevenson, *A Man Called Intrepid: The Secret War* (New York: Harcourt and Brace Jovanovich, 1976), 294.
23. Cull, *Selling War,* 66.
24. Richard W. Steele, "The Pulse of the People. Franklin D. Roosevelt and the Gauging of American Public Opinion," *Journal of Contemporary History*, Vol. 9, No. 4 (October 1974), 195–216.
25. Martin Gilbert, *Churchill and America* (New York: Free Press, 2005), 186.
26. Mahl, *Desperate Deception,* 70.
27. William Stevenson, *A Man Called Intrepid: The Secret War,* 127.
28. *The New York Times,* October 14, 1939, 10.
29. Winston S. Churchill, *Never Give In: The Best of Winston Churchill's Speeches* (New York: Hyperion, 2003), 57.
30. *The New York Times,* October 14, 1939, 10.
31. Cole, *Roosevelt and the Isolationists,* 328–29.
32. *The New York Times,* October 27, 1939, 14.
33. Black, *Roosevelt,* 537.
34. C. A. Lindbergh, *Autobiography,* 192–93.
35. Gilbert, *The Second World War,* 31–49.
36. Ibid., 45.
37. Lash, *Roosevelt and Churchill,* 131.
38. Morgan, *FDR,* 522–23.
39. Freidel, *Roosevelt,* 336.
40. *The New York Times,* May 17, 1940, 10.
41. Berg, *Lindbergh,* 399.
42. *The New York Times,* May 20, 1940, 8.
43. Freidel, *Franklin D. Roosevelt,* 323.
44. Morgan, *FDR,* 523.
45. *The New York Times,* May 23, 1940, 1.
46. Loewenheim, Francis L. et. al. (eds.) *Roosevelt and Churchill: Their Secret Wartime Correspondence* (New York: E. P. Dutton, 1975), 97.
47. Elliott Roosevelt and James Brough, *A Rendezvous With Destiny: The Roosevelts of the White House* (New York: G. P. Putnam's Sons, 1975), 261.
48. Lash, *Roosevelt and Churchill,* 142.

49. John Morton Blum, *Roosevelt and Morgenthau* (Boston: Houghton Mifflin Company, 1970), 318–19.

50. Morgan, *FDR,* 523.

51. Ickes, *Diaries Vol. III,* 182.

52. James MacGregor Burns, *Roosevelt: The Soldier of Freedom* (New York: Harcourt Brace Jovanovich, 1970), 6.

53. C. A. Lindbergh, *Autobiography,* 193.

54. *The New York Times,* May 27, 1940, 12.

55. William L. Shirer, *The Collapse of the Third Republic* (New York: Simon and Schuster, 1969), 26.

56. *The New York Times,* July 19, 1940, 2.

57. *The New York Times,* April 24, 1941, 12.

58. Robert B. Stinnett, *Day of Deceit* (New York: The Free Press, 2000), 4.

59. James P. Duffy, *Hitler Slept Late and Other Blunders That Cost Him the War* (New York: Praeger Publishers, 1991), 27.

60. Gilbert, *The Second World War,* 73.

61. Blum, *Roosevelt and Morgenthau,* 320.

62. Lash, *Roosevelt and Churchill,* 148–49.

63. Ibid., 149.

64. Roosevelt, *A Rendezvous with Destiny,* 261.

65. Blum, *Roosevelt and Morgenthau,* 321.

66. Browder, *Independent,* 149.

67. Ickes, *Diaries, Vol. III,* 214–15.

68. Ickes *Diaries, Vol. III,* 202.

69. *The New York Times,* June 11, 1940, 6.

70. Ibid., 1.

71. *The New York Times,* June 12, 1940, 12.

72. *The New York Times,* June 13, 1940, 22.

73. Lash, *Roosevelt and Churchill,* 151–52.

74. Ibid., 170.

75. *The New York Times,* June 21, 1940, 1.

76. Ibid., 4.

77. Morgan, *FDR,* 528.

78. Patrick J. Buchanan, *A Republic, Not an Empire: Reclaiming America's Destiny* (Washington, D.C.: Regnery Publishing, 1999) 269–70.

79. Henry Kissinger, *Diplomacy* (New York: Simon and Schuster, 1994), 388.

80. Lash, *Roosevelt and Churchill,* 257–59.

81. Black, *Roosevelt,* 577.
82. Mahl, *Desperate Deception,* 70, 75.
83. Thomas Parrish, *To Keep the British Isles Afloat: FDR's Men in Churchill's London, 1941* (New York: HarperCollins Publishers, 2009), 92.
84. Loewenheim, *Wartime Correspondence,* 94–95.
85. Ibid., 99.
86. Ibid., 105.
87. Freidel, *Roosevelt,* 334.
88. Blum, *Roosevelt and Morgenthau,* 326.
89. Ibid., 328.
90. Gilbert, *Churchill and America,* 189.
91. Loewenheim, *Wartime Correspondence,* 108–9.
92. Black, *Roosevelt,* 577.
93. Robert H. Jackson, *That Man: An Insider's Portrait of Franklin D. Roosevelt* (New York: Oxford University Press, 2003), 74.
94. Justus D. Doenecke, "Edwin M. Borchard, John Bassett Moore, and Opposition to American Intervention in World War II," *The Journal of Libertarian Studies* Vol. VI, No. 1 (Winter 1982) 17.
95. Marks, *Wind Over Sand,* 162.
96. Black, *Roosevelt,* 578.
97. Ibid.
98. Smith, *FDR,* 468.
99. Morgan, *FDR,* 526.
100. Black, *FDR,* 578
101. Smith *FDR,* 470–71.
102. *The New York Times,* September 4, 1940, 13.
103. Ibid., 16.
104. *The New York Times,* September 6, 1940, 2.
105. Winston S. Churchill, *The Second World War, Volume 2: Their Finest Hour* (New York: Houghton Mifflin Company, 1949), 358.
106. *Time* Magazine, October 19, 1942.
107. *The New York Times,* September 15, 1940, 78.
108. Bureau of Labor Statistics, U. S. Department of Labor.
109. Burns, *Roosevelt,* 54.
110. C. A. Lindbergh, "What Substitute for War?" *The Reader's Digest* (May, 1940) 43–47.
111. C. A. Lindbergh, *Wartime Journals,* 382–83.
112. *The New York Times,* August 5, 1940, 4.
113. *The New York Times,* August 6, 1940, 6.

114. *The New York Times*, August 7, 1940, 11.
115. Mahl, *Desperate Deception*, 109.
116. Berg, *Lindbergh*, 410.
117. Brendan Gill, *Many Masks: A Life of Frank Lloyd Wright* (New York: Da Capo Press, 1998) 404.
118. *The New York Times*, October 15, 1940, 1.
119. *The New York Times*, October 17, 1940, 28, 10.
120. Berg, *Lindbergh*, 409.
121. C. A Lindbergh, *Wartime Journals*, 411.
122. Berg, *Lindbergh*, 413.

Chapter 8

1. Morgan, *FDR*, 579.
2. Ickes, *Diaries, Vol. III*, 367.
3. Lash, *Roosevelt and Churchill*, 260n.
4. *The New York Times*, November 24, 1940, 1.
5. Loewenheim, *Roosevelt and Churchill*, 125.
6. Churchill, *Their Finest Hour*, 501.
7. Ibid., 501; Sherwood, *Roosevelt and Hopkins*, 223–24.
8. Blum, *Roosevelt and Morgenthau*, 347.
9. *The New York Times*, December 18, 1940, 1.
10. Freidel, *FDR*, 359.
11. Ibid., December 30, 1940, 6.
12. Blum, *Roosevelt and Morgenthau*, 349.: Cole, *Roosevelt and the Isolationists,*414.
13. Gilbert, *Churchill and Roosevelt*, 212.
14. Cole, *Roosevelt and the Isolationists*, 417–19.
15. *The New York Times*, January 24, 1941, 7.
16. Berg, *Lindbergh*, 412.
17. Ibid., 415.
18. *The New York Times*, February 7, 1941, 6.
19. Ibid., 1.
20. Freidel, *FDR*, 363–64.
21. W. Averell Harriman and Elie Abel, *Special Envoy to Churchill and Stalin, 1941-1946* (New York: Random House, 1975), 18–19.
22. Gilbert, *Churchill and America*, 217–19.
23. Robert G. L. Waite, *The Psychopathic God: Adolf Hitler* (New York: Da Capo Press, 1993), 409–10.
24. Burns, *Roosevelt*, 53.

25. Susan A. Brewer, *Why America Fights: Patriotism and Propaganda from the Philippines to Iraq* (New York: Oxford University Press, 2009), 92.
26. Walter Johnson (ed.), *Selected Letters of William Allen White, 1899-1943* (New York: Henry Holt and Company, 1947), 416–17.
27. *The New York Times*, December 25, 1940, 14.
28. *The New York Times*, December 29, 1940, 10.
29. Doris Kearns Goodwin, *No Ordinary Time: Franklin and Eleanor Roosevelt: The Home Front in World War II* (New York: Simon and Schuster, 1995), 204.
30. Cole, *Roosevelt and the Isolationists*, 420–21.
31. Ian Kershaw, *Fateful Choices: Ten Decisions That Changed the World, 1940-1941* (New York: Penguin Press, 2007), 232.
32. Cole, *Roosevelt and the Isolationists*, 421–22.
33. *The New York Times*, June 24, 1941, 1.
34. Cole, *Roosevelt and the Isolationists*, 460.
35. Mosley, *Lindbergh*, 280.
36. Ickes, *Diaries, Vol. III*, 474.
37. *The New York Times*, April 14, 1941, 19.
38. *The New York Times*, April 15, 1941, 9.
39. *The New York Times*, April 18, 1941, 8.
40. Shirer, *The Rise and Fall*, 882.
41. Hanson W. Baldwin, *The Crucial Years, 1939-1941* (New York: Harper & Row Publishers, 1976), 199.
42. *The New York Times*, April 20, 1941, 21.
43. *The New York Times*, April 19, 1941, 8.
44. Berg, *Lindbergh*, 418.
45. *The Washington Post*, April 25, 1941, 3.
46. Ibid., 21.
47. Ibid.
48. Freidel, *Roosevelt*, 366.
49. Mosley, *Lindbergh*, 283.
50. Cole, *Roosevelt and the Isolationists*, 461.
51. *The New York Times*, April 26, 1941, 5; *The Washington Post*, April 26, 1941, 2.
52. C. A. Lindbergh, *Wartime Journals*, 478–79.
53. A. M. Lindbergh, *War Within and Without,*179–80.
54. C. A. Lindbergh, *Wartime Journals*, 480.
55. *The Washington Post*, April 29, 1941, 1.
56. *The Washington Post*, April 30, 1941, 3.

57. *The New York Times*, April 29, 1941, 18.
58. *The Washington Post*, April 30, 1941, 3.
59. *The Washington Post*, April 26, 1941, 1; *The New York Times*, April 26, 1941, 1.
60. *The New York Times*, May 24, 1941, 7.
61. *The New York Times*, May 30, 1941, 1.
62. Freidel, *Roosevelt*, 372
63. Gilbert, *Churchill and America*, 234.

Chapter 9

1. Cole, *Charles A. Lindbergh*, 129.
2. Ronald Kessler, *The Bureau: The Secret History of the FBI* (New York: St. Martin's, 2003), 65–66.
3. Ibid., 66.
4. Victor Lasky, *It Didn't Start With Watergate* (New York: The Dial Press, 1977), 154.
5. Richard W. Steele, "Franklin D. Roosevelt and His Foreign Policy Critics," *Political Science Quarterly*, Vol. 94, No. 1 (Spring 1979), 21.
6. Burns, *Roosevelt*, 217.
7. Steele, "Franklin D. Roosevelt," 22.
8. Ickes, *Diaries Vol. III*, 396, and Steele, "Franklin D. Roosevelt," 21–22.
9. Fleming, *The New Dealer's War*, 301–3.
10. Cole, *Charles A. Lindbergh*, 129.
11. Athan G. Theoharis, ed., *The FBI: A Comprehensive Reference Guide* (Phoenix: The Oryx Press, 1999), 18.
12. Black, *Roosevelt*, 536–37.
13. Theoharis, *The FBI*, 18.
14. Stevenson, *A Man Called Intrepid*, 294.
15. Steele, "Franklin D. Roosevelt," 20.
16. *The New York Times*, August 23, 1940, 5.
17. Steele, "Franklin D Roosevelt," 20.
18. Susan A. Brewer, *Why Americans Fight: Patriotism and War Propaganda from the Philippines to Iraq*, 91.
19. Steele, "Franklin D. Roosevelt," 31–32.
20. Justus D. Doenecke, "American Isolationism, 1939-1941," *The Journal of Libertarian Studies* Vol. VI, Nos. 3–4 (Summer/Fall, 1982), 203. Morgan, *FDR*, 504.
21. Anne Morrow Lindbergh, *War Within and Without: Diaries and Letters, 1939-1944*, 96, 411.

22. Robert E. Sherwood, *Roosevelt and Hopkins: An Intimate History* (New York: Harper & Brothers, 1948), 127.

23. Ibid., 130.

24. *The New York Times*, August 26, 1940, 9.

25. Sherwood, *Roosevelt and Hopkins*, 152–53.

26. Ibid.

27. Ruth Sarles, *A Story of America First: the Men and Women Who Opposed U.S. Intervention in World War II* (Westport, CT: Praeger Publishers, 2003), 12.

28. Sarles, *America First*, lviii.

29. *Life*, November 6, 1939, 25.

30. Morgan, *FDR*, 581.

31. Michele Flynn Stenehjem, *An American First: John T. Flynn and the America First Committee* (New Rochelle: Arlington House, 1976), 121.

32. Hessen, *Berlin Alert*, viii.

33. Mosley, *Lindbergh*, 269–70.

34. Hessen, *Berlin Alert*, xviii–xix, 33–34.

35. Ibid., 36–42.

36. Ibid., viii.

37. Berg, *Lindbergh*, 420.

38. Cole *The Battle Against Intervention*, 152.

39. Robert Smith Thompson, *A Time for War: Franklin Delano Roosevelt and the Path to Pearl Harbor* (New York: Prentice Hall Press, 1991), 241.

40. *The New York Times*, May 24, 1941, 7.

41. *The New York Times*, May 30, 1941, 1.

42. *The New York Times*, September 12, 1941, 1.

43. James P. Duffy, *The Sinking of The Laconia and The U-boat War* (Santa Barbara: Praeger, 2009); Marks, *Wind over Sand*, 166; Clay Blair, *Hitler's U-boat War: The Hunters, 1939-1942* (New York: Random House, 1996), 360.

44. Robert Dallek, *Franklin D. Roosevelt and American Foreign Policy, 1932-1945* (New York: Oxford University Press, 1979), 287.

45. C. A. Lindbergh, *Wartime Journals*, 537.

46. Charles A. Lindbergh, Des Moines Speech; transcript available at: http://www.pbs.org/wgbh/amex/lindbergh/filmmore/reference/primary/des-moinesspeech.html [accessed August 19, 2010].

47. Berg, *Lindbergh*, 426.

48. Charles A. Lindbergh, Des Moines Speech, *op. cit.*

49. A. M. Lindbergh, *War Within and Without,* 220-221.
50. *The New York Times,* September 13, 1941, 1.
51. Lindbergh, Program description, PBS; available at: www.pbs.org/wgbh/amex/lindbergh/filmmore/description.html [accessed August 19, 2010].
52. Robert H. Jackson, *That Man: An Insider's Portrait of Franklin D. Roosevelt* (New York: Oxford University Press, 2003), 109.
53. Lasky, *It Didn't Start With Watergate,* 150.
54. Ickes, *Diaries, Vol. II,* 676.
55. Johnson, *A History of The Jews,* 504.
56. Tifft, et al, *The Trust,* 171.
57. Freidel, *Roosevelt,* 296.
58. Morgan, *FDR,* 509.
59. Ibid., 553.
60. Fleming, *The New Dealer's War,* 267.
61. Gordon Thomas & Max Morgan Witts, *Voyage of the Damned* (New York: Stein and Day Publishers, 1974); Black, *Roosevelt,* 493–94.
62. Morgan, *FDR,* 508.
63. David S. Wyman, *The Abandonment of the Jews: America and the Holocaust, 1941-1945* (New York: Pantheon Books, 1984), 312.
64. Morgan, *FDR,* 23.
65. Ward, *A First-Class Temperament,* 251.
66. Morgan, *FDR,* 508–9.
67. *The New York Times,* April 20, 1980, 68.
68. Berg, *Lindbergh,*429.
69. Brendan Gill, *Many Masks: A Life of Frank Lloyd Wright,* 405.

Chapter 10

1. C. A. Lindbergh, *Wartime Journals,* 560.
2. Sarles, *America First,* 121–24.
3. Berg, *Lindbergh,* 431.
4. Ibid., December 8, 1941, 44.
5. Dallek, *Franklin D. Roosevelt,* 312.
6. Bailey & Ryan, *Hitler vs. Roosevelt,* 227.
7. C. A. Lindbergh, *Wartime Journals,* 561.
8. *The New York Times,* December 10, 1941, 1; Bailey & Ryan, *Hitler vs. Roosevelt,* 246–47.
9. C. A. Lindbergh, *Wartime Journals,* 566–67.
10. Cole, *Roosevelt and the Isolationists,* 508; Sarles *America First,* 171.
11. Arnold, *Global Mission,* 359.

12. Cole, *Roosevelt and the Isolationists,* 509.
13. C. A. Lindbergh, *Wartime Journals,* 570–71.
14. *The New York Times,* December 31, 1941, 3.
15. FDR Library, Stephen T. Early Collection Box 10, Charles A. Lindbergh folder.
16. R. Cort Kirkwood, "Dauntless High Flyer," *The New American,* August 20, 2007, 35–38.
17. Berg, *Lindbergh,* 436.
18. FDR Library, Stephen T. Early Collection Box 10, Charles A. Lindbergh folder.
19. Mosley, *Lindbergh,* 309–10.
20. Berg, *Lindbergh,* 437.
21. *The New York Times,* December 31, 1941, 16.
22. Ibid., 3.
23. Cole, *Lindbergh and the Battle Against Intervention,* 214.
24. C. A. Lindbergh, *Wartime Journals,* 578–81. Mosley, *Lindbergh,* 310.
25. Ibid., 581–84.
26. Ibid., 587–606; Berg, *Lindbergh,* 437–38.
27. Cole, *Lindbergh and the Battle Against Intervention,* 220.
28. C. A. Lindbergh, *Wartime Journals,* 607–927. Berg, *Lindbergh,* 438–544.
29. Jonathan Yardley, "Homeland Insecurity," *The Washington Post,* October 3, 2004, BW02.
30. Thomas Fleming, "Unlucky to Elect Lindy," *The Wall Street Journal,* October 7, 2004, D12.
31. Ross Douthat, "It Didn't Happen Here," *Policy Review,* February–March, 2005.
32. Bill Kauffman, "Heil to the Chief," *The American Conservative,* September 27, 2004; available at: http://www.amconmag.com/article/2004/sep/27/00028/ [accessed August 20, 2010].

INDEX